THE PATH TO EUROPEAN UNION

*From the Marshall Plan
to the Common Market*

HANS A. SCHMITT

For centuries Europeans of every class and country have sought to fulfill a dream—the dream of European union. This dream is as old as the spires of Mont Saint-Michel and Chartres, but only since yesterday has the vision of one Europe begun to emerge as a definite and distinct reality.

Only after millions had perished in two world wars, only after the old order in Europe had collapsed entirely, only after the continent had been brought to the brink of chaos, only then did Europeans finally realize that unity was no longer merely a utopian ideal: it was imperative if a new Europe was to rise from the ashes of the old. With this realization and with promulgation of George C. Marshall's plan for a long-term European recovery program in June 1947, Europe reached a turning point in its history: overnight the centuries-old dream of European unity became the destiny—and the salvation—of postwar Europe; it must unite or perish.

In this book—the first complete historical account of the developments which may ultimately result in a United States of Europe—Professor Schmitt traces the spectacular advances made along the road toward union in a mere decade, the years between the Marshall Plan and the emergence of the Common Market.

Schmitt's book opens with a brief survey of the perspective from which "the latest and broadest European revolution" must be viewed: Europe's weariness of violent revolution, the nature of previous plans to unify the continent, and in post-World War II terms, the economic and political antecedents of present-day "European institutions."

In the second section of his survey of European integration, Schmitt describes the genesis of the Schuman Plan and the negotiations which eventually led to the establishment of the European Coal and Steel Community (ECSC) in 1952. Having personally interviewed many of the negotiators who brought the ECSC into being, he gives a detailed account of the steps which brought the Schuman Plan "from vision to reality." He then presents a thorough analysis of each of the institutions comprising the ECSC, including the High Authority, the Council of Ministers, and the Common Assembly.

The fourth and final section of THE PATH TO EUROPEAN UNION traces the events leading from the collapse of the proposed European Defense Community in 1954 to "the second launching of European union." This so-called "relaunching" of Europe culminated in 1957 with the signing of the Rome treaties which established Euratom and the Common Market.

Schmitt concludes his vivid and valuable survey of postwar European institutions with a concise analysis of what has been accomplished since the Common Market became a thriving concern and what still must be done in order to achieve the union for which so many Europeans have worked so hard and so long.

The Path to European Union
From the Marshall Plan to the Common Market

Hans A. Schmitt

The Path to
European Union

*From the Marshall Plan
to the Common Market*

Louisiana State University Press
Baton Rouge

Copyright 1962 by
Louisiana State University Press
Library of Congress Catalogue Card Number: 62–18669
Manufactured in the United States of America by
Franklin Printing Company, Inc.
Designed by Ernst A. Seemann

This Book is dedicated to
Christopher René
born in Luxembourg on April 18, 1957,
and the memory of
R. A. H.
died in Luxembourg on April 18, 1961

Foreword

SINCE 1956 I HAVE HAD THE OPPORTUNITY OF OBSERVING AT FIRST hand the rapid growth of the European integration movement which got its forward thrust from the Schuman Plan. Professor Schmitt has focussed his attention on the origins of the Schuman Plan and the institutions which it produced in the European Coal and Steel Community. It is perhaps a natural phenomenon, however, that this earliest facet of the tryptique formed by the European Communities has come to be overshadowed in the popular mind by the potential of its younger brother—the European Economic Community, or the "Common Market."

In the short space of twelve years Europe has indeed gone far and fast. The Common Market has imposed itself on the world as a major economic power. Its success has finally brought the United Kingdom and other European countries to come knocking at its door. The six Member States, conscious of the practical impossibility of planning their joint economic future without taking account of intimately related foreign policy, have generated renewed discussion looking to closer political ties among the Community members. And there is now the broader perspective of a cooperative partnership between the United States and an increasingly cohesive Europe—a partnership stretching across the Atlantic but open toward other friendly countries.

However, the European Coal and Steel Community was the forerunner. It created the cohesive precedent among its sovereign Member States. It provided the initial means for linking Western Germany intimately with the West and laid the bases for permanent Franco-German reconciliation. It brought forth the new form of common institutions that served as models for the Common Market and for Euratom. History will doubtless remember the European Coal and Steel Community not so much for what it accomplished for the coal and steel industries, however significant those results may be, but rather for showing the path to the goal of a United Europe.

Professor Schmitt has performed a service in his scholarly documentation of a decisive page in the history of European integration, and he has placed it in perspective against the early postwar development of European cooperation, the great debate about the European Defense Community, its ultimate failure, and the subsequent relaunching of the European integration movement. In particular, he has succeeded in capturing the pioneering atmosphere of Luxembourg during the formative period of the Community. One may agree or disagree with his incisive views on events, men and institutions; I feel sure they will serve to provoke thought and reflection about a movement which is having an increasingly significant impact on the world in which we live.

Brussels, July 19, 1962　　W. WALTON BUTTERWORTH
American Ambassador
to the European Communities

Preface

WE LIVE AMIDST CONTINUOUS REVOLUTION. EVER SINCE THE EVENTS OF 1776 and 1789 few cultures have been able to resist the temptations of upheaval. Once one *status quo* perished in the fires of insurrection, no order remained sacred for long.

What is today true throughout the world has applied to Europe for more than 175 years. After the revolution in France, revolts and attempted revolts occured almost every decade. The years 1799, 1820, 1830, 1848, 1860, and 1863 are a selected catalog of banner years during which new and precarious systems were pushed to the edge of existence or snuffed out altogether. Then the fever seemed to subside. Except for the Bosnian and Bulgarian massacres, the seventies, eighties, and nineties were relatively quiet. But the twentieth century brought new and even more devastating explosions. The year 1905 witnessed the end of autocracy under Nicholas II. The revolutions of 1917 in Russia and 1918 in Austria and Germany might be explained by the first World War, but what previous war had unleashed such a chain reaction of domestic violence?

By 1920, the heat generated by continuous political fission threatened revolution as a creative process altogether. With Mussolini, Hitler, Tito, the Algerian colonels in 1958, and a new generation of Turkish generals in 1960 came a wave of revolution for its own sake. As early as 1922 Carl J. Burckhardt had shrewdly observed the phenomenon in young Italian Blackshirts: the symptoms were burning eyes and flushed cheeks, a sense of inarticulate power, the exhilaration of being in the ascendancy . . . but no aims. These were advocates of the dangerous life for its own sake, the riders of the wave of the future. But waves, Burckhardt reflected, have no steering gear. When and how they are spent, no one can foretell. Even the Bolsheviks had a program and a gospel. Their successors on the streets of Rome, Berlin, and Belgrade were propelled by the energies of the moment and guided by the expediencies of the day. The history of revolutions from 1789 to 1960 was a descent from the Declaration of the Rights of Man to the dogma of the gutter: when in doubt, shoot!

Popular government depreciated in the same manner. Once tradition had been rejected, revolution trod on the heel of revolution. While European monarchy took a thousand years to dissipate its credit, parliamentary democracy achieved the same in less than a century. Popular government, particularly when divested of royal curlicues, quickly lost glamor and purpose. Only America, without a dynastic tradition, could invest the Presidency with the hallowed air formerly associated with hereditary office. In the old world presidents became dictators, who produced no permanent order since they could not transfer to their successor what loyalty they themselves might have commanded. Weak executives became figures of fun and derision. Popular attention came to be concentrated on the disillusioning rites of parliamentary life, which produced indifference and apathy that would finally yield to the electrifying approach of the brutal usurper.

In 170 years two new concepts, the national state and popular government, supplanted the dynastic order and an aristocratic society, only to reveal themselves inadequate substitutes. Nationalism brought Europe an anarchy that recalled and excelled the turmoil of the religious wars of the sixteenth and seventeenth centuries. And when World War II ended in 1945, there was no one left in Europe strong enough to make peace. The ship was too rotten to sail, yet not leaky enough to sink. The short and tragic ascendancy of Hitler over Europe shook the faith in popular government without making a case for dictatorship. In 1815 there had been an old regime still capable of replacing the temporarily discredited principles of revolution. In 1945 everything seemed to have been destroyed. The old monarchies were beyond revival, the popular, national states too weak and corrupt to command widespread and enthusiastic allegiance. Finally, a civilization which for the better part of a century had lived on the factory, instead of the land, had to pick up amidst unprecedented material destruction.

A new beginning had to be found. In 1945 only the United States and the Soviet Union had survived as political and ideological powers. The secularized version of Eastern autocracy did not inspire confidence for long. Those whom it engulfed were too weary to resist. Among the countries to the West, communism soon lost its support, or, as in France, became involved in new Gallican controversies of its own. West of the Elbe, there was at first nothing but a frantic effort to live from day to day. After the larders had been replenished, houses rebuilt, transport restored, and production revived, complete dependence on America appeared undignified and unnecessary.

At this point it might be said that Europe came to and began to consider anew the question of union. After everything had gone as wrong as it could, after every illusion had been lost, after an entire continent had managed to live a thousand years in a century, only then was the European ready to sift through a long register of trial and error. Now perhaps history might permit a synthesis between tradition and revolution in which the old world could survive.

The progress toward Western European Union described in this book appears to the writer as a fusion between the conservative and the revolutionary. It seems conservative because it abandons the ethnic exclusiveness of the modern national state. It breaks new ground because it refuses to return to the dynastic state whose policy was constant expansion of the royal patrimony. The European community of the future will have to attempt survival in a politically static multinational commonwealth, held together by common cultural values and shared political and economic institutions. The weaknesses of a fairly rigid political system must be counterbalanced by a dynamic economy and with ideological drive. The new Europe must conquer in peace, or it will be conquered in turn.

Since this latest and broadest European revolution is far from complete, what follows is a progress report on the first experimental phase. Its purpose is to draw attention to a unique development by placing a short decade into historical context. The story contains gaps, the assessments are tentative. Much of what has been accomplished looks to the future for vindication. Much still remains to be done.

In acknowledging his various debts to friends and colleagues who have aided him along the way, the author wishes to reverse customary procedure by beginning with his wife. This book was her idea. Upon her suggestion, I successfully applied for a postdoctoral grant from the United States Government under the Fulbright Act, which permitted spending the academic year 1956-57 in Luxembourg, and studying "Little Europe" at first hand. The research was completed with the help of further grants from the Faculty Research Councils at the University of Oklahoma and Tulane University.

A great many persons have a claim on my gratitude. Insofar as they were themselves part of my narrative, they have preferred to remain anonymous as benefactors. Some of them will appear in the footnotes at the proper time. A special debt is owed to the Director of the Information Division, Common Assembly, European Coal and Steel Community, M. G. d'Arvisenet, and his indefatigable library staff, above all M. Fernand Lemmer, Signorina Ivana Ascenso and Mme. Juliette Lanser. It is also a pleasure to recall several days spent at the hospitable Institut Royal des Relations Internationales in Brussels and in the company of its able and gracious director, Dr. Emmanuel Coppieters. At the United States Department of State, Dr. Taylor Parks provided valuable guidance and assistance. A similar accolade is due the former reference librarian at the University of Oklahoma, Miss Opal Carr, and her counterpart at Tulane University, Mrs. Dorothy Whittemore. Among colleagues, Professor John L. Snell of Tulane provided constructive and penetrating criticism in the early stages of writing. Finally the author wishes to thank three fellow-historians, Professors Charles L. Delzell of Vanderbilt University, C. Grove Haines of the Johns Hopkins University's School of Advanced International Studies, and Peter d'A. Jones of Smith College. These three scholars subjected his manuscript to a thorough and searching review. Now that his and their work is done, there remains nothing for the undersigned to do except to claim sole possession of all errors that may mar this volume.

HANS A. SCHMITT

Tulane University
New Orleans, Louisiana

Table of Contents

PART ONE

THE SETTING

CHAPTER ONE

Pioneers of European Union

EUROPE'S SEARCH FOR UNION AFTER WORLD WAR II WAS NOT SOLELY the fruit of her latest disasters. Its beginnings can be identified amidst the chaos of feudalism. For several centuries papal claims to universal authority furnished an ordering principle. What stronger bond could exist between civilized men than the postulates of the Prince of Peace? But the break between Eastern and Western Christianity in 1054 betrayed the trust of the faithful, and the schism of the fourteenth century nearly destroyed it. The permanent rift of religion annihilated what was left of a united Christian Europe.

Men and women, harassed by the extortions of the lord of the manor, began to seek protection under the territorial prince. This next best solution revealed a conflict between unity and diversity which Ludwig Dehio has described as the basis of occidental history: on the one hand "unitary tendencies which never led to complete union;" on the other "fragmenting tendencies that never progressed to complete dissolution."[1] The countryside was now freed of strife from castle to castle. Political consolidations brought forth states strong enough to defend their boundaries and to maintain respect for the law. But at the same time the rivalry over boroughs and counties was replaced by competition for larger stakes. At the end of the fifteenth century, Italy became the ground on which Habsburg and Valois warred inconclusively for continental supremacy. Later the Low Countries and Germany furnished the battlefield, but the issue remained the same. The great princes committed on a grand scale what robber barons had perpetrated from behind the fastness of their mountain haunts.

[1]Ludwig Dehio, *Gleichgewicht oder Hegemonie, Betrachtungen über ein Grundproblem der neueren Staatengeschichte* (Krefeld, 1948), 21.

3

European unity was sought again, both by the meek who needed protection against the new anarchy and the mighty who saw it as a short-cut to their hegemonic ambitions. The utopias of the sixteenth and seventeenth centuries did little, however, to further the cause of order. Few plans detailed elaborate European institutions.[2] Inevitably peace was to be entrusted to a gathering of kings, princes, or ambassadors who represented the rapacious interests which accounted for the perpetual turmoil.[3]

The most striking suggestions originated in seventeenth-century England. Richard Zouche, a professor at Oxford, contended in 1650 that local governors should be allowed to bypass their rulers and send embassies to any peace congress that proposed to discuss matters concerning their province.[4] More novel was the pacifist impulse of the Quakers, who were unconcerned with the preservation of the dynastic interest. These brave sectarians were the first to apostrophize international organization as a cure for war between rulers.[5] In 1693 William Penn called for a European parliament, not a democratic gathering but an institution representing peoples rather than princes.[6] John Bellers, his coreligionist, wished to divide Europe into one hundred constituencies, each to send one representative to a European senate.[7]

[2]Ellinor von Puttkamer, *"Historische Pläne europäischer Verfassungsbildung,"* Völkerrechtliche und staatsrechtliche Abhandlungen Carl Bilfinger zum 75. Geburtstag gewidmet (Cologne, 1954), 360.

[3]For the most complete catalog of these projects, see Jacob Ter Meulen, *Der Gedanke der internationalen Organisation in seiner Entwicklung,* Vol. I: 1300-1800 (The Hague, 1917); Christian L. Lange, *Histoire du Internationalisme,* Vol. I (Oslo, 1919), and Edith Wynner and Georgia Lloyd, *Searchlight on Peace Plans* (New York, 1944); while Sylvester J. Hemleben, *Plans for World Peace Through Six Centuries* (Chicago, 1943), is more selective and less routine. Elizabeth V. Souleyman, *The Vision of World Peace in Seventeenth and Eighteenth Century France* (New York, 1941), is an excellent treatment of a significant segment of the same subject.

[4]Richard Zouche, *An Exposition of Fecial Law and Procedure, or of Law Between Nations, and Questions Concerning the Same,* tr. J. L. Brierly (Washington, D.C., 1911), II, 90.

[5]Sir George N. Clark, *War and Society in the Seventeenth Century* (Cambridge, 1958), 14.

[6]William Penn, *An Essay Toward the Present and Future Peace of Europe, by the Establishment of an European Dyet, Parliament or Estates* (Old South Leaflets, No. 75) (Boston, n.d.), 6-8.

[7]A. Ruth Fry (ed.), *John Bellers, 1654-1725, Quaker, Economist and Social Reformer* (London, 1935), 93.

On the continent such advanced notions gained no support. Neither the Abbé Saint-Pierre, whose project for the pacification of Europe elicited both praise and ridicule at the Peace of Utrecht, nor the Italian Cardinal Alberoni, were prepared to go beyond the ambassadorial congress. Before 1789, the contributions of the Age of Enlightenment were meager. Political life simply did not keep pace with the progress of the mind. The contemporaries of Leibniz and Montesquieu in the princely chancellories were strapped into the strait jacket of dynastic war and diplomacy. Spanish, Austrian, Polish, and Bavarian successions—the task of finding the right throne for the right prince—kept armies and diplomats in constant agitation. Voltaire, the self-styled conservative in politics, assured his contemporaries that "by and by a Republic of Letters was being born in Europe, despite wars and despite diverse religions."[8] He merely confirmed that Europe, if it existed at all, was confined to the realm of the mind. Plans for European organization were notable only for the increasingly frequent appeal to the principle of arbitration. A court was to replace the diplomatic conference as the agent of peace. But as late as 1787, an anonymous project still specified that the judges were to be selected by the sovereigns themselves.[9] European organization existed solely for emergencies, and European government had no significant advocates.

For a short time the French revolution seemed to testify that freedom from dynastic control had invested mankind with the keys to universal peace and order. In 1791, men of goodwill listened to the rhapsodic exhortations of Constantin François Volney: "Let us banish all tyranny . . . let us form but one society . . . and soon mankind will have but one constitution . . . but one law, that of nature; one code, that of reason; one throne, that of justice; one altar, that of union."[10] Immanuel Kant had never accepted the utopia of the philosopher-king because "possession of power despoils reason of clear judgment."[11] He greeted the revolution as an end to immoral government, which forced peoples into war against

[8]Federico Chabod, "L'idea di Europa," *Rassegna d'Italia*, II, No. 4 (1947), 15.

[9]Ter Meulen, I, 282-83.

[10]Constantin François Volney, *Oeuvres complètes* (Paris, 1846), 37.

[11]Karl Vorlaender, *Kant und der Gedanke des Völkerbundes* (Leipzig, 1919), 47.

their will. The subject had ceased to be the property of the ruler. Whatever evil men wrought henceforth, they did on their own responsibility. In February 1793, Condorcet, on the threshold of suicide, gamely announced to the world that France was fighting for the liberty of all and that there were only two nations: freemen and slaves.[12]

Kant's was the most modest and rational assessment of the blessings of the new order, yet even he had believed that popular governments would not go to war for sheer aggrandizement nor to avenge mere verbal insults. This assumption went the way of many other illusion when the Revolution exposed the cloven hoof of ambition. Volney himself had not been satisfied merely to prophesy the coming of one law, one justice, and one union. He had also announced one "lawgiving people," the French nation.[13] Would their legislative service be provided gratis? Anacharsis Cloots gave an answer to such suspicions: after the events of 1789, mankind, animated by the spark of French civilization and led by French daring, would build a universal republic.[14] More and more the price of freedom appeared to be French hegemony.

Following a quarter century which saw the ideals of revolution corrupted by Napoleonic generalship, Europe relapsed into a coma. The Comte de Saint-Simon was the first to plead for continental democracy, complete with House of Lords and Chamber of Deputies.[15] But just as Saint-Pierre had vainly preached his sermons at Utrecht, so the eccentric French aristocrat harangued deaf ears at Vienna. His plan fell between two stools. The conservative forces, briefly reasserting themselves, attempted the restoration of a European order on dynastic foundations. Their Europe was controlled by Metternich and supported by the Quadruple Alliance of Czar, Emperor, King of Prussia, and the Lords of Westminster.[16] The revolution, on the other hand, looked toward the self-governing nation. Mazzini, for instance, like Cloots and Condorcet, was

[12]A. Condorcet-O'Connor and M. F. Arago (eds.), *Oeuvres de Condorcet* (Paris, 1847), XII, 526.

[13]Volney, *Oeuvres complètes*, 30.

[14]Anacharsis Cloots, *La république universelle ou adresse aux "tyrannicides"* (Paris, 1792), 9, 40-41.

[15]Laszlo Ledermann, *Fédération internationale, idées d'hier, possibilités de demain* (Neuchâtel, 1950), 56-60.

[16]The European aspects of this restoration are detailed in Hans W. Schmalz,

to play the European tune, but only after he had failed to free Italy.

The idealistic fringe, too, was curiously unimaginative. At the end of their rainbow stood a League of Nations, no great union of peoples. The American peace crusader William Ladd returned to the shopworn idea of a meeting of ambassadors. Constantin Pecqueur, far ahead of his time as advocate of social justice,[17] exhausted his European imagination in projects of international arbitration rather than international government.

The consolidating influence of the national impulse must not be denied. By 1834, the German Customs Union had razed the paralyzing economic barriers between thirty-eight German states. Italy, much more successfully than the Empire to the north, ultimately built *one* state where there had been several before. But the goal of political revolt in the nationalist era was independence. While its most spectacular victories resulted in the fusion of small fragments into larger commonwealths, elsewhere it sought to break up large empires with equal enthusiasm. The problems of European organization had become irrelevant.

The champions of continental union toiled on, but in obscurity. For a time, in the 1860's they found an eminent sponsor in Napoleon III, who was ever willing to outdo his uncle without taking his risks. Under his benevolent patronage, a League for Peace and Freedom was founded, and at its first meeting in 1869, Victor Hugo eulogized the United States of Europe. Before the year was out, a German, Eduard Loewenthal, had founded the League for the Union of Europe.[18] This group miraculously survived the Franco-Prussian war, and under the leadership of Charles Lemonnier, it maintained a fitful stream of activity and publicity until 1914. Though far removed from the main stage of political life, the League bore witness to a high-minded tenacity that refused to let Europe die in the minds of men.

There was to be no progress without disaster. Between 1870 and 1914, wars and rumors of wars populated a gallery of nightmares,

---

Versuche einer gesamteuropäischen Organisation, 1815-1820 (Untersuchungen zur allgemeinen Geschichte, Heft 10) (Aarau, 1940).

[17] Leo Loubère, "The Intellectual Origins of French Jacobin Socialism," *International Review of Social History,* IV (1959), 427-28.

[18] Otto Guglia, *Kampf um Europa* (Vienna, 1954), 36-37.

but they never materialized. It was hard, therefore, to mobilize millions for peace while peace prevailed. Europe was prospering fitfully while conquering the world. She was not in need of restoration or reorganization. The ever-present uneasiness was appeased by the installation at The Hague of an International Court of Arbitration. Few wanted to proceed beyond this modest achievement since it did not appear necessary.

At first it seemed as if the First World War had been sufficient warning. The agenda of the Paris Peace Conference included peace *and* its maintenance. The League of Nations was more elaborate and ambitious than the Quadruple Alliance, its functions far more encompassing than those of the Hague Court. But the partisans of European unity at once recognized the obvious, that the new compact, too, first and foremost established an organ of world arbitration, which was irrelevant to the European question. In 1918, when Wilson's Fourteen Points were still merely an object of discussion, Luigi Einaudi compared them to "the American Articles of Confederation and insisted that . . . Europe really needed a replica of the American Constitution."[19] The determined minority of "Europeans" saw no justification for resting on its laurels.

Some optimistically expected to gain their ends through the League itself. Several French statesmen, including Edouard Herriot and Aristide Briand, tried this approach. On September 5, 1929, the latter—then Foreign Minister—presented at Geneva a plan which proposed a federal organization of European states, to be endowed with real political powers. A subsequent French memorandum proposed two agencies: a legislative conference and an executive committee. Yet no one had the courage to advocate concrete inroads on national sovereignty. Apart from this weakness, the scheme ran into other difficulties. Following the death in October 1929 of Briand's colleague at the German Foreign Office, Gustav Stresemann, and the staggering Nazi gains in the elections of September 1930, France's eastern neighbor could no longer be counted on. England had never supported the memorandum, and the cautiously polite applause of the lesser European powers ta-

[19]Charles F. Delzell, "The European Federalist Movement in Italy: First Phase," *The Journal of Modern History*, XXXII (1960), 241.

pered into silence after this discouraging turn. A year after Stresemann's demise Briand himself fell from office and soon after retired from politics altogether.

Depression stalked Europe. Economic barriers rose to accentu-
ate political divisions. Each rise in unemployment brought forth
new measures of protectionist panic. Every piece of bad news on
the market contributed to the further throttling of European industry and commerce. The Briand proposal was dead before its author
went to his grave in 1932.[20] It was ominous and ironical that in this
very year a vague young man named Alfred Rosenberg stood before an international gathering at the Italian Royal Academy to
present his version of the European "mystique." Once his turgid
prose was stripped of its pseudometaphysical baggage, the message
turned out to be nothing but a four-power condominium of the
continent, composed of Britain, France, Germany, and Italy. The
timid effort of Aristide Briand had not even succeeded in laying
the ghost of the Quadruple Alliance.

A private center of activity was the Pan-European movement of
Count Richard Coudenhove-Kalergi. It was well financed, occupied offices in Vienna's historic *Hofburg*, and claimed a profusion
of distinguished sponsors and illustrious honorary presidents. Pillars of the League, as well as raucous dissidents like Benito Mussolini, professed benevolent interest. Branches sprang up all over
Europe. Within ten years after the armistice, the European cause
had become the rallying center of all opponents of sin. But, recalls
the founder with disarming frankness, "by the autumn of 1928 the
balance sheet of the Pan-European movement reflected a curious
contradiction. In five years the movement had grown from a snow-
ball to an avalanche—and yet it had no influence on governmental
policy."[21]

The Pan-Europeans were jubilant when at last Briand went before the League of Nations with his proposal. His failure, therefore,
cast them into an abyss of despair. Europe having failed its first
test at the bar of diplomacy, the avalanche began to melt rapidly

[20]Rudolf von Albertini, "Aristide Briand's Union Européenne und der Schuman Plan," *Schweizer Monatshefte*, XXX (1950), 483-91.
[21]Richard Coudenhove-Kalergi, *Kampf um Europa: Aus meinem Leben*
(Zürich, 1949), 177.

in the sun of new hatreds. Hitler's advent to power crushed the movement's biggest cell in Berlin. After the ephemeral triumph of 1929, Coudenhove-Kalergi's organization was "a heap of rubble."[22]

The vision of the Austrian magnate had been carried aloft by a strong pacifism that flourished in the wake of the First World War. After 1933, the dread of war alone survived. It clung to peace at any price, having lost the momentum of political reformation. Stripped of all creative elements, the quest for Europe had foundered in anxiety, an anxiety which led back to conflict and another attempt at European unification, brutal and practical, but which was wholly devoid of principle or system.

Hitler's National-Socialism had no European message. But it succeeded in selling itself as the bulwark against bolshevism, thus claiming a civilizing mission that went beyond the mere revival of German power. By 1938 the British Conservative government accepted the principle of an anti-Communist partnership in Europe. To the German Führer, this facade was a useful deceit, equally effective in pulling the wool over the eyes of Chamberlain and Halifax as well as a faithful acolyte like Rosenberg. Hitler's immediate ambitions were more specific and more limited. Ahead lay the conquest of Austria and Czechoslovakia, and the victories of 1940 and 1941 were as much a surprise to the victor as to his victims. Only the fall of France brought European control once more within the grasp of one power. Yet the dream which this catastrophe awakened in German hearts was not called "Europe." It was symbolized by a new weekly, *Das Reich*, first issued by the Propaganda Ministry in May 1940.[23] The new rule of Europe was to be a nazified edition of the Holy Roman Empire.

History was summoned to dress the new expediency with the mantle of righteousness. Even before the attack on Russia, no less a scholar than Paul Herre obligingly reviewed German history "in the service of Europe." Beginning with the Frankish kings, those representatives of the "Christian, Romano-Germanic Occident,"

[22]*Ibid.*, 181.
[23]Paul Kluke, "Nationalsozialistische Europaideologie," *Vierteljahreshefte für Zeitgeschichte*, III (1955), 249-50.

he paid tribute to the unifying functions of the medieval empire. Its stabilizing influence, he claimed, disappeared under the successor hegemony of England and France. Nationalism distorted the features of Europe. The peace of Versailles, finally, trampled its interests under foot.[24] Since 1919, Herre insisted, overseas interests had ruled the old world: the United States, the British Commonwealth, and even France, 60 per cent of whose subjects lived on other continents. Now resurrection was at hand. Greater Germany, wrought single-handedly by Hitler, marked the turning point. Pacts with Russia and Japan had fixed for the first time Europe's fluid eastern boundary. In the southeast, the partnership with Italy had brought order into what had been borderland chaos.[25]

Events quickly dated Herre's book. The invasion of Russia in the summer of 1941 destroyed the fleeting stability in the East and pushed the boundaries of the Reich towards Leningrad, Moscow, the Volga, and the Caucasus. National Socialism resumed its pose as protector of Western civilization against the barbarism of the East. Once more allowed to feed on the diet of cliches that had swelled the movement to herculean proportions, the Nazi imagination cantered over the Russian steppes, exultantly relieved from the nightmare of Soviet partnership. Even Hitler, who had generally left pronouncements of visionary idealism to lesser party spokesmen in earlier years, joyfully described the Eastern Front as the melting pot from which a "European" race was to pour forth. Yet about the empire which this race was to inherit there was only silence, punctuated by an increasingly monotonous drum-fire of platitudes. To millions of victims, no amount of conjuring with the ghosts of Charlemagne, Frederick Barbarossa, and Frederick the Great could conceal the inauguration of a new continental system. Nazi Europe's one unequivocal characteristic was the material exploitation of the occupied by the occupier. Now and then Walther Funk, Germany's minister of Economic Affairs, tried to beautify the economic conquest as a prelude to economic integration,[26] but the attempt visibly lacked conviction.

[24]Paul Herre, *Deutschland und die europäische Ordnung* (Berlin, 1941), 7, 55-56.
[25]*Ibid.*, 178-95.
[26]"Das Reich und Europa," *Zeitschrift für Politik*, XXXII (1942), 196.

Professorial parrots, several of whom were occupants of chairs at once-respectable universities, tirelessly wrote variations on the pseudo-European theme.[27] Paul Herre set the tone in 1941 when hope was at its highest. Friedrich Stieve echoed him in 1944 to keep up flagging spirits.[28] After the Ardennes offensive had failed and defeat became inevitable, Walter Frank still shrieked invocations of "Teutonic knights . . . in Poland, the Hanseatic League at Bergen," and "Charlemagne at the Pyrenees."[29]

It was a "line," not an idea. Shoddy parallels, sloppy generalizations, distorted judgments were the ingredients of the European cocktail brewed by Nazi publicists. Hitler had no European policy and was not interested in formulating one. On November 6, 1940, a directive of the Propaganda Ministry, designed to cut down talk about "Europe," stated bluntly: "Above all we are fighting not for a new European order, but for the defense and preservation of our vital interests."[30] This was the real theme of German policy.

In the privacy of his headquarters, Hitler used "European" and "German" synonymously. Of Russia he said: "We'll take away its character of an Asiatic steppe, we'll *Europeanize* it." Roads were to be constructed from the center of the continent "to the southernmost point of the Crimea and to the Caucasus." *German* towns were to dot them. "Our" colonists would settle the regions around them.[31] To Europeanize and to Germanize were one and the same, to be Europe-minded meant the espousal of German ambitions. Even if one took the protestations of continental solidarity at their face value, it was clear that their purpose was conquest, not order. How close could any order be to the heart of a man who believed "that a peace which lasts for more than twenty-five years is harmful to a nation?"[32]

During the last campaigns, when the German manpower barrel

[27]Egmont Zechlin, "Die europäische Ordnung und die Ozeane," in *ibid.*, 154-55, went a step farther and interpreted the German conquest of Europe as the prelude to German control of the seas.

[28]*Deutsche Tat für Europa: Von Armin bis Hitler* (Potsdam, 1944), 11.

[29]*Adolf Hitler, Vollender des Reiches: Deutsche Geschichte und deutsche Gegenwart* (n. l., 1944), 41. The text indicates that this essay was written in the last week of December 1944.

[30]Kluke, "Nationalsozialistische," *loc. cit.*, 259.

[31]*Hitler's Table Talk, 1941-44* (London, 1953), 68. Italics supplied.

[32]*Ibid.*, 661.

was empty, when foreign auxiliaries had to be thrown into the line in growing numbers, the front did become a melting-pot of sorts. But the underlying principle, again, was not Europe *in extremis*, but the cynical reflection: "For every foreigner who dies in battle, no German mother needs to weep."[33] Hitler's evil dream of an enslaved Continent came and went, exacting terrifying sacrifice and leaving only the memory of an equally terrifying nightmare. Above all, it was a propagandistic device, conceived in a spirit of "blasphemous arrogance."[34]

Hitler's machination tarnished the European ideal. His opponents bent every effort to destroy his continental system and then cut down to size Germany's hastily inflated aspirations. Ahead of them lay the task of solving a German problem. A Pan-European question, if it was recognized, does not seem to have been the object of systematic international discussion during the war.

In Washington the deliberations of a State Department Sub-Committee on European Organization revealed no enthusiasm for European unity. Meeting irregularly during 1943 and 1944, the group was to study "proposals for the organization of Europe on a regional or other group basis." It was to investigate whether there was a real desire for union. Did Europe wish "to return to the state of affairs prevailing prior to the present war," or was it "inclined to try something different?"[35] Several members felt that there was little indication of a changed attitude among European statesmen, and added the significant consideration that European union was not especially desirable from the American point of view.

The reservations of the United States were in part economic. Removal of internal trade barriers on the Continent might injure American trade. National tariffs might be replaced by equally onerous European restrictions. But more important in their impact on the committee's thinking loomed the lessons of current German control. A power strong enough to unite the Continent was dangerous per se. Although a vigorous world organization might check

[33]Kluke, "Nationalsozialistische," *loc. cit.*, 268.

[34]Hans Rothfels, "Zehn Jahre danach," *Vierteljahreshefte für Zeitgeschichte*, III (1955), 235.

[35]United States, Department of State, Sub-Committee on European Organization, "Chronological Minutes, June 4, 1943," p. 2, hereafter cited as SEO.

it, a decisive imbalance of power in Europe would, in turn, jeopardize the new League of Nations.

Another school of thought argued, to the contrary, that a united European economy would raise income and increase the demand for American goods. "Caution and reserve," rather than opposition were recommended as the most fruitful attitude toward a European customs union.[36] This segment of the subcommittee also refused to reject political consolidation out of hand. After the defeat of Germany some kind of political reorganization of the Continent appeared essential in order to prevent "non-European" conquest.

The subcommittee agreed on the following set of particulars under which European union might be compatible with American interests:

1) The organs of the union should be democratic and provide opportunity for periodic reconsideration of the scheme by its members.

2) No European state was to be merged with another against the wishes of its citizens.

3) "Each European nation [should] remain a diplomatic entity and . . . maintain a separate representation in a world organization."[37]

The State Department group was foresighted enough to devote special attention to Eastern Europe. The members clearly expected special conditions to arise from what some of them described as a "Soviet Monroe Doctrine." Trouble appeared possible but not inevitable. American diplomacy, it was agreed, should oppose the formation of any bloc "hostile toward any major power" or "prejudicial to the success of a wider system . . . predicated upon a strong world organization."[38]

This general formula may leave the mistaken impression that the subcommittee was at sea concerning Soviet ambitions. Nothing could be further from the truth. Some of its members were students of the Balkans and knew its problems. They warned their colleagues in unmistakable terms, identifying and pinpointing centers

[36]SEO, "Analytical Minutes, October 29, 1943," p. 2.
[37]SEO, "Document R 63c, January 7, 1944," p. 3.
[38]SEO, "Analytical Minutes, February 18, 1944," p. 3.

of future crisis. One of the ablest participants prophetically "considered that the future of Czechoslovakia would be [the] acid test of the ability of the Soviet system to exist side by side with a non-Soviet system without attempting to dominate its internal affairs." Although he did not necessarily consider the mounting differences over Poland's future insignificant, he predicted that "in the case of Czechoslovakia there would be better grounds for judging the long-run compatibility or incompatibility of the two systems."[39]

After its sixteenth meeting the subcommittee adjourned sine die on March 31, 1944. There is no indication that it provided the United States with a working doctrine on the European question. At the end of the war, its reservations, born of German excesses, vanished with victory. When the time for the Czech diagnosis had arrived, other symptoms had presaged what the *coup d'état* of 1948 in Prague merely confirmed. The swiftly-changing scene invested the problem of European union with an urgency, both economic and political, which the members of the group could not have foreseen. The postwar era put before the United States different problems and forced upon her new and summary decisions.

Meanwhile, regardless of the use and abuse of the European idea by the great contenders, their victims and satellites often regarded it as the ultimate rescue from their tribulations. As early as 1942, *Combat*, the official organ of the French resistance, proclaimed its support of a United States of Europe. Winston Churchill backed this stand with his plan for the postwar formation of a number of regional councils, a Council of Europe among them.[40] His text found favor among a growing number of French underground groups, and European union became a part of their gospel of rebellion. Contact with like-minded patriots in the Netherlands revealed harmony on this issue. Italian exiles, led by Count Carlo Sforza, spoke out for a truly new order after the war. In Rome, Eugenio Colorni distributed the first issue of his clandestine newspaper *L'Unità Europea* two months ahead of the overthrow of

[39]SEO, "Analytical Minutes, March 3, 1944," p. 3.
[40]Richard W. Van Alstyne, *American Crisis Diplomacy, the Quest for Collective Security, 1918-1952* (Stanford, 1952), 85.

Mussolini. Though this fearless pioneer was murdered before the liberation of the Italian capital, European federalism in Italy spread to the ranks of the Christian Democrats, who were to become its most effective agents. On the eve of liberation, the quest for Europe extended throughout western and southern occupied Europe.[41]

The many threads of this European resistance joined on Swiss soil, and leaders from eight countries met in Geneva in the spring of 1944 to discuss the future of their world. They issued a joint declaration which described federation as the only means of European survival and the only method through which Germany could rejoin the European family. Federated Europe was to rise above the old national framework. Its government must be responsible to the peoples rather than to the governments of member states. Federal authorities were to wield powers comparable to those which reposed in the hands of the U. S. government: regulation of interstate commerce, diplomatic relations with non-European powers, and responsibility for the defense of the continent.[42]

Clearly European union commanded more support than some American diplomats anticipated. But when Germany collapsed and speculative questions of the future became present urgency, Europe was still far away. British and Soviet views, so different on many issues, were equally unaccommodating. France, whose resistance had given so much substance to the idea, was too preoccupied with domestic grief to provide continental leadership. Until America became converted to the cause, peace brought a visible deceleration of the European momentum. Before the panaceas of tomorrow could be brought to fruition, the bare existence of today had to be assured. Without necessities there would be no survival, without survival no Europe in any form.

[41]Carl H. Pegg, "Die Résistance als Träger der europäischen Einigungsbestrebungen in Frankreich während des zweiten Weltkrieges," *Europa-Archiv*, VII (1952), 5197-5201.
[42]*Ibid.*, 5202; Delzell, 248-49.

CHAPTER TWO

American Aid and Economic
Union: 1945-1950

MAY IS A BEAUTIFUL MONTH IN EUROPE, AND TO MILLIONS OF WAR-wracked Europeans, none could compare with the May of 1945. As the bells rang in another peace, eyes went up to a cloudless sky, fearlessly and unsearchingly for the first time in almost six years. In countless cities, trucks unloaded their often pathetic freight of pale and emaciated men, returning to the arms of their families after years of involuntary servitude or worse. Every manner of rolling stock was winding through the countryside, bedecked with flags and flowers, crowded with returning internees. The ruins were still there, communications and industry still paralyzed, but even in defeated Germany the bottom had been reached. The terrifying worst was over; henceforth there was only one way for Europe to travel—upward.

A year of feverish surface reconstruction followed: the rubble was pushed aside or piled together, trains resumed their schedules, schools re-opened, and theaters and concert-halls were crowded once more. But anyone who viewed the quickening pace of everyday European life as true recovery was mistaken. Will Clayton, U. S. Under Secretary of State, accurately described what happened in Europe between 1945 and 1947: "At first the recovery went even faster than after World War I." But after American loans and aid, together with UNRRA relief, had guided Europe through its first postwar winter, after another summer had passed and the days were shortening once more, "things went wrong. The hidden damage began to show." Like an injured man, who has been so busy aiding others that he could not stop to consider damage to himself, Europe stopped, caught her breath, and suddenly

17

collapsed from delayed shock. Secondary symptoms aggravated the feebleness of the patient. A severe winter was followed by drought, "floods washed away topsoil and drowned livestock." Nature seemed intent on robbing the Continent of the little that was left.[1]

By 1947 it became evident that Europe was too depleted to provide the capital resources for long-range reconstruction. Immense purchases in the United States were necessary to spark the motor, but none of the potential buyers possessed significant dollar reserves or sufficient U. S. markets to obtain them. In Great Britain, coal was burned faster than it could be mined; Britain's days as a major exporter of this basic fuel were obviously past. Billions of dollars in foreign investments had been sold in order to maintain the military effort. Now she must import large stores of raw materials to revive an industry dependent on the export of increased quantities in order to pay for these abnormally large purchases.

France's financial position deteriorated rapidly during 1946. Gold reserves were evaporating more quickly than anticipated, and credit melted like snow in the sun. In September 1947, two years after the coming of peace, the government was forced to restrict buying abroad while curtailing the basic bread ration at home. In the Low Countries able-bodied young people besieged American and Canadian consulates, anxious to leave homelands in which they saw no future. Following the liquidation of the United Nations Relief and Recovery Administration, Eastern Europe faced a famine as disastrous as any wrought by the war.

Apart from furnishing a major part of the capital for UNRRA, the United States was providing aid to individual countries and responding to individual emergencies. Large credits had been granted Great Britain in 1946, but under conditions that prevented a solution of her exchange problem.[2] In 1947 Congress passed the European Interim Aid Act to support the faltering economies of Austria, France, and Italy. Yet even as this measure was enacted,

[1] Will Clayton, "Is the Marshall Plan 'Operation Rat Hole'?" *Saturday Evening Post,* November 29, 1947.

[2] John H. Ferguson, "The Anglo-American Financial Agreements and Our Foreign Policy," *The Yale Law Journal,* LV (1946), 1145-53.

the need for comprehensive rather than particular measures had become manifest if Western Europe, at any rate, was to survive.[3]

The end of the stop-gap age and the beginning of planned aid came on February 21, 1947, when the British government confidentially informed Washington that it was about to end assistance and to relinquish responsibility for Greece and Turkey. This decision, more than anything that had happened since 1939, clearly revealed to the United States that the past was dead. Not a shadow of the balance of power remained in Europe. Indeed, there was no power left to balance. "Great Britain was exhausted and impoverished. Germany did not exist; France was barely alive; defeated Italy did not count; and the smaller countries were not important."[4] If this collapse had been accepted as final, poverty on a scale even larger than in war-time would have become the attribute of peace. Despair would have led to incalculable disasters. The population of the enfeebled continent would have revolted and would, in all probability, have lost its recently-restored freedom to Russia.

Humanitarian and political imperatives called for American action at a time when an inexperienced president faced a Congress dominated by the opposition. It was fortunate that the crisis first awakened in Harry S Truman that penchant for skillful directness which was to become the hallmark of his administration. Six days after the stunning British disclosure, congressional leaders were briefed on the Greek and Turkish dilemma. The impact of the chief executive's homespun eloquence was evident when Arthur H. Vandenberg, the Republican leader in the Senate, wrote on March 13: "The President . . . faces facts and so must Congress."[5] Both parties agreed to uphold what came to be known as the Truman Doctrine. The act authorizing aid to the two abandoned nations was signed into law on May 22, 1947. But this historic turning point was not the result of the crisis in the eastern Mediterranean alone. Between the enunciation and enactment of the Truman Doctrine lay the crucial Moscow Conference on Germany (March 10-April 24,

[3]United States, Department of State, *Outline of a European Recovery Program* (Washington, 1949), II, 1.
[4]Joseph M. Jones, *The Fifteen Weeks* (New York, 1955), 41.
[5]Arthur H. Vandenberg, Jr., *The Private Papers of Senator Vandenberg* (Boston, 1952), 343.

1947), which failed to bring agreement and convinced Secretary of State George Marshall that the Soviet Union was counting on a total collapse in Western Europe, to be followed by the communization of countries like France and Italy (from whose governments Communists were eliminated only in the course of the year).

Marshall was shocked into the realization that the Soviet Union was in effect suspending meaningful negotiations until a situation completely to her advantage had materialized. His experience convinced American policy-makers that action in the Levant was merely a first and peripheral step in a desperate struggle to prevent what appeared to be unmitigated catastrophe. On the second anniversary of peace in Europe, Under Secretary of State Dean Acheson presented the somber picture to a receptive audience at the Delta Council in Cleveland, Mississippi. State Department officials, charged with drafting details of a sweeping aid scheme, were instructed to think about it in European terms. On May 20, the *New York Times* referred to the emerging effort as a "Continental Plan." Terms like "economic unification" and "European economic federation" were freely used at all levels.[6]

At the end of May, the Secretary of State accepted an invitation from Harvard University to address an alumni meeting. He decided to take the opportunity to launch his European recovery plan. Despite advice to the contrary from his top counselors, including Acheson, who feared poor press coverage, he had his staff work on a speech which was to reflect the thoughts of Charles Bohlen, Will Clayton, and ultimately his own. These remarks, delivered on June 5, marked a new beginning in American diplomacy. In a departure from the script, Marshall emphatically, and perhaps unknowingly, turned his back on the apprehensions voiced by the Sub-Committee on European Organization in 1944. This was no time to fear a united Europe, he said. This was no time for aid to individual countries on a piecemeal basis "from crisis to crisis . . . The program should be a joint one, agreed to by a number, if not all, European nations."[7]

[6]Jones, *Fifteen Weeks*, 231-48.
[7]For a complete text of the address, the writer is indebted to Professor Forrest Pogue, who allowed him to listen to a recording of its delivery, which is preserved among the Marshall Papers.

The phrase "all European nations" was uttered without qualifications. Did it include the Soviet Union? An English historian of the cold war, writing in 1955, considered it "doubtful whether America ever seriously contemplated applying the Marshall proposals to the Soviet Union." According to him, "American financiers" and Congress would not have approved, unless the Plan was linked "closely with the Truman Doctrine."[8] It is true that public hostility against the USSR was to reach new heights after the seizure of Czechoslovakia, and that the astronomic sums necessary for Russian reconstruction would never have been appropriated by the Eightieth or any other Congress. But the architects of European aid wisely refused a premature commitment on this ticklish question. For the time being, they avoided speaking on this issue for two reasons: 1) the Marshall Plan, they were convinced, must be more than a passive reaction to Communist pressure, and 2) it must never be identified as a deliberate attempt to divide Europe. Since it would require the participants to reveal their economic and financial conditions, and since it would have been a departure indeed had the Soviet Union agreed to give unrestricted publicity to her troubles, it was safe to assume that the Bolsheviks would reject it. Washington could afford to be silent.

The State Department, therefore, adopted George Kennan's advice to "play it straight."

If the Russians were inclined to participate, we should confront them with the old Marxist maxim, "from each according to his ability, to each according to his need," and ask them *to share fully the burdens as well as the benefits of a common recovery program.* This would put the Russians in the position of making a contribution to a revival of Europe's economy or of foregoing the benefits of a program supported by the United States . . . we should not take the responsibility for defining the area that would receive American aid.[9]

Secretary Marshall's address nevertheless did exclude without naming "any nation attempting to foster adverse economic conditions in order to gain politically from the hunger and misery of others." Were Russia to agree to cooperate she would naturally

[8]Kenneth Ingram, *History of the Cold War* (New York, 1955), 61.
[9]Jones, *Fifteen Weeks,* 255.

have to abandon such a policy. Her very decision presumably would have qualified her as a recipient and partner. As another State Department official, close to these events, pointed out recently: "There was nothing said or done or *even felt* during that period to suggest that the offer was not quite honest, and it was explicitly recognized that there would be advantages and disadvantages to Russian participation and advantages and disadvantages to Russia's boycotting a cooperative plan involving non-Communist Europe."[10]

As Kennan predicted, the United States did not have to slam the door in anybody's face. Russia refused to come in. At the Big Four meeting in Paris, on July 2, 1947, Mr. Molotov, after arriving with a company of 80 Soviet experts, suddenly turned and announced that foreign aid should play only a secondary role in the reconstruction of the Continent, and he rejected the Marshall Plan as an attack on the economic independence of Europe's nations. His stand proved to be binding for the satellites, and the venture of cooperative rehabilitation was finally supported by only sixteen countries.[11] Czechoslovakia accepted at first, but changed her mind after Stalin had told Foreign Minister Jan Masaryk in unmistakable terms where her economic and political interests lay. Spain, on the other hand, was not invited.

Thus the Marshall Plan divided Europe after all. But evidence does not point an accusing finger at the United States. Europe needed help, and the American government offered to supply it, secretly apprehensive perhaps of possible Russian acceptance and its effect on Congress and public opinion. The USSR resolved the dilemma by refusing to participate, a refusal which also committed the nations under her control. Even if the United States had wanted to divide Europe, which she clearly did not, the Soviet Union would have done it for her.

After the withdrawal of the Communist powers, the sixteen remaining countries continued their deliberations. On July 16, they formed the Committee of European Economic Cooperation and

[10]Joseph M. Jones to writer, December 4, 1961.
[11]Austria, Belgium, Denmark, France, Greece, Iceland, Ireland, Italy, Luxembourg, Netherlands, Norway, Portugal, Sweden, Switzerland, Turkey, and

charged it with the task of drawing up a four year recovery program. The first step toward European economic consolidation had been taken. On April 16, 1948, two weeks after Congress had provided the working capital by an appropriation of five billion, the European recipients signed the Convention for European Economic Cooperation.[12]

Responding to the American concept of a multilateral settlement for continental problems, the signatories went beyond finding ways and means to spend American dollars. They recognized the interdependence of prosperity and advocated efforts to achieve a maximum exchange of goods, services, and capital. A free trade area was their ultimate declared objective. To attain it, the contracting parties promised to put their houses in order, develop production, stabilize currency, and make the most efficient use of manpower resources.[13]

With the signing of this convention, the Organization for European Economic Cooperation (OEEC) was born. It was directed by a Council of Ministers, responsible for all administrative decisions including those committing governments. Agreement had to be unanimous; the hoary customs of international life, in other words, continued to be observed. The rule of total consensus could be suspended, but it never was. A dissenting member might abstain and not be bound by a measure agreed to and executed by the rest.[14]

The members of the Council belonged, of course, to national cabinets and could only meet infrequently and then for a limited time. During the interim, an executive committee of seven, elected annually, provided continuity of action. It could not make policy; its job was to clear away the inevitable underbrush of detail before a question went before the ministers. A good deal of the technical preliminaries, in turn, went from the executive group to various

---

the United Kingdom; William C. Mallalieu, "The Origin of the Marshall Plan; a Study in Policy Formation and National Leadership," *Political Science Quarterly*, LXXIII (1958), 483-91.

[12]Van Alstyne, *American Crisis Diplomacy*, 155.

[13]OEEC, *The Organization for European Economic Cooperation, History and Structure* (Paris, 1953), 9-12.

[14]There was precedent for this suspension of unanimity in the history of the Central Commission of the Rhine whose measures bound only members who had voted for them: Antoine Ferrier, *La liberté de navigation sur le Rhin de Bâle à la mer* (Winterthur, 1955), 54.

expert committees, representing all members. This substructure operated vertically and horizontally. Under the former heading, economic, monetary, and social problems received attention while the horizontal organization divided committees by sectors of production.[15] Finally, there was the inevitable secretariat to discharge current administrative tasks.

The OEEC recognized European unity in distress. It undertook joint inquiries, pooled administrative and technical skills, and provided joint deliberation. Members' requests for funds had to be modified in accordance with the total amount forthcoming from Washington. Yet, in the final analysis, American aid went to the sixteen governments, not to the Organization. The political framework of Western Europe, which had been completely restored in 1945, was in no way modified by the OEEC.[16] Altiero Spinelli, veteran European federalist of the Italian Resistance, chided both England and Europe for their failure to use the Marshall Plan to unite Europe, and went on: "If the American government had seen through the false European spirit of the British, and had granted the aids contingent on the creation of political federal institutions on the continent, we would now have European union, since no serious opposition could have been given [sic] by the forces favoring maintenance of sovereignty except, of course, Great Britain . . . ."[17]

Despite its orthodox structure, the OEEC got things done. In 1949 production figures for Western Europe equalled those of 1938, even though two nations—Germany and Greece—failed to reach base-year levels.[18] In July the Organization attacked import controls. All signatories agreed to remove restrictions on at least 50 per cent "of their trade on *private account* with other participants . . . " by the end of the year, and to raise this percentage to 60 during the following twelve months.[19] Response and execution showed that they meant what they put their hand to. On raw ma-

[15]A special energy commission was organized in June 1955. It consisted of eight members only, chosen on the basis of personal qualifications.

[16]A recent assessment of OEEC activities may be found in M. Margaret Ball, *NATO and the European Union Movement* (New York, 1959), 217-52.

[17]C. Grove Haines (ed.), *European Integration* (Baltimore, 1957), 54; For a different view see Lincoln Gordon, "The Organization for European Economic Cooperation," *International Organization*, X (1956), 2.

[18]OEEC, *European Recovery programme, Second Report* (Paris, 1950).

[19]*Ibid.*, 19. Italics supplied.

terials the quotas were quickly exceeded. While some nations failed to exempt more than one quarter of their trade in manufactured goods, others went all the way. The Second Report of the OEEC was justified in boasting that "a twenty year trend in European commercial policy has been reversed."[20]

Still, the exchange of goods was bound to lag, unless accompanied by the free movement of currency. Ever since the Great Depression, the effort to increase European trade had run aground on problems of monetary exchange. In order to protect ailing domestic industries, governments had added currency controls to the traditional barriers of high duties and import quotas. After World War II, these restrictions reappeared An attempt was made to modify them with bilateral currency agreements. Such agreements might raise the volume of trade between two partners, but they could not cure a resulting monetary imbalance. If one party was left with a substantial cash surplus, it still found no way to dispose of it unless it continually increased its orders with the partner-nation. Once trade between two nations reached the saturation point, the greater purchaser of the two was bound to be saddled with large quantities of indisposable paper.

From the very outset, the OEEC had recognized this problem as an important hindrance to the liberalization of trade. Until 1950, a series of annual agreements had attempted to level the differences in purchasing power between currencies. The last of these, dated September 1949, had charged the Bank of International Settlements with the recording and possible offsetting of balances originating in OEEC countries and held by member national banks. But credit and trade deficits remained the subject of bilateral negotiations. One member country could not "settle its deficits with a second by drawing on its surplus with a third."[21]

The European Payments Union, founded July 1, 1950, was to launch a multilateral attack on the currency dilemma. It aimed to eliminate all restrictions and discriminations which could be justified by monetary exigencies. The first step was the consolidation

[20]*Ibid.*, 224.

[21]OEEC, *At Work for Europe* (Paris, 1957), 52; Kurt F. Flexner, "The Creation of the European Payments Union," *Political Science Quarterly*, LXXII (1957), 243-59, describes the negotiations between the United States and her European partners that led to the creation of the EPU.

of all trade balances between sixteen countries. To the deficit or surplus which any of them might have acquired in a bilateral partnership would be added the balances, negative or positive, with the remaining OEEC associates. If the final sum showed a surplus, the Union would be the debtor. If the reverse turned out to be the case, the country in question would owe the Union. The EPU was to be the clearing house of sixteen European nations.

Once compounded, these debts had to be settled. At the outset each country received a paper credit equivalent to 20 per cent of the cash value of its foreign trade for 1949.[22] To the Union went a credit of 60 per cent of that amount from each participant. The discrepancy of 40 per cent was to be settled by a combination of gold payments and paper transactions. If a member became the Union's creditor to the extent of one fifth of the initial cash quota, the EPU might settle its credit accordingly. But once this minimum was exceeded, settlement was made half in credit, half in gold. If the reverse happened and a country had used up its initial credit and incurred additional debts, accounting was effected by the following sliding scale:

| | Settlement by | |
Debt in per cent of quota	*Credit*	*Gold*
40	36	4
60	48	12
80	56	24
100	60	40
120	60	60*

*Percentages above 100 had to be settled entirely in gold.

Since Union debts to members required a higher percentage of gold payments than demanded by the reverse situation, the EPU might have to pay out more gold than it took in. For this eventuality, a working capital fund of 400 million dollars was furnished by the United States through the Economic Cooperation Administration.

It was accurately predicted that the shifting ratio of gold and credit settlements would provide an incentive to keep debts to the Union to a minimum. At the same time the system was intended to cushion the shock of any sudden reversal in a nation's balance

[22] EPU, *First Annual Report of the Managing Board* (Paris, 1951), 14.

of trade. Abruptly changing conditions could be met by stages of gradual adjustment.[23]

Unlike the parent organization, the European Payments Union was not organized to represent each national interest. Its managing board was composed of seven members, individually appointed by the Council of Ministers, but always including nationals of the major participants.[24] Decisions were reached by simple majority vote. The jurisdiction of the board encompassed the operation, administration, and execution of the agreement. Its edicts were binding upon all member states and could not be appealed unless they conflicted with the agreement under which the EPU had been organized.[25] The contracting powers delegated to this management the accounting of their trade balances with each other. This was the second significant reversal of established commercial policy.

But achievement had its limits, and disappointments were not lacking. Liberalization applied to purchases on private account at a time when many governments were still buying large quantities of food. The OEEC had no control over these transactions. Moreover, it had confined its assault to *quantitative* restrictions. Tariffs, for instance, were not modified.

American capital raised production, irrespective of demand. "The money which the Americans thought they were giving to help the Europeans to overcome economic nationalism served only to reconstitute old national economies, instead of creating one market and one European economy," warned Spinelli.[26] His voice, in fact, echoed the OEEC's 1950 report which cautioned against "massive investments in each country over a wide range of industries, that had to be made without full regard to development in other countries." Duplication of effort was one failing of postwar reconstructions.[27] Aggravation of competition was another. Once the production levels of 1938 had been passed, the problems of selling and distributing rose accordingly. Before the demands of World War II

[23]Robert Marjolin, *Europe and the United States in the World Economy* (Durham, N.C., 1953), 69-70.
[24]Gordon, "Organization for European Economic Cooperation," *loc. cit.*, 7.
[25]OEEC, *A European Payments Union and the Rules of Commercial Policy to be Followed by Member Countries. Document approved by the Council of OEEC on July 7, 1950* (Paris, 1950), 14.
[26]Haines, *European Integration,* 54.   [27]Second report, 218-19.

had extracted everything men and machines could furnish, Europe had suffered from glut and unemployment. Now she faced more of the same. The danger was compounded by the dogged attempt to close the "dollar gap" by providing more and more goods for export to the United States. The greater the success of that effort, the greater became European dependence on a steady level of business activity in North America.[28] A recession across the Atlantic, added to mounting competition on the Continent, would have mushroomed into a disaster which an industrially overtaxed Europe could not have survived—and which it could do little to prevent.

The OEEC's "continuous confrontation of views" and the "grappling with the tasks of common concern" might teach governments in an unprecedented manner "to take into consideration the international consequences and repercussions of their national policies."[29] But it did not permit the assumption that they were preparing to meet these constant threats. As long as the governments remained sole masters of their economies, one danger would be tackled by sixteen unrelated, partial cures. The fact remained that after lip service had been paid to the truth of international economic interdependence, each nation returned to the assiduous fattening of the domestic herd. Hence the meeting of the European Movement at The Hague in 1948 called for genuine integration, and others joined the chorus demanding that reconstruction "must flow into the channels most beneficial for Western Europe as a whole."[30]

Integrated international economic planning was largely virgin territory. In March 1948, France and Italy had agreed in principle to establish a customs union, but their parliaments never ratified the scheme. Consequently, a premature agreement between these two powers and the Low Countries to merge their markets collapsed. A similar project, broached between the United Kingdom and the Scandinavian countries, proved equally abortive.

In 1950 the only persistent and systematic effort towards eco-

[28]*Ibid.*, 25.
[29]Council of Europe, *The Present State of Economic Integration in Western Europe* (Strasbourg, 1955), 30-31.
[30]*Second report,* 219.

nomic integration was Benelux, an attempt to join the economies of
Holland, Belgium, and the Grand-Duchy of Luxembourg. First
conceived in 1943, and initiated by the Customs Convention of
1944, it had made disappointingly slow progress and had experienced all the frustrations of its immediate predecessor, the economic union of Belgium and Luxembourg in 1919.[31] The customs
union did not go into effect until January 1, 1948. In 1950 full integration was nowhere in sight.

There were good reasons for a number of delays. Benelux had
begun as an unequal partnership. The last winter of the war had
ravaged Holland while Belgium's economically important areas
had been spared. With peace Holland lost her colonies; Belgium
retained hers. Holland had depended on German markets for agricultural exports. The temporary loss of these markets and supplies
from the same source produced a determined effort to industria-
lize, increasing at the same time competition with Belgium. The
two nations were worlds apart in economic policy: Holland believed in planned austerity; Belgium, America's only creditor in
Europe at war's end, had indulged in spendthrift recklessness, en-
joying to the full a unique, though none too stable, prosperity.
Only a draconic decision in 1946 to negotiate a tariff union, even if
every dike in the Low Countries should give way to the waters,
kept the two partners from drifting hopelessly apart.

The tariff agreement of 1947 accentuated old and produced new
perplexities. Increased competition with Dutch agriculture hit
some Belgian areas, notably East and West Flanders. Holland's
new industries proved unexpectedly vigorous rivals. Lower wages,
in fact, allowed the Dutch to buy semi-finished textiles in Belgium,
complete the manufacturing process, and sell the cloth at competitive prices south of the border.[32]

To the diversity of economic structures were added differences
in law and procedure. Belgium figured tariffs ad valorem; Holland
levied specific duties. Belgium's excise taxes were part of the toll

[31] James E. Meade, *The Belgium-Luxembourg Economic Union, 1921-1939.
Lessons from an Experiment* (Essays in International Finance, No. 25)
(Princeton, 1956), 9-19.

[32] Floor Peeters, "Benelux—Ideal und Wirklichkeit," *Politische Bildung*, VI
(1953), 58-63. For a discussion of the limited nature of the Customs Convention, see F. Gunther Eyck, "Benelux in the Balance," *Political Science Quarterly*, LXIX (1954), 70-71.

while they were paid separately in Holland. The classification of goods at customs varied between the two countries.[33] Even after the tariff convention had been signed, the slow decontrolling of the Dutch economy allowed only a piecemeal integration of the two systems. By the time this had been accomplished, different economic responses to the Korean War boom created new difficulties which are beyond the scope of this chapter.[34]

Nevertheless, the Benelux tariff union eventually cancelled all duties among Belgium, Luxembourg, and the Netherlands. Imports from third countries were subject to identical levies. Trade within the area rose impressively, and unhampered circulation of capital and labor entered the realm of possibilities. The laborious integration of an area of less than 25,000 square miles provided a host of valuable lessons. Subsequently more ambitious projects reflected the knowledge gained from this experience.

The first step toward a new Europe had been made by the American aid proposals. Responding to this generous and shrewd impulse, sixteen European countries banded together to increase its effect by their thorough study of needs and the adoption of common policies that would assure their satisfaction. This association of powers worked within the orthodox framework of international organization. The governments remained in the driver's seat. Though they communicated their requests to a common organization, the ultimate use of their slice of the aid-pie was determined by the national interest. Members pledged a certain degree of trade liberalization, but retained control over tariffs which would let restrictions in by the back door. For the settlement of international accounts they embraced multilateralism and created an independent technical board. But the intimate union of economies, which had been expected on both sides of the Atlantic, had not materialized under the OEEC.

In 1950, Benelux was the only operating scheme for economic integration. A customs union had been born, but economic policy

[33]J. E. Meade, "Benelux: The Formulation of the Common Customs," *Economica*, XXIII (1956), 201-13.

[34]J. E. Meade, "The Building of Benelux," *The Banker*, CVI (1956), 760.

remained in the sphere of national control. Benelux operated on unanimous consent no less than the association of Marshall Plan beneficiaries. In the tripartite as well as the multipartite setting, compliance and enforcement rested with the governments. The union could not be more dynamic than the most timid among its members.

1950 brought new remedies. These cures reflected more than economic frustration. Political integration was also in the wind, and the history of the early '50's cannot be fully understood without a review of its first achievements and failures.

CHAPTER THREE

Toward Political Union: 1945-1950

AS GOVERNMENTS REPLACED RESISTANCE ORGANIZATIONS IN THE LIB-erated areas, restoration of national sovereignty supplanted war-born notions of European unity. This was reasonable enough. A new order, one that was orderly as well as new, could not germi-nate in the chaos left behind by the German armies. There had to be government pure and simple before the peoples of Europe could decide the large question of continental unity.

The European dialogue was publicly and actively revived by Sir Winston Churchill in a speech at Zurich University on September 19, 1946. Gazing upon a "vast quivering mass of tormented, hun-gry, careworn and bewildered human beings," listening to "a babel of voices" among the victors, and beholding "the sullen silence of despair among the defeated," the former prime minister proposed "to create the European family" and to "build a kind of United States of Europe." To these eloquent generalities that harkened back to earlier speeches on the subject of regional organization, Churchill added at least one concrete proposal, which was at the same time a revealing reservation: Europe was to grow around the powerful core of a Franco-German partnership; it would obviously not include Great Britain.

The new manifesto found an instant echo among the survivors of Pan-Europeanism. It exercised a strong appeal on utopians. To-gether with the leaders of the European cells of the resistance, they hastened to form a multiplicity of European movements.[1] Despite their number and diversity, they kept sight of the ultimate goal and

[1] For a list of the most important of these, see Arnold J. Zurcher, *The Strug-gle to Unite Europe, 1940-1958* (New York, 1958), 21-23; Lucien de Ste. Lorette, *L'idée d'union fédérale européenne* (Paris, 1955), 113-27.

in December 1947 joined under the *International Committee of Movements for European Unity.*[2]

This tightening of the reins put an early stop to the proliferation of private initiatives toward United Europe and coincided with the end of a period of drift in international politics.

Hitler's dream of a breakup of the grand alliance had proved vain, but not unfounded. Without a common enemy, the future of the Big Four was uncertain. The 1946 crisis in Iran, followed by the eastern Mediterranean complications of the next year, ushered in a new alignment of power. The founding of the Cominform in September 1947 was Russia's consistent though inadequate answer to the Truman Doctrine and the Marshall Plan. After another allied conference on Germany ended in failure, the Communist seizure of power in Prague engulfed one of the last countries in Europe that had tried to survive as an ally of the Soviet Union and a friend of the West. An important bridge had been burned.

These rapid developments demanded an equally swift adjustment in many foreign offices. Secretary of State James F. Byrnes' 1946 proposal for a forty-year quadruple alliance against Germany was rejected by the Soviet Union, which was less concerned with German revival than the continued American presence on the Continent. This refusal and its sequels quickly rendered it academic. Leaders of the West European bloc, who had considered Churchill's recommendation of a Franco-German reconciliation premature, if not absurd, now realized that a limited German recovery was necessary if her neighbors were to survive. The Anglo-French alliance of Dunkirk, signed March 4, 1947 and directed against a future resurgence of German power, had become outdated in a matter of months.

At this point, British Foreign Secretary Ernest Bevin called for a union of the West, the replacement of political bilateralism by a multi-power agreement which would contain further Russian gains. His first simple prescription was to extend the Dunkirk treaty to the Benelux countries. But the ensuing negotiation, swayed in all likelihood by events in Prague, revealed a desire on the part of most participants to make this more a defensive partnership than a

[2]Julius G. Boetticher, *Europa erwacht. Die europäische Bewegung von der Utopie zur Wirklichkeit* (Vienna, 1950), 12-13.

military alliance. As a result, the Treaty of Brussels, signed March 17, 1948, called for "collective self-defense *and* . . . economic, social and cultural collaboration."[3]

Yet even the initiative of Britain's first Labor Foreign Secretary brought but limited progress. The most concrete and direct provisions of the alliance were still military. An attack on one of the participants in *Europe* would obligate the other partners to render "all the military and other aid and assistance in their power."[4] The provisions on "economic, social and cultural collaboration" were more vague. Social collaboration alone, a delicate phase of international affairs in which spectacular advances have been notably slow, produced the Social Security Convention of 1949, granting equal benefits for all member nationals residing in the territory of one of the signatories. This agreement broke new ground and opened avenues to further accomplishment. On the other hand, the promise to eliminate conflict in national economic policies, coordinate production, and develop commercial exchanges remained just that. Since these problems were shortly consigned to the OEEC, they quickly disappeared from the agenda of the Brussels Treaty agencies. In the cultural sphere the treaty was supplemented by a number of exchange agreements, but intellectual exchange in the West had not encountered notable obstacles for some time. Its emphasis here reflected the desire for an ideological counterthrust to communism, a goal still best accomplished by example rather than by preachments and programs.

After all was said and done, the spirit of Brussels was the same as that of the OEEC. Its implementation was entrusted to a Consultative Council of foreign ministers, a secretariat, and a number of committees. In keeping with Article Seven, which required that the work of the Council should "be so organized as to be able to exercise its functions continuously," a permanent commission, composed of the members' ambassadors in London and a Foreign Office representative of corresponding rank, was to carry on work between Council sessions.

The primary military tasks were assigned to the Western Union Defense Organization, established in September 1948, at Fon-

[3]S. I. P. van Campen, *The Quest for Security* (The Hague, 1956), 32, 50.
[4]Council of Europe, *European Yearbook* (The Hague, 1955-   ), I, 208-209. This volume provides texts of all major European agreements then in force.

tainebleau near Paris. Three commanders of land, sea, and air forces were appointed to guide its work. Since the pact had nowhere provided for such a hierarchy, this development was obscure and puzzling. These leaders had no forces under their immediate jurisdiction, and they led no troops. Their tables of organization were certainly not needed to enable the signatories to "afford the party attacked all the military and other aid and assistance," promised by Article Four. What the Fontainebleau apparatus *did* register was the fluidity of circumstances which had called it into being. Even the Brussels Pact had named Germany, rather than Soviet Russia, as a specific potential enemy. As thinking on this question altered under the dramatic impact of events, and with the reorientation of United States policy toward the former enemy, ideas and plans changed. At the end of this succession of shifts came the quick supersession of the Brussels Treaty by the North Atlantic Treaty Organization.

Three days after the signing of the Brussels Pact, the Soviet Union walked out of the Allied Control Council for Germany in Berlin. June saw the blockade of the former German capital. France, at last persuaded that the nursing of recent grievances was no longer expedient, joined her zone of occupation to those of the United States and Britain, and the division of Germany into two parts was accomplished. As the USSR was tightening her political and economic control beyond the line of demarcation, it was time for a similar effort on the western side.[5]

The two forces facing each other across the territory of their former foe demonstrated the failure of the United Nations to provide a comprehensive security system. A regional response to universal failure was called for.

The first such reaction was expressed in the remarks of Prime Minister Louis St. Laurent before the Canadian House of Commons on April 29, 1948. While he advocated a regional pact, he assured his audience that this would not mean "sacrificing the universality of the United Nations." The same desire, to meet the Russian challenge effectively without abandoning the quest for world order, rang through the Vandenberg resolution, passed overwhelmingly by the United States Senate in June: it envisaged an "associa-

[5]Ball, *NATO and the European Union Movement*, 12-14.

tion of the United States with such regional and other collective arrangements as are based on continuous and effective self-help and mutual aid."[6] This emphasis on "regional and other collective arrangements" superseded an earlier Bevin formula which favored a series of European defense pacts to be backed by the United States and Canada. The American pronouncement was shortly followed by the opening of negotiations in Washington by the host country, its northern neighbor, and the Brussels powers. Before the final drafting of a new treaty, these charter participants were joined by Norway (which had just rejected a non-aggression pact with the Soviet Union) Denmark, Iceland, Italy, and Portugal. On April 4, 1949, as the United States Marine Band played "I Got Plenty O' Nothin' " and "It Ain't Necessarily So," this group of nations signed the NATO pact.[7]

The new defense structure, while somewhat more elaborate than the Brussels predecessor, followed similar patterns: a council of ministers, a defense committee at the ministerial level to be advised by the chiefs of staff, a financial and economic committee, and five regional planning groups. The Military Production and Supply Board, renamed Military Production Board after the outbreak of the Korean War, was to be responsible to the Council.[8]

On paper, Western union had been replaced by a North Atlantic concept. The new agreement affirmed in the military sphere what the Marshall Plan had pointed out in the economic sector: the necessity of American participation in all phases of the European quest for survival. At the same time, the American signature under the NATO treaty did not indicate United States amalgamation with Western Europe. It affirmed certain links while limiting American obligations. The control of Congress over war and peace remained unimpaired, regardless of treaty commitments, and the latter did not include the dispatch of large troop contingents across the Atlantic.

In some respects the objectives of NATO, though similar to those

[6]Arthur C. Turner, *Bulwark of the West, Implications and Problems of NATO* (Toronto, 1953), 9-11.
[7]Lester Pearson, "NATO: Retrospect and Prospect," *International Journal*, XIII (1958), 80.
[8]Greece and Turkey joined NATO in 1952.

of the Brussels Pact, were stated more vigorously. An armed attack
against one or more of the signatories "in Europe or North America" would be considered an attack on all. But there was no provision for any continuously functioning apparatus. Article Four
merely called for consultation "whenever in the opinion of any of
the signatories the territorial integrity, political independence or
security of any of the parties is threatened."[9] The Council was to be
organized so that it could meet promptly, but not permanently. The
social and economic objectives were stated without spirit or conviction. The contracting parties went on record as favoring "stability and well-being" and expressed a desire to eliminate economic
conflict among themselves.[10] Once, in 1952, at Lisbon, it was suggested that the migration of European labor be facilitated, so that
depressed areas like Italy might relieve the labor shortage elsewhere, notably in Germany and Belgium. But the meeting shied
away from any action.[11] Its only accomplishment was the admission
of Greece and Turkey, neither of them, properly speaking, members of the Atlantic community.[12]

Some of NATO's organizational shortcomings were soon put to
the test by the war in Korea and remedied. In 1950 the five regional
groups were abolished and replaced by the Supreme Allied Commander Europe, stationed in Paris, and the Supreme Allied Commander Atlantic in Norfolk, Virginia. The Defense Committee
gave way to the Council Deputies under American chairmanship,
and a permanent secretariat was organized in 1952. But NATO
needed more than a civil service and a revision of the committee
structure. Here, as in the OEEC, the great lack was effective policy
coordination. Economic planning alone could determine the extent
to which each member might commit resources to the common defense. A joint foreign policy was indispensable, for without it military cooperation was meaningless. The failure to examine conflicts
of interest among the members at the very outset came close to kill-

[9]Ben T. Moore, *NATO and the Future of Europe* (New York, 1958), 26-27.
[10]The need for more action in these areas has recently been stressed in Lincoln Gordon, "NATO and European Integration," *World Politics*, X (1958),
219-31.
[11]Turner, *Bulwark of the West*, 97.
[12]Wolfgang Friedmann, "New Tasks for NATO," *International Journal*, XI
(1956), 157-58.

ing NATO during the Suez crisis in 1956.[13] Estimates of its success have varied accordingly. Paul-Henri Spaak has pronounced it a complete success because of the USSR's failure to expand in Europe since its founding.[14] Others have pointed out that its "sword" has been so exclusively in American hands as to call the very existance of Atlantic *community* in question.[15]

The European defense treaties of the postwar era moved timidly and hesitantly toward a true European reorganization. They constituted an orthodox effort to preserve what was left after Hitler and Stalin had done their evil work. Their contribution was not without value, but to a generation looking for more than a simple repetition of the past, it was not enough.

The first significant step beyond intergovernmental cooperation was taken in 1948 by the great congress at The Hague—"a cross between a Frankfurt Assembly and a Barnum-Bailey circus"—convoked by the International Committee of Movements for European Unity. Here, at last, the summary demand was made to create a supranational government superimposed on a European federation, or, as Paul-Henri Spaak put it, a pooling of governments. Henri Brugmans set the tone for the assembly when he postulated: "Nothing can be accomplished without European unity." The resolutions of the congress demanded economic integration: amalgamation of national economies, uniform currencies, and free circulation of capital and labor. They demanded political integration: above all the immediate convocation of a European parliament recruited from the national legislatures, or elected by them.[16]

[13]Royal Institute of International Affairs, *NATO's Role in the Free World* (London, 1952), 104, drew attention to this problem when there was still time to do something about it.

[14]Paul-Henri Spaak, "NATO and the Communist Challenge," *International Journal*, XIII (1958), 245.

[15]Pearson, "NATO: Retrospect and Prospect," *loc. cit.*, 82-83; Charles G. McClintock and Dale J. Hekhuis, "European Community Deterrence; its Organization, Utility and Political Feasibility," *The Journal of Conflict Resolution*, V (1961), 231.

[16]"Dokumente zum europäischen Kongress im Haag, vom 7. bis 11. Mai, 1948," *Europa-Archiv*, III (1948), 1442-45; Clarence C. Walton, "The Hague 'Congress of Europe:' A Case Study of Public Opinion," *The Western Political Quarterly*, XII (1959), 738-52.

These proposals circulated first among the Brussels powers and subsequently among the other governments of Western Europe. In October a Committee for the Study of European Unity was formed under the aegis of the Brussels Pact. It labored to reconcile a Franco-Belgian proposal for a European parliament with a British countersuggestion for a European council of ministers to be convoked at irregular intervals to discuss matters of common concern. On February 5, 1949, a compromise was reached which attempted to encompass both views. It called for the ministerial council on the one hand, meeting in secret, and an advisory assembly meeting in public on the other. A statute, creating these two bodies, was signed at Westminster three months later by the Brussels powers, Ireland, Italy, and the three Scandinavian nations.[17] The circle was subsequently widened by Greece and Turkey in 1949, Iceland in 1950, Germany in 1951, and Austria in 1956.

The composing of differences between France and England over Europe's future was fragile indeed. The treaty text called in question whether it had actually been reached. The official French version stated the Council of Europe's aim to be the establishment of a "closer union," while the English translation spoke of "the desire to achieve greater unity." For this reason "the French-speaking observers who come to Strasbourg are on the whole more inclined to the view that the aim of the council is political union . . . whereas the English speaking representatives tend to believe in unity of purpose or common action . . . between separate and independent states."[18]

Either way, the Council of Europe realized only a modest share of the hopes voiced at The Hague. Its feeble powers were assumed to reside in the Committee of Ministers. Composed of one member from each country, once again most commonly the foreign minister who was spending more and more time "on the road," it alone could initiate decisions. The language which conferred this authority was tortured at that; it merely bade them "consider the action required to further the aims of the Council of Europe, including the conclusion of conventions . . . and the adoption by governments

[17]A. H. Robertson, *The Council of Europe; Its Structure, Functions, and Achievements* (London, 1956), 5-7; Frederick L. Schuman, "The Council of Europe," *American Political Science Review*, XLV (1951), 727-29.

[18]Robertson, *The Council of Europe*, 15.

of a common policy with regard to particular matters." This nebulous phraseology was further diluted by the next paragraph: "In *appropriate* cases the conclusions of the committee *may* take the form of recommendations to the governments of members, and the committee *may* request the governments of members to inform it of the action taken by them with regard to such recommendations."[19] Thus the Committee of Ministers *might* recommend decisions, which no one need take seriously. Since this was plainly a waste of time, it developed very little initiative. In the words of one indignant observer, it was "not really in any sense a responsible body . . . not an organ at all."[20] Whatever happened at the Council of Europe after it became settled in Strasbourg originated in the Consultative Assembly.[21]

This Assembly was composed of representatives chosen by the participating governments in a variety of ways. In Great Britain, Iceland, and Belgium, they were designated by the government through the Minister of Foreign Affairs. Though taken from ranks of parliament, they had quasi-diplomatic status. In Denmark the parliamentary groups each appointed their alloted share of the delegation while in France, Germany, Italy, and Sweden the selection was made by the parliaments outright. Parliamentary selection, subject to ministerial confirmation, was the norm in Holland and Greece.[22] Seats were distributed as shown on page 42.

Even the smallest participants sent a minimum of three members, so that the three major moderate political directions—Christian, Socialist, and Liberal—could be represented. One Luxembourger sat for each 100,000 of his fellow citizens while the ratio was closer to 1 to 3,000,000 in the case of Germany, France, and the United Kingdom. Since the Assembly was purely consultative, and at first could not even fix its agenda, these inequities were no issue.

The optimistic and zealous European spirit, in fact, moved off into other directions immediately. To break the tradition of nation-

[19]Italics supplied.
[20]Kenneth Lindsay, *European Assemblies, the Experimental Period, 1949-1959* (London, 1960), xx.
[21]Robertson, *The Council of Europe*, 34.
[22]Michel Moushkély, "Le mandat des représentants à l'Assemblée Consultative du Conseil de l'Europe," *Revue du Droit Public et de la Science Politique en France et à l'étranger,* LVIII (1952), 665. This publication will hereafter be cited RDP.

Number	Country	Total
18	France	
18	Germany	
18	Italy	
18	United Kingdom	72
10	Turkey	10
7	Belgium	
7	Greece	
7	Netherlands	21
6	Austria	
	Sweden	12
5	Denmark	
5	Norway	10
4	Ireland	4
3	Iceland	
3	Luxembourg	6
		135

al divisions in international gatherings, it ruled that members were to sit in alphabetical order. This put the European loyalties of some under a novel and unexpected strain. Winston Churchill sat, possibly for the first time, next to Laborite Hugh Dalton. Former Greek premier Constantin Tsaldaris rubbed elbows with his compatriot Evangelos Tsirinokos whom he had once put in jail.[23] The heat of possible national rivalries erupting on the international scene was lessened, however, by organizing the Assembly along party rather than national lines. While facilities for national delegations were provided, British Conservatives and Laborites demanded, and got, separate offices.[24] Christian Democratic, Socialist, and Liberal groups organized, and, though only intermittently vocal, became models of their kind for future European parliaments. The extent to which they livened up the proceedings of the Consultative Assembly was debatable, since its first and uppermost problem was not so much to organize as to find something to do.

Article twenty-two of the statute signed at Westminster in the spring of 1949 stipulated that the Assembly might debate matters within its competence. But it excluded defense problems *in toto* and all economic questions which came under the jurisdiction of the OEEC. When one remembers that Marshall Plan aid and the evolving defense picture in NATO were major concerns of political

[23]Kenneth Lindsay, *Towards a European Parliament* (Strasbourg, 1957), 67.
[24]Lindsay, *European Assemblies*, 63-65.

leaders throughout Europe in 1949, this said in effect: the Consultative Assembly may meet and talk, but not about anything important.

Commendably, the Assembly countered with a rebellious spirit.
Two such unlikely revolutionaries as Winston Churchill and
Harold Macmillan pressed so successfully in the very first session
that the Assembly became the master of its order of business. This
demand was grudgingly accepted by the governments, and article
twenty-three was amended to state that the Assembly could fix
its agenda, but without expanding its jurisdiction.[25] Encouraged,
the members obtained reforms in other matters of organization and
administration, especially in the realm of liaison with the ministers.[26] Yet victories of substance failed to follow. Much time during
that vigorous first session was devoted to a discussion of a closer
economic union among European powers. The events of 1950 were
to give added significance to what was said and proposed at Strasbourg. But the immediate result was a rap on the knuckles from
the Committee of Ministers, which passed the resulting recommendations to the OEEC, pointedly emphasizing who had jurisdiction
in these matters.[27]

Undaunted, the Assembly (whose second session convened after
the outbreak of the Korean War) ventured to treat defense policies.
For the first time, the concept of a European army took shape in
discussion, and a resolution by Winston Churchill called for the
creation of integrated forces. A vocal minority, notably from Britain and Scandinavia, opposed him and went on to point to the dangers inherent in public discussion of a topic customarily shrouded
in deepest secrecy.[28] Yet the issue would not be denied, and the impossibility of keeping parliamentarians from speaking when they
had a mind to was affirmed. German rearmament was another
issue, and French socialist Guy Mollet launched into a disquisition

[25]Karl Carstens, *Das Recht des Europarats* (Berlin, 1957), 110; Jean Boulouis, "Les rapports de l'Assemblée Consultative et du Comité des Ministres du
Conseil de l'Europe," *RDP,* LVIII (1952), 110-12.
[26]Ball, *NATO and The European Union Movement,* 163-71.
[27]Council of Europe, Consultative Assembly, First Session, *Documents—
Working Papers* (Strasbourg, 1949), 29-30, 32, 41, 43-44.
[28]Carstens, *Das Recht des Europarats,* 65-66; Clarence C. Walton, "Background for the European Defense Community," *Political Science Quarterly,*
LXVIII (1953), 42-52.

on the European army as a pre-condition for German military revival. To his critics, the speaker replied that the Assembly indeed
could not discuss organization and techniques of defense, but that
it must deal with the political implications of defense policy. Once
the barrier had been breached by these two assaults, everyone
joined in the discussion, albeit disapprovingly. The ministers, of
course, had the last word when they refused to accept the Assembly's recommendations on a subject which it was not legally competent to discuss.[29]

In time, members became more and more irritated by this "dis-
agreeable surprise of meeting ministers whom they had invested,
whom they could overthrow at home, but over whom they had no
power on the European level."[30] At Strasbourg the ministers alone
could carry proposals to the seats of power. To circumvent their
interposition, the parliamentarians decided in many instances to
bring their European frustrations before national parliaments. The
President of the Assembly, instead of addressing recommendations
to the Committee, communicated with national legislatures. Eventually the texts of Assembly resolutions were forwarded to the national parliaments as a matter of routine.[31] The spectacular emergence of the presiding officer as a leader as well as a chairman could
be ascribed to the forceful personality of Belgium's Paul-Henri
Spaak, who occupied the chair during the first two years of the Assembly's history.[32] He provided the leadership necessary to prove
that the Strasbourg gathering need not accept statutory impotence.
It could not render decisions, but it could and did bring forth a
wealth of ideas. It established the first continuous setting for regular interparliamentary work, and many of its inhibited desires were
subsequently satisfied elsewhere.[33] Economic integration, military
integration, and political integration, generalizations and particulars, might succeed or founder in the years to come, but they received their first airing at the *Maison d'Europe* in the Alsatian capi-

[29]Zurcher, *The Struggle to Unite Europe*, 60-61.

[30]Boulouis, "Les rapports de l'Assemblée Consultative," *loc. cit.*, 107.

[31]Carstens, *Das Recht des Europarats*, 150-51.

[32]Michel Moushkély, "Le Président de l'Assemblée Consultative du Conseil
de l'Europe," *RDP*, LVIII (1952), 359.

[33]Dusan Sidjanski, "Le Conseil de l'Europe et son évolution," *L'Europe naissante*, III, No. 2 (1956), 28.

tal. The intergovernmental pattern of European cooperation had been broken. Despite endless disappointments, "the ceaseless cold war between Assembly and Ministers,"[34] even the eventual stagnation of this first European parliament—for it was never to be endowed with decision-making attributes—mark it nonetheless as another significant departure in the history of postwar Europe. It fell pitifully short of the luminous expectations that had emerged at The Hague;[35] it might be merely a "simulacrum of a European parliament and not the real thing."[36] But among the political experiments of the decade, the Council of Europe, rather than the Brussels Pact and NATO, alone held the germ of development. The events of 1950 were to bear this out.

[34]Lindsay, *European Parliaments*, 60.

[35]Best expressed in the concluding pages of Pierre Duclos, *La réforme du Conseil de l'Europe* (Bibliothèque de textes et études fédéralistes, Vol. II) (Paris, 1958), 246-49.

[36]P. J. S. Serrarens, "La construction sociale de l'Europe," *Droit social*, XVII (1954), 627.

PART TWO

THE SCHUMAN PLAN: FROM VISION TO REALITY

PART TWO

THE SCHUMAN PLAN:
FROM VISION TO
REALITY

CHAPTER FOUR

The Genesis

AT FOUR O'CLOCK ON THE AFTERNOON OF MAY 9, 1950, ROBERT SCHU-man, Foreign Minister of France, held a press conference which may have marked a new epoch in the history of Europe. After active participation in various private efforts to further the union of Europe, Schuman had become convinced that the time for vain talk had passed and that only bold action could save the cause. Hence he proposed a "limited but decisive" plan. He suggested that Franco-German coal and steel production be placed under the control of a "common high authority," and invited the other countries of Europe to join their resources with this pool. His project would eliminate the threat of future conflict between these two arch-rivals while paving the way for their economic integration. Germany and other interested nations were exhorted to begin negotiations immediately.

The Schuman declaration was the last in a series of events precipitated by Europe's continuing economic and political crisis. On the eve of the Korean war, the continent faced a recession. Orders for steel were dropping sharply. Heavy industry was by nature inflexible, and its current expansion under the Marshall Plan could not be controlled from one day to the next. Planning for recovery on a national scale, it has been noted before, had resulted in much duplication of effort.[1] Plants under construction since 1949 would soon produce an additional eight million tons of steel, for which there was no demand in the foreseeable future. This impending surfeit of a basic commodity conjured up the specter of a staggering depression. American aid might actually hasten its coming, unless Europeans themselves added to U. S. capital the ability to correct the structural defects of their economy. The rumored re-

[1] See above, 27-28.

vival of the prewar International Steel Cartel was a by-product of crisis. France's noted economist, the deputy André Philip, called the attention of the National Assembly to this ominous return to the discredited ways of the past when he warned: "A large number of steel producers of different nationalities have become accustomed to meeting and having tea together. . . . I must admit to a certain uneasiness. It is not yet a cartel, but the contacts, the preparatory negotiations are clearly in the air."[2] Protective discrimination was once more becoming national policy. The European market was breaking up again into its helpless political components. Planning, even at its most intelligent and successful, as in the case of the Monnet scheme for the modernization and rationalization of French industry, still stopped at the border. It increased national production beyond national need and revived cut-throat competition on the world market.

Hand-in-hand with these disturbing economic symptoms went an understandable restlessness on the part of labor. The over-supply of goods first reduced working hours, then employment. The prospect of bread lines struck particular terror in the hearts of those union leaders who, since the darkest days of 1947, had begun to hope, not unreasonably, that they could guide their supporters to the good life instead of losing them to the methods and principles of communism.

A more concrete, though not necessarily more important, contributing issue was Germany. The deep wound near Europe's heart had not yet healed. At the end of the war, the Allies had merely agreed to eschew anything that would "maintain or strengthen the German economy." No consensus had been obtained on whether to maintain or destroy the German state. The mere announcement by Marshal Stalin on May 9, 1945 that Russia did not favor dismemberment provided no base for a policy.[3] At Potsdam the historic question had been raised: "What is Germany?" Innumerable conferences gave no answer.

[2]Pierre Gerbet, "La genèse du Plan Schuman," *Revue Française de Science Politique*, VI (1956), 529, still the best account, was followed in this chapter, unless indicated otherwise. For a good summary of the economic causes of the Schuman Plan, see Henri Rieben, *Des ententes des maîtres de forges au Plan Schuman* (Lausanne, 1954), 314-21.

[3]John L. Snell, *Wartime Origins of the East-West Dilemma over Germany* (New Orleans, 1959), 181-84.

Meanwhile, the widening gulf between the former allies divided Germany, despite lip service to the principle of her unity. Here, as in other European problem areas, matters did not move; they drifted. Notwithstanding the expressions of sympathy and understanding from Secretary of State James Byrnes in his Stuttgart speech of September 6, 1946, the American policy of decentralization on the national level and development of responsibility on the local level was continued. The fusion of the British and American zones, decided in December, was only economic. Three weeks before the Prague *coup d'état*, a State Department memorandum on German reparations still warned against any policy that might be interpreted as "a callous disregard for the moral issues at stake and for the superior rights of the victims over the aggressor."[4] To what extent in this instance, again, the showing of the Soviet hand had functioned as a catalyst cannot be proved by the chronology of events. On February 6, the Bizonal charter reversed the policy of division. A week later the Russians conferred corresponding powers on the German Economic Commission in their sector. Three weeks later the Czech government in Prague was communized. In March the Reds left the Allied Control Council in Berlin. Their interference with traffic in and out of the city began, ironically enough, on Bismarck's birthday, April 1.[5]

As the chicaneries over the movement of vehicles in and out of the former German capital broadened into a blockade, two Germanies took the place of four. On September 1, 1948, the deliberations over a basic law for *Western* Germany—the American, British, and French zones—began, and on the fourth anniversary of VE Day, the *Grundgesetz* of the present Federal Republic was adopted. Meanwhile, the area had been welcomed into the OEEC, and with the election of President Theodor Heuss, a Germany sovereign except in military and foreign affairs had been reborn.

This limited political revival solved few old problems, and it raised some new ones. In the Atlantic arena, the issue of rearmament moved quickly to the forefront. Of immediate significance

[4]United States, Department of State, *Germany 1947-1949, the Story in Documents* (Washington, 1950), 377.
[5]Ernst Deuerlein, *Die Einheit Deutschlands* (Frankfurt, 1957), 176-77, attributes the 'new course' after 1948 to the events in Prague, but his evidence is far from conclusive.

for "little Europe" was the end of the dismantling of German industry, which was stopped once and for all in November 1949. It
was clearly incompatible with German sovereignty, but did it signify that her industry could now move full steam ahead? Division had
simplified the question somewhat. All of Silesia was in Polish
hands. The Saar was autonomous under French governance. This
left the mines and mills of the lower Rhine and the Ruhr valley.[6]
Since 1945, Britain and the United States had successfully defended them against Soviet demands for four-power control. At the
same time, the utopia of an agrarian Germany, producing only pots
and pans, had been discarded when an export quota of fifteen million tons of coal was set for the May 1945-April 1946 period in order
to assure German survival.[7] As soon as these industries resumed
even limited production, the specter of reviving economic power
severely frightened the French. In May 1946, Georges Bidault had
demanded that the Rhineland be put under his government's economic and political control.[8] This demand was no more successful
than the Russian scheme for four-power control. Until the French
agreed to join their zones with those of Britain and the United
States, there was, in fact, no practical way of achieving it, and once
this was done, the take-over by the French could be successfully
resisted by American and British authorities. But American respon-
siveness to the apprehensions of her major continental ally, to
which were joined those of the Benelux countries, called for some
measure of compromise.

This compromise was the International Ruhr Authority, devised
in June and established in December 1948. It imposed international control without internationalization. Its executive body was a
council on which every occupying power had three and the Benelux countries one vote each. Decisions were made by majority bal-
lot. Its mission was twofold:

    1) to avoid the misuse of "the resources of the Ruhr . . . for ag-
       gression in the future."

---

[6]These produced "9/10 of total German coke production" and "about 4/5 of
all German hard coal." Hans Schrepfer, *Der Nordwesten* (Vol. I of N. Krebs
[ed.] *Landeskunde von Deutschland*) (Berlin, 1935), 139.
   [7]Snell, *Wartime Origins of the East-West Dilemma*, 201-11.
   [8]Vandenberg, *The Private Papers of Senator Vandenberg*, 281.

2) "to assure to the countries cooperating . . . equitable access to the coal, coke, and steel of the Ruhr."

It expressed to perfection the abiding fear of Germany's resiliant but indispensable might. After the adoption of the Bonn Basic Law, Germany joined the Authority by accepting the "rights and obligations arising out of the Ruhr agreement."[9]

The dilemma persisted: was this arrangement compatible with sovereignty, even if its exercise excluded control over diplomatic and military affairs? In the newly expanded Ruhr council, Germany was assigned three votes. Numerically her position was equal to that of the United States, Britain, and France. Yet a more realistic appraisal had to recognize that she held three out of a total of fifteen votes in a directorate controlling industry on German soil, operated by German labor and management, and predominantly fueled by German capital. Alien policies would control them, regardless of the three German protest votes, unless she could obtain the support of two occupying powers, or of one occupying power and two Benelux countries.

The International Ruhr Authority expressed an uneasy transition, even before the advocacy of German rearmament, particularly in the United States, removed other limitations on the sovereignty of the Federal Republic. Yet what could replace it under prevailing circumstances? Students of history recalled past schemes which had sought to effect a merger of French and German heavy industry.[10] It had been implicitly advocated by Lord Keynes in his sweeping indictment of the Treaty of Versailles and by the then Lord Mayor of Cologne, Konrad Adenauer, during the Ruhr occupation.[11] Concurrently, the German industrialist, Hugo Stinnes, had approached French financial interests with a plan for a Franco-German combine to rebuild the devastated regions between the Rhine and the Marne.[12] Paul Reynaud claimed to have "advocated the linking up of France's heavy industry with that of Germany"

[9]Georges Kaekenbeek, "The International Authority for the Ruhr and the Schuman Plan," *Transactions for the Grotius Society,* XXXVII (1952), 4-8.

[10]Felix Stoessinger, "Geschichte und Verfassung des Schumann-Plans," *Neue Schweizer Rundschau,* XIX (1951-52), 417.

[11]William Diebold, Jr., *The Schuman Plan, a Study in Economic Cooperation* (New York, 1959), 25-26.

[12]George W. F. Hallgarten, *Hitler, Reichswehr und Industrie* (Frankfurt, 1955), 13-16.

"on the morrow of the First World War," and blamed Raymond Poincaré for successfully opposing a meeting with Hugo Stinnes towards this end.[13]

After the Second World War, the idea reappeared and would not be denied. Winston Churchill saw as early as 1946 that a Franco-German reconciliation was indispensable for European recovery. André Philip subsequently presented similar views to a hostile National Assembly in Paris. The first prominent German to lend his support to this gigantic merger seems to have been the late Karl Arnold, who was Minister-President of North-Rhine-Westphalia at the time. His scheme was frankly conceived to liquidate the International Ruhr Authority, but in a manner acceptable to France. Instead of the one-sided international control of German industry, he proposed an international "association of convenience" which encompassed the German Ruhr, French Lorraine, and the heavy industries of Belgium and Luxembourg. In short, Karl Arnold advocated a true Europeanization of heavy industry.[14]

Early in 1950, the West German government began to examine this extension of international supervision in connection with two other sensitive problems. On March 3, France had concluded an agreement with the Saar, recognizing the region's political autonomy and affirming its economic union with the Fourth Republic. This coincided with an invitation asking Germany to join the Council of Europe. Chancellor Adenauer's government faced a difficult decision. Joining the Council of Europe, whose membership included the Saar, could have been interpreted as recognition of the Saarbrücken government as well as an acceptance of the loss of an important province in the west. At the same time, the invitation to Strasbourg was appreciated as an important step in the gradual recovery of that international equality which alone could make the Federal Republic meaningfully sovereign.

What course were Franco-German relations to take from here? On March 5, Chancellor Adenauer told a press conference that France's unilateral action in the Saar was "a heavy blow to the

[13]Paul Reynaud, *In the Thick of the Fight, 1930-1945*, tr. James D. Lambert (New York, 1955), 1.

[14]Karl Arnold, *Deutsche Beiträge zur Verwirklichung der Europa-Idee* (Politeia, Bonner Universitätsreden zu öffentlichen Fragen, I) (Krefeld, n. d.), 17.

cause of Franco-German understanding." French reaction was instantaneous. Foreign Minister Schuman pointed out that the Saar statute was as provisional as the Federal Republic. The March agreement should not be regarded as an obstacle to the restoration of normal, cordial relations. Adenauer did not comment on the first part of the French rejoinder; however, in a subsequent interview on March 21, he promptly seized on the second, suggesting that "a beginning should be made with an economic and customs union between the two countries."[15] Press conferences were a curious and novel avenue of diplomatic communication. But German foreign affairs were still the province of the Allied High Commissioners, and no other official channel of intercourse existed.

The question of joining the Council of Europe also called for a decision. On May 9, 1950, at eleven a.m., a cabinet meeting was convened to settle it. As it was about to begin, an official of the French Foreign Office arrived at Bonn to inform the German Chancellor of Schuman's impending press conference that afternoon. The official answer to Adenauer's proposal had arrived. With an economic juncture to be espoused by France, two decisions were taken forthwith: one to go to Strasbourg to join the Council of Europe; the other to go to Paris to negotiate on the Schuman proposal.

Actually, the Schuman Plan had not been drafted in reply to Adenauer's appeal. On March 21, the date of the Chancellor's second press conference on Franco-German relations, Robert Schuman was as unaware of its formal existence as his German vis-à-vis. At that time, the project was still locked in the safe of the French State Planning Office. The head of that office was a brilliant, creative technician, then outside the public limelight. His name was Jean Monnet.

Monnet was the son of a cognac merchant. Born to wealth, he was also born to adventure, and he left school at the age of sixteen to begin a spectacular career as salesman of the family product on both sides of the Atlantic. During the First World War, he was a member of various economic missions to Britain. He so impressed his hosts that they subsequently recommended him, then scarcely thirty-one, to become Assistant Secretary General of the League of

---

[15]Paul Weymar, *Adenauer, His Authorized Biography*, tr. Peter de Mendelsohn (New York, 1957), 318-26.

Nations. He left this disheartening employment after only two years and returned to the House of Monnet, which was then in straits almost as dire as the League, and succeeded in curing its ills with greater effect and dispatch.

Between 1925 and 1940, Monnet's economic and financial talents were put to work on a bewildering variety of tasks. He reorganized the finances of Poland and Rumania, acted as adviser to Chiang-Kai-shek, and liquidated the affairs of "match king" Ivar Kreuger. Upon the renewed outbreak of war, he became chairman of the Anglo-French Coordinating Committee and was the author of Winston Churchill's famous proposal of 1940 to unite the British and French commonwealths for the duration.

After the fall of France, Monnet went to America, where he contributed his experience and optimism to the shaping of Roosevelt's victory program. He was appointed to public office in France for the first time in 1945, when he became Commissioner under the Plan for the Reconstruction of Key Industries, usually known as the Monnet Plan.[16] His achievements there were impressive: by 1955 French overall industrial production had risen to twice what it was in 1938. Nevertheless, the world owes Monnet a far greater debt for the development of another plan, a plan which was to bear the name of Robert Schuman.

Plans, economic plans in particular, were not in short supply at mid-century. The concerns which animated Monnet, and Schuman after him, were uppermost in the best minds of Western Europe. In a single day—August 24, 1949—no less than three projects proposing economic union among its members were laid before the Council of Europe. The most important of the three, in view of later events, was a resolution signed and co-sponsored by Schuman and Bidault, urging a study of basic European industries and advocating legislation which would facilitate the free movement of investment capital from one country to another. After its adoption by the Assembly, this project was implemented by the economic committee, which finally went on record in favor of "commercial enterprises, public or private, exempt from tariffs, which could function simultaneously in several member states. An Office of European

---

[16]Shepard Clough, "Economic Planning in a Capitalist Society: France from Monnet to Hirsch," *Political Science Quarterly*, LXXI (1956), 542-49.

Companies would be attached to the Council of Europe, which would supervise them."[17]

American hope that the Marshall Plan would usher in an age of greater European unity was neither dead nor dormant. On October 31, 1949, ECA Administrator Paul Hoffman told a gathering of the OEEC that a European program for "effective and lasting integration" would have to include the following measures:

"1) substantial coordination of fiscal and monetary policies by the countries,

2) the means to effect necessary adjustments of exchange rates,

3) provisions for cushioning temporary disturbances in the flow of trade and payments between countries, and

4) insurance against the imposition of restrictive commercial policies which would thwart the integration measures."[18]

This intervention is significant because it may have engendered the notion that the subsequent Schuman Plan was of American, rather than French, origin. Actually, Hoffman said nothing about supranational institutions and refrained from alluding to the Benelux agony, which illustrated so well that a customs union without "constitution" was likely to founder.[19] The goal of the American planner was a payments union, not an economic community.

Even after the negotiations for the Schuman Plan had begun, but before their issue could be foretold, other plans continued to see the light of day. The Petsche Plan envisioned an organization to channel scarce capital to those areas where it was most needed. The Pella Plan sought a broad integration of the European consumer market. On June 15, 1950, the Netherlands delegation to the OEEC presented a memorandum, which, in accordance with prevalent fashion, came to be known as the Stikker Plan. It advocated a speeding up of liberalization, and then total economic integration by sectors, if necessary, before liberalization had been completed. To smooth out inevitable difficulties, a European Integration Fund was to finance rationalization of those industries which in their

[17]Council of Europe, Consultative Assembly, Second Session, *Reports* (Strasbourg, 1950), II, 610-12; III, 801-05.

[18]United States, Economic Cooperation Administration, *Second report to Congress* (Washington, D.C., 1950), 3; Flexner, "Creation of the European Payments Union," *loc. cit.*, 242.

[19]Lincoln Gordon, "Myth and Reality of European Integration," *Yale Review*, XLV (1955), 83-84.

present condition could not survive without protective tariffs. What shocked Stikker's audience into refusal was the proviso that some decisions of the Council of Ministers could be made by simple majority vote.[20]

With the notable exception of the Schuman plan, none of these proposals ever became more than an item in the files. But then none of their authors ever moved European public opinion as did Robert Schuman. The reason for this was that none of them had so well-wrought a product, and none of them—this is of the utmost importance—knew how to display it quite like Schuman. Of what value was the unveiling of a scheme before a forum, like the Consultative Assembly, which could do no more than recommend its adoption to a powerless Committee of Ministers? The most likely fate of a plan in Strasbourg was to have it talked to death before it could come to life.

This fate had befallen Schuman's own European company project. Timing and procedure were, therefore, the new plan's first great asset. It was the brainchild of the compact, disciplined staff of the French Planning Office, working in complete secrecy and setting its own pace. No outside pressures disturbed the work, and no leaks brought about premature disclosure. Thus the first effective attack on Europe's economic problems on an international scale was not launched by an irresponsible international gathering, but by a national government firmly committed to its purpose.

Monnet's planning was the fruit of prevalent apprehensions. Growing East-West tensions are said to have convinced him that Soviet aggression as well as preventive American action might occur. In either case a divided Europe would first vacillate and then suffer helplessly between the contenders. United, on the other hand, it might close the source of the conflict by standing up to either one. In common with other thoughtful Europeans, Monnet "was convinced that the European countries could not solve their difficult problems within their own borders alone . . . some new form of relationship should be established between France and Germany and the nations of Europe, other than relations based on

---

[20]OEEC, "Plan d'action pour l'intégration économique de l'Europe, Memorandum de la délégation des Pays-Bas." (OEEC Document C [50] 159, Paris, 1950), 1-5.

the rules of national sovereignty." One way "was to start with one particular problem and have France and Germany agree to transfer for this problem to common institutions the power that in the past they exercised on the basis of their national sovereignty."[21]

Integration entrusted to a control organ independent of national supervision was at the heart of Monnet's thinking. Without the acceptance of the supranational principle, there could be no new start. But the birth and history of the Council of Europe had demonstrated to him that no government in Europe was ready to abdicate in the political sphere. A less sensitive area must be found to put the new approach to the test. Considering the objectives of Franco-German amalgamation, coal and steel suggested themselves as promising test objects. French ore and German coal might complement one another, although they had not done so in the past. Rivalries in the two sectors had, however, contributed immeasurably to the tensions between the two, and even if the economic results of the merger were unpredictable, its political and psychological value could be expected to be considerable. Finally, coal and steel were basic industries. They supported the economic health of Europe, and their integration was thus the logical point of departure for a general economic union.

Spade work in the French Planning Office was completed on May 3, 1950. Despite persistent rumors to the contrary, there is no evidence whatsoever that the plan was the subject of international negotiations of any kind, on any level, before that date. Assertions that Monnet discussed in 1949 with English friends the revival of the Anglo-French union of 1940 on the economic level lack authoritative confirmation. Throughout 1949 and 1950, however, he did discuss his general ideas in private conversations with American acquaintances in Paris, but no conversations with German partners took place. When the blueprint at last left Monnet's office, it went to Premier Georges Bidault and his Foreign Minister, Robert Schuman. The former apparently failed to grasp the significances of the project. The latter at once made it his own. At this point it became *his* plan.

Robert Schuman was then sixty-four years old, well past the age of youthful enthusiasms. Born in Luxembourg and reared in Metz,

[21]Gerbet, "La genèse du Plan Schuman," *loc. cit.*, 538-43.

where he had opened law offices in 1910, he had been an officer in the German Imperial Army during World War I. From 1919 until 1940 he represented a constituency of the department of the Moselle in the Chamber, affiliating with the moderate URD *(Union Républicaine Démocratique)*. His career had been unspectacular, and not until 1940 did he enter a French cabinet (as undersecretary of state in charge of the refugee problem). After voting for summary powers, he refused to join the Pétain government and was arrested by the Germans. He escaped his captors in 1942 and spent two more years in hiding. Following the liberation of Metz in October 1944, he returned to his home town. He resumed his seat in the National Assembly a year later, and as a leading figure in the Catholic MRP *(Mouvement Républicain Populaire)*, he emerged at last as a national leader. At the time Monnet presented his plan, Schuman had headed the Foreign Office for almost three years.[22]

To appreciate Robert Schuman's contribution to the cause of European integration, one must recapitulate the conditions under which the plan was launched. Formulated in complete secrecy in the Planning Office, it was now entrusted to the persuasiveness of one man, born in the borderlands where the two merging countries had clashed so often. No other member of the Bidault cabinet had received so much as a carbon copy; neither industry nor financial circles in France had been consulted; and no attempt had been made to prepare the ground in parliament.

Battle-scarred parliamentarian though he might be, Schuman approved of this secrecy. Parliament, he felt, must deal with the finished product. Its function was to legislate, not to advise. Nor was he opposed to being the sole recipient, with Bidault, of M. Monnet's confidences. Unconcerned with economic affairs on a day-by-day basis, he believed that his office would be able to strike out more boldly than the technical departments.[23] This seemingly imprudent offensive was perhaps also a tribute to Jean Monnet's audacity. He may well have realized that the Foreign

[22]A satisfactory resume of Schuman's career is Charles Ledré, *Robert Schuman, pélérin de l'Europe* (Paris, 1954).

[23]Robert Schuman, "Origines et élaboration du 'Plan Schuman,'" *Les Cahiers de Bruges,* III (1953), 276.

Minister would surrender economic jurisdictions more readily than the colleagues of Industrial Production, Finance or Economic Affairs. In any event, Schuman immediately accepted full political responsibility for the enterprise and undertook to present it to the cabinet, where he did not anticipate strong opposition. It took only two meetings of the ministers to overcome all objections.

The first foreign statesman to be informed of the impending step was the American Secretary of State, Dean Acheson. On May 7, he arrived in the French capital, three days before a Big Three conference scheduled for London. Schuman called on him at the American Embassy, where the two conferred in the presence of the ambassador. A cabinet decision apparently had not been reached, for both David Bruce and the Secretary remember that Schuman merely described the project as having been discussed with his colleagues. He asked Acheson "to keep this communication in absolute confidence for thirty-six hours and, thereafter, to inform only the President until public announcement was made." The exchange was purely informative and constituted no request for American approval. Schuman wanted the United States "to know about the proposal, so that [she] would not be taken by surprise, [and] would have an understanding of its broad aims and potentialities . . ." He hoped that Acheson might agree to advise his government to favor it.[24] The entire conversation was primarily a display of courtesy. Considering American assumptions in the launching of the Marshall Plan, her policy on European recovery since that time, and the growing isolationist demands in Congress that no further aid should be granted until Europe was united, objections from Washington were most unlikely.

It seems that the French cabinet adopted the Schuman Plan on May 8, for on this day other governments were approached. In the case of Germany a personal letter from Schuman to Chancellor Adenauer was carried to Bonn, where it arrived on the morning of the 9th. The Federal Republic's prior agreement in principle was needed. Without it the announcement would have been meaningless. German assent was obtained immediately, and the famous press conference in Paris took place as scheduled. Two days later Schuman followed Acheson to London. The English accorded him

[24]Dean G. Acheson to writer, November 19, 1957.

a decidedly chilly reception, but American reaction more than compensated for their reserve. He had the approval that counted: the Schuman Plan was on its way.

The entire sequence of events constitutes one of the most unconventional maneuvers in the history of modern diplomacy. An age which had substituted the boorishness of shirtsleeve politics for the devious secrecy of the professional negotiator and replaced private ceremonial politeness with the frequent exchange of informal public insults confronted a promising alternative: the tight-lipped discretion of the diligent planner, coupled with the undiplomatic directness of the statesman who recognized his historic opportunity.

CHAPTER FIVE

From the Schuman Plan
to the European Coal
and Steel Community[1]

THE GOVERNMENTS OF WESTERN EUROPE HAD BEEN GIVEN ADVANCE
notice of the Schuman proposal, but businessmen read about it in
the newspapers. Their response was nevertheless generally favorable. No serious objections came from the Low Countries, although
Dutch coal and steel people had some doubts about whether the
plan would actually work,[2] and some Belgian industrialists became
openly worried after the gradual closing of some mines had been
predicted.[3] Conservative German apprehensions over a possible
conflict between European economic integration and their rearmament under Atlantic defense plans[4] were easily stilled by the en-
thralling prospect of ending the degrading tutelage exercised by
the International Ruhr Authority.[5] In Italy the fear of free market
competition was assuaged by the hope of finding in the partner

---

[1] The sequence of events from May 9, 1950 to the signature of the treaty on
April 18, 1951 has been chronicled by Georges Goriely in his unpublished
study, *Naissance de la Communauté Europeénne du Charbon et l'Acier*, a copy
of which was kindly put at the writer's disposal by the Press division of the
ECSC. The ratification debates are described by Henry L. Mason, *The European Coal and Steel Community, Experiment in Supranationalism* (The
Hague, 1955), 10-33.

[2] *Nieuwe Rotterdamse Courant*, May 11, 1950.

[3] Charles D. de Lespaul, "L'industrie charbonnierè et le plan Schuman,"
Bulletin de l'Institut de Recherches Économiques et Sociales, XVII (1951),
217-58, is a good example of this viewpoint.

[4] *Deutsche Zeitung*, June 10, 1950.

[5] Friedrich Lemmer, "Über den Schuman-Plan," *Deutsche Rundschau*,
LXXVII (1951), 392. That this advantage was also appreciated by some socialists can be seen from Heinz Potthoff, "Von der Ruhrbehörde zum Schumanplan," *Recht-Staat-Wirtschaft*, III (1951), 244.

countries work opportunities for the peninsula's unemployed.[6] Only French business interests were miffed by the secrecy with which the Planning Office had spun its web and concerned that a powerful international agency might curtail its freedom to an extent which their government had never managed.[7] Everywhere, however, thoughtful observers agreed that this complex scheme was really beyond judgment until it actually had been tried.[8]

A far more definite pattern of assent and dissent emerged in the political arena. Extreme Right and Left fought the plan every step of the way. In France, M. Schuman's failure to consult the deputies before speaking to the world prompted the Gaullists to submit a resolution which would have enjoined the government from sitting down at the bargaining table until the plan had received the National Assembly's formal approval. The Committee on Foreign Relations defeated the motion by one vote, despite its support by the powerful Communist membership. In June 1950, leaders of France's General Federation of Labor met with other Communist dignitaries in Berlin to discuss tactics for fighting European integration. The result was the manifesto of July 4, in which Communist parties of six West European countries—Germany, France, Italy, Holland, Belgium, and Luxembourg—attacked the proposal on the grounds that it was dictated by American imperialists in preparation for war against the Soviet Union and the people's democracies.[9] Everywhere the extreme Left now posed as defender of that national interest betrayed by Schuman, "the servant of the '*Comité des Forges*'," and by Adenauer, the "friend of Krupp."[10] The specific enemy varied from country to country. In France Communist propaganda, in unwitting conjunction with the Gaullist, Gaston Palewski, conjured up the specter of German economic domination. In Belgium it predicted the wholesale deportation of

---

[6]ECSC, CA, *Die Debatte über den EGKS-Vertrag in den nationalen Parlamenten* (Luxembourg, 1958), 94-96.

[7]*Le Monde,* May 22, 1950; see on this subject H. W. Ehrmann, "The French Trade Associations and the Ratification of the Schuman Plan," *World Politics,* VI (1954), 453-81, and by the same author *Organized Business in France* (Princeton, 1957), 407-08.

[8]Lemmer, Über den Schuman-Plan," *loc. cit.,* 387, was one such neutral voice.

[9]*Le Drapeau Rouge* (Brussels), July 4, 1950.   [10]*Ibid.,* September 22, 1950.

unemployed miners to the Aachen pits. East of the Rhine it fore-
saw continuing enslavement by Allied interests.

The parties of the Center stood solidly behind Schuman in spite
of reservations among some business groups. Notable divisions
occurred, however, within the Socialist movement. To begin with,
the parties in Belgium, France, Italy, and the Netherlands en-
dorsed the plan. The Dutch Labor Party and the Italian followers
of Giuseppe Saragat held firm throughout the bargaining and constituent phase. In France support had been predicated on eventual
British participation. Disappointment of this hope lessened enthusiasm, but led to no change in policy.[11] In Belgium, however, Paul-
Henri Spaak's spokesmanship of integration was not universally
accepted. The Belgian Federation of Labor demanded that the
treaty should give equal weight to social and economic problems.
It struck a responsive chord in timid hearts when it insisted that
free-enterprise Belgium could not join Schuman's Grand Design
without disaster. A "new deal" for the country's mines was described as essential if the coal industry was to survive without protective tariffs.[12] Articulate, though not unanimous, opposition
came from the German Social Democrats. The bitter personal feud
between their leader, Kurt Schumacher, and Konrad Adenauer assured rejection of any measure bearing the latter's stamp of approval. Schumacher's assertion that his party's "solution remained
Europe, not Europe, Inc.," was glib rather than convincing. Party
rank and file and organized labor took a more positive view, and
union leaders in general successfully defied the political cadre on
this issue.[13] In the case of Germany's and Belgium's socialists, the
road from the Schuman Plan to the European Coal and Steel Community was a thorny peregrination, accompanied by much inner
conflict and soul-searching.

[11]See Ramadier's comments in the National Assembly as reported in *Le
Monde*, July 27, 1950. During the ratification debates Felix Gouin demanded
an early accord between the community and the United Kingdom. ECSC, CA,
Die Debatte . . . , 30-31.

[12]*Le Peuple*, May 16, 1950.

[13]Cf., the report of the German correspondent of the *Neue Zürcher Zeitung*,
May 12, 1950. For more detailed analysis of the reactions of the SPD and the
unions see Karl-Wilhelm Ulrich, "Réactions allemandes," *Documents*, No. 6
(1951), 526-35. As late as 1957 a SPD member of the Bundestag complained
bitterly to this writer that Adenauer had "bought" the Unions with the promise of co-determination in industrial management.

The French Foreign Office, meanwhile, began to look for partners in integration. Since the original proposal had dealt with the fusion of French and German heavy industry, Jean Monnet arrived in Bonn on May 23 to open talks with both the Allied High Commissioners and Chancellor Adenauer. His visit was very well received in Germany since it underlined French sincerity and emphasized the decisive role assigned to the young Federal Republic. Following agreement on preliminaries, France three days later asked the remaining Western European countries, including Great Britain, to indicate a similar readiness to begin conversations. The response was rapid, and on June 3, Germany, France, Italy, Holland, Belgium, and Luxembourg agreed to deliberate on the basis of the French draft.

Britain's refusal to join the chorus of assent came as no surprise to the initiated. Had there been hope, would not Jean Monnet have crossed the Channel before he crossed the Rhine? London refused to accept Schuman's supranational principle, which would have removed control of key industries from the sphere of national jurisdiction. Though it was a Labor government which assumed responsibility for this refusal, it reflected an attitude shared by Britons of all political hues. Winston Churchill's early interest in European union notwithstanding, events proved time and again that such a stand could be expected only from British statesmen out of office. In the summer of 1950, at any rate, His Majesty's Government insisted that it could not take part if this implied prior acceptance of a supranational authority. Schuman and Monnet did not yield. They spurned compromise on this issue, and the conference began and finished its labors without the British.

Proceedings opened in Paris on June 20, 1950. Their history will be hard to trace, even after all participants have told their story, because the only documentary evidence of the conference is contained in a series of drafts that tell little about the progression of the talks. But their broad course has long ceased to be a secret. Although a working document prepared by Jean Monnet urged that the conferees confine themselves to creating institutions with wide powers, postponing considerations of functional details and technical problems until a later date, strong dissent from almost every quarter led to a different course of action. This resistance was in considerable part a defiance of the author's autocratic personality. As *Commissaire général* of the French Planning Office, Jean Monnet was one of the most independent operators in his country's administration. Moreover, he expected to be appointed to the presidency of the organization which would emerge from the discussions just begun. Hence he wanted to secure for this office the greatest possible freedom and reserve for himself and future collaborators full control of operations. The other delegations understood what he was after and insisted on a precise treaty instrument. They not only distrusted the studied vagueness of Monnet's initial text; they were also alarmed by the generous interpretations given to it by his associates.

The inevitable compromises were not invariably losses. On the positive side, the treaty became a thoughtful and precise tool for the operations of the Community, reflecting the consensus of six nations rather than the planning genius of a few enthusiastic technocrats. On the negative side, the immediate stemming of Monnet's drive allowed a multiplicity of parochial interests to try to whittle away at the grandeur of his conception. After the first stunning impact of the announcement had worn off, industrial groups, labor unions, ministers of transport, economics, and finance—in short, everybody who had something to lose, or thought he had—came with a bill of particulars which "had" to be taken into account before the work was finished.

As a result, negotiations moved forward on two levels. The chief delegates made the decisions. This group was dominated by Monnet himself, Secretary of State Walter Hallstein of Germany, a genuine supporter of integration, and Dirk Spierenburg of the Netherlands. These three men pushed successfully for the substantial acceptance of the supranational principle while the heads of the other delegations confined themselves to fighting the rearguard action of national interests. The "horse-trading" was done in the so-called *commission des six,* headed by Étienne Hirsch, who later succeeded Monnet as head of the French Planning Office. Three of its members—C. B. Balladore-Pallieri (Italy), F. Vinck (Belgium), and R. Hamburger (Netherlands)—were to become directors of the High Authority.[14] Under this *modus operandi* the representatives

[14]In discussing some of these initial conflicts here and elsewhere, the writer

of the six governments took ten months to produce an expertly
fashioned instrument of one hundred articles. Their work provided
answers to both institutional and technical problems and set forth
in solid detail the purpose and range of the European Coal and
Steel Community.

The original Schuman Plan had provided for a High Authority
endowed with extensive general powers and a parliamentary control organ to be called the Common Assembly. In the face of opposition, led by the Low Countries, the institutional structure of
the community-to-be was spelled out in much greater detail. This
vanguard of the smaller nations not only insisted on a long bill of
particulars, describing the powers of the High Authority, but also
demanded a Council of Ministers to maintain effective liaison between national and supranational institutions. The Belgian delegation, which has generally been credited with leading this charge,
argued in its support that all federal organizations included a body
representing the component states. The Belgians further contended
that in an enterprise of partial integration omission of this feature
would lead to unqualified disaster. Since it was recognized that
many advocates of European union associated such councils with
delay and inertia, the proposal was modified to provide that the
ministers under the Schuman Plan would in most instances *not* operate under the unanimity rule. These mitigating conditions made
the "necessary evil" acceptable to all.[15]

Both Germany and the Benelux countries demanded the creation of a Court of Justice before whom acts of the High Authority
could be challenged on the basis of the treaty. This additional curtailment of executive power was accepted, but it did not end the
controversy over composition and prerogatives of the High Authority. With the small nations once more in the vanguard, the original
proposal limiting this body to five members and leaving a description of its functions to later deliberations was overridden. Unanimity was not reached until April 1951, when the number was fixed
at nine, giving each participating country at least one seat, but not

---

had the benefit of contact with some of the negotiators whose information was
available on condition that the source of information not be divulged.

[15]Fernand Dehousse, "Belgique," *Notre Europe*, Nos. 11 and 12 (1952), 95
explains the Belgian stand on this issue.

more than two. Simultaneously, it was decided that the High Authority would raise its operating capital by a levy on coal and steel production: it would have the power to borrow money, and it could amass a reserve fund to finance the redeployment of surplus labor.

Outlining the scope of the activities of the Common Assembly produced only minor difficulties. As the parliament of an organization confronting questions of considerable technical intricacy, its deliberative role was confined to an annual review of community policies. Its chief weapon was to be the right of forcing the High Authority to resign, following a vote of nonconfidence approved by a two-third majority. All delegations agreed to allow the governments to retain the basic legislative task of amending the treaty. They were drafting an international compact, not a constitution; they were providing for a parliament, not a legislature. Yet harmony on this point led to a serious oversight: in its relations with the Assembly, the High Authority would have to account for past actions. Its future policies, on the other hand, would be beyond the grasp of assembly control.

The negotiators, instead of dealing with this substantial question of structure and policy, wrangled endlessly over the status of the Saar. On May 9, 1950, it will be recalled, the Germans had agreed to join the Consultative Assembly of the Council of Europe. They thus accepted, temporarily at least, membership in an organization where this productive valley was represented by a separate delegation. Now they took legitimate advantage of the indispensable part assigned them in the forming of the new community and refused to accept a similar settlement for the Common Assembly. The mines and foundries of the Saar would have to be covered by the treaty. That much was clear. But who was to speak and sign for them? France insisted that binding action should be taken by her government, which represented the territory in international affairs. Adenauer feared that this would prejudice Germany's future claims and might imply that Germany accepted France's control of the Saar's foreign relations. Personal negotiations with Schuman resulted in a purely negative solution, publicized in an exchange which stipulated that "the French Government does not consider the signature by the Federal Government of the Treaty . . . to constitute recognition by the Federal government of the present status of the Saar." This compromise was later crowned by the peaceful transfer of the region to Germany, thereby proving the extent to which Germany and France had become capable of burying the past.

At the outset of the parley, the French had also been compelled to accept the fact that the signing of a treaty would have to be preceded by a lengthy explanation of the technical details of community operations. As early as June 23, the conference agreed that the effect of the plan on the national economies would have to be studied. " 'We must know where we are going,' this is the common preoccupation," reported a Belgian newspaper.[16] The principle of supranationality had been accepted before the first meeting in Paris. The opening of a common market for coal and steel was likewise supported by the six powers. Yet the implementation of these ideas raised a number of vexing questions. French and German views differed on the speed with which the markets were to be unified. The Paris government persisted in favoring the immediate abolition of tariffs and trade restrictions since this had been one of the key points of the Schuman Plan.[17] German opposition rested on the fear that a common market would raise steel prices because it also required the abolition of national price controls. On November 4, 1950, the recently appointed minister of the interior for the Federal Republic, Robert Lehr, described the Schuman Plan as a measure designed to protect Germany's competitors abroad while steeping her economy in inflation at home.[18] His statement voiced the apprehensions of enterprises using half-finished steel products, essential for reconstruction and export, who anticipated the ruination of both their domestic and foreign business. It is unlikely that Chancellor Adenauer shared these reservations, or that the Germans in Paris consistently opposed the French on this issue.

But incidents like the Lehr speech, unexplained and inexplicable at best, were viewed with the utmost seriousness, particularly by American observers. Up to November 10, 1950, U. S. comments on the Schuman negotiations had been "exclusively and informally" transmitted to the French. Henceforth, the need "for additional U. S. action designed particularly to assist in removing these obstacles

[16]*Le Soir* (Brussels), June 24, 1950.   [17]*Ibid.*, November 2, 1950.
[18]*Neue Zürcher Zeitung,* November 5, 1950.

to agreement" was recognized. Above all, it was deemed necessary to emphasize in Bonn that continued support of the Schuman Plan was in the German interest while the growing support of some steel producers for a private steel cartel was not. Original American enthusiasm for the Schuman Plan had rested on the desire to "pave the way for full integration of Western Germany into Western Europe."[19] If Germans were to turn their back on this project, "it might even be desirable to go to [the] point of making clear to them [that the] U. S. will not support further expansion [of] steel plant, unless Germany reaffirms its original position."[20] The German delegation in Paris, although it was no doubt sensitive to the fluctuations of domestic opinion, had done nothing to justify this attitude. The French approach to and conception of a common market prevailed, without prolonged toe-to-toe combat.

Consequently, all delegations were forced to deal with the effects that the opening of a unified market might have on the Belgian coal industry. High costs of labor and of operation, resulting from extensive and prolonged exploitation of areas such as the Borinage, had raised prices substantially above the West European average. Belgian mines could not compete with those of Germany, France, and Holland. Free trade might force their closing and result in considerable unemployment. Although a few Belgian observers challenged such gloomy prophesies, pointing out that a large percentage of Belgian mine labor came from abroad,[21] the Brussels government insisted on special protection as condition of eventual signature. It wanted a five-year grace period, during which her coal prices would be kept artificially competitive through a subsidy fund maintained by contributions from Germany and Holland, whose coal sold below the community average. The Germans understandably took a dim view of this plan. Belgium was prospering, and the crisis in this sector was not representative of her general economic condition; on the contrary, it could be directly blamed on reckless and inefficient methods of exploi-

[19]United States, Department of State, "The Current Status of the Schuman Plan, DRE Divisional Report 1.6, September 8, 1950." 7.

[20]United States, Department of State, "Telegram prepared by ECA for clearance in the Department of State to Embassy Paris, November 10, 1950."

[21]Cf., the interview of the Belgian deputy Delattre (Mons) in *Le Monde,* November 20, 1950.

tation. A Dutch newspaper at the time reported a German counter-offer to employ idle Belgian miners in Germany.[22] Neutral negotiators have since denied that this thought was ever entertained by the German delegation. They have pointed out that the difficulties encountered by industrial resettlement projects within Belgium were sufficiently well known and in themselves would have been enough to doom any "deportation" scheme. The record shows that the Germans finally withdrew their objections, and the Belgian entrepreneur won his case.

The Belgian victory was accepted with mixed feelings. The ensuing subsidy regimen benefited the Belgian mine owner, who could continue to milk an aging cow at the expense of his government and the more efficient industries of neighboring countries. Some conference participants have insisted to this day that Belgium should have entered the common market without reservation, and that the funds expended to shore up her moribund mines could have been used to better advantage by training Belgian miners for other jobs and paying them a subsidy during transitional unemployment. These critics have rested their verdict on the belief that the days of the coal industry in Belgium were numbered regardless of all efforts to postpone the inevitable.

A heated controversy developed over treaty provisions dealing with the control of cartels and monopolies. Jean Monnet and his staff believed in the creation of genuine competition in heavy industry. They therefore advocated that the treaty prohibit the establishment or continuation of economic combinations in restraint of trade. This viewpoint, modeled on American theory and practice, was new to most Europeans, but it was stubbornly defended by the French delegation, whose members recalled that past cartels had *reduced* production, whereas the Schuman Plan intended to increase it. German and Belgian negotiators objected that this meant undue regulation of business activities and would promote jurisdictional conflicts with the national governments. But France perservered for reasons that cannot be explained on grounds of principle alone. Her delegates knew that unless some limitations were imposed upon the future formations of cartels, fear of German re-

[22]*Nieuwe Rotterdamse Courant*, December 11, 1950.

covery would defeat the treaty in the National Assembly.[23] This hard fact may explain why a German delegation, committed to the Schuman Plan, gave in once again and accepted the French proposal as a basis for negotiation.[24] There is evidence of some American pressure to achieve harmony,[25] but above all it seems clear that the Bonn representatives were bent upon the liquidation of the International Ruhr Authority, hoping that this would give German industry more freedom than it could otherwise enjoy under any circumstances.

In parallel negotiations with the occupying powers on the same subject, Germany agreed to abolish within two years the coal sales monopoly in the Ruhr, to prohibit a specified group of large steel concerns from controlling more than 75 per cent of their coal supply, and to continue the de-concentration of large industrial combines. A detailed agreement, recognizing twenty-eight steel producers, the largest of whom—Dortmund-Hoerde—had an annual capacity of less than three million tons, provided the blueprint of a decentralized production structure. The majority of French opinion was, therefore, satisfied when Schuman explained this plan to the Foreign Relations Committee of the Council of the Republic, and added that "the treaty would not weaken the guarantee and controls now in effect in Germany." This satisfaction grew out of the totally mistaken impression that the European Coal and Steel Community would replace the Allies as watchdog in the Ruhr. The wall of incomprehension between a complex technical project and Paris parliamentarians was all but insurmountable. Senator Michel Debré, the leading opponent of the Plan in the upper house, warned his colleagues of their error. That he was one of a minute faction of politicians who actually read the treaty is perhaps less surprising than the apparent French belief that Germany would support the Schuman Plan even if it contained provisions that continued to place her industry in a particular and inferior position. What Germany claimed, and won, was the formal assurance that the International Ruhr Authority would be dissolved as soon as the European Coal and Steel Community was born. Allied legislation in

[23]*Le Monde*, June 21, 1950.   [24]*Ibid.*, November 18, 1950.
[25]*Ibid.*, March 5, 1951 and April 13, 1951; *The Times* (London), March 6, 1951.

regard to German cartels was nowhere mentioned in the pact. Nor did it contain any other specific allusions to German industry. It merely affirmed that the community would watch over business organizations in restraint of trade while keeping silent on *recon-centrations* that fell short of that specification. These provisions would apply to *all* member countries.

Finally there was the problem of the proposed common market's geographic scope. From the outset it had been agreed that Tunis, Algeria, and Morocco were to be excluded.[26] Italy, exceedingly dependent on iron ore from Algeria, protested and demanded the inclusion of its departments or a special agreement assuring her supply. After she had made her signature contingent on the redress of this grievance, a meeting between Premiers René Pleven and Alcide de Gasperi led to the agreement of Santa Margherita on February 14, 1951, which guaranteed Italy continued access to France's North African iron ore and removed the entire question from the Paris agenda.

It was clear to all participants that the European Coal and Steel Community would exercise substantial economic functions. But in addition the Schuman Plan had definite social objectives, among them "equality of progress in the improvement of working conditions for the workers of the coal and steel industries."[27] Did this mean that the High Authority would be empowered to prescribe uniform wage scales for the new common market? Countries like Belgium and Luxembourg, whose salaries were at least reputed to be high, favored this interpretation. Since a new supranational authority certainly would not set out by alienating labor through a reduction of pay rates, it might under this provision raise minimum salaries in the other countries. This would slow the competitive tempo of the common market by equalizing one element of production costs.[28] By the same token, Germany, Italy, and the Netherlands feared that raises in the coal and steel industries would upset the delicate balance of their closely regulated economies. They were joined by trade unions throughout the community, who did not want direction of the wage structure on an industry-wide basis,

[26]*La libre Belgique,* November 8, 1950.
[27]Goriely, *Naissance de la Communauté Europeénne,* 45.
[28]Leon Metzler, *Le Plan Schuman dans la perspective luxembourgeoise* (Luxembourg, 1951), 44.

but preferred to bargain with governments and employer representatives on the national level. The apprehensions of the low salary areas were well founded. A wave of increases in two industries would force governments to unshackle wages and prices elsewhere and contribute to inflationary pressures.

The debate on the pay issue was complicated by the absence of any sound comparative wage statistics or international indices of purchasing power, without which a valid policy was unthinkable. For the time being, it was therefore inevitable that the community's control over salaries would be quite restricted. High Authority action in this sector was confined to providing advice in emergencies. It was a foretaste of the problems of partial integration. In an area in which the governments retained legal control and public responsibility, the High Authority could not also assume exclusive jurisdiction. The same doctrine prevailed in the discussion of labor mobility in the common market. Here the shoe was on the other foot, and Italy—a country with low wages but an overabundance of workers—favored maximum freedom of migration. Germany, on the other hand, opposed such a policy on two counts: she could not afford to lose her highly skilled put poorly paid workers, nor could she replace them with relatively untrained Italian migrants whose job-preparation would be complicated by language problems. The negotiators found no exit from this impasse and merely recommended that restrictions of movement be eliminated, "subject to the limitations imposed by the fundamental needs of health and public order." These would, of course, be determined by the national administrations.

The social question yielded one dividend, however. From the point of view of national arithmetic, the composition of the nine-member High Authority was fraught with complexities. After it had been agreed that France and Germany should each nominate two members, and the remaining countries one, a vacancy remained. Would its incumbent be an Italian or a Benelux national? In order to avoid conferring this distinction on one, and thereby offend the sensibilities of the other three, it was decided that the ninth oligarch was to be proposed by labor and coöpted by the other eight. This procedure was not incorporated into the treaty, but it became part of the unwritten law of the community.

Details of organization kept delegations and foreign ministers in feverish activity until the last moment. The choice of the community capital was the subject of several fruitless sessions, some of which lasted all night. No decision emerged, and Luxembourg became the *siège provisoire* when the treaty was signed by all six partners on April 18, 1951. "Printed in Louis XIV type with German ink on Dutch vellum," it was to be "bound in Belgian parchment and adorned with a marker of Italian silk."[29] Each member thus made a contribution which, it was hoped, would be symbolic of a similar harmony of effort and function in the community.

One great battle had been fought and won. Now the result of eleven months of negotiation had to be guided through the treacherous and turbulent shallows of parliamentary debate.

In countries where opposition was confined to the Communists, the treaty was ratified in due course. Holland accordingly passed it first and with the most substantial majorities.[30] Luxembourg's Chamber was the last legislative body to debate it, waiting until May 1952, but this was due to a comparatively involved constitutional procedure. Once begun, adoption was a foregone conclusion, since France, Germany, and Belgium had by then ratified.[31] In Italy's Chamber of Deputies, the combined forces of communism and neo-Fascism could not prevent a decisive 265 to 98 vote in favor of the treaty.

The Communists everywhere persisted in casting themselves as champions of national sovereignty. In Holland and Luxembourg they had the field to themselves. Elsewhere their efforts were seconded by the apprehensions of the Right. In France, where the Constitution of 1946 permitted the signing of international agreements involving reciprocal renunciation of sovereignty, Gaullist representatives maintained that Germany was not yet sovereign and therefore was unable to match French concessions in this regard.[32] Among the majority of the National Assembly, which fa-

[29]*The Times* (London), April 18, 1951.
[30]36-2 in the first, 62-6 in the second chamber.
[31]G. D. of Luxembourg, Chambre des Députés, *Session ordinaire de 1951-52*, 1611.
[32]Anon., "La ratification du traité instituant la Communauté Europeénne

vored the agreement, this was taken as the argument of ingenuous obstructionism, and it made no apparent converts. In the Belgian Senate, in turn, non-Communist objections to the impending transfer of sovereignty were answered no less deviously by Foreign Minister Paul van Zeeland. He maintained that a treaty freely entered into was a legitimate exercise, rather than a limitation, of sovereignty. The constitution nowhere prohibited it, and members should be guided solely by the merits of the issue and their country's interest.[33]

Exchanges of this kind must not be taken to indicate a widespread and vigorous constitutional debate. Treaties inevitably involve some surrender of sovereignty, so that the problem was one of quantity rather than principle. In Italy the question was not raised. In Holland the constitutional paragraph dealing with national sovereignty was amended *after* the treaty had been ratified to avoid possible later complications. In Germany, as in France, the constitution expressly permitted commitments of the nature specified in the treaty establishing the European Coal and Steel Community. It was rightly pointed out in the Luxembourg Chamber that the idea of unlimited sovereignty for small nations was anachronistic regardless of constitutional law. The same viewpoint animated the remarks of Senator Dehousse of Belgium, who told his colleagues that the "poor girl," Belgium's Constitution, had been violated so many times in the past that her virtue was becoming the object of growing public indifference.[34]

There remained, however, a good deal of general suspicion concerning the manner in which the powers of the new community might be used, and there also remained the abiding distrust between Frenchmen and Germans. In France the widespread fear of the powerful High Authority, formulated at the outset by an apprehensive business community, had not abated. German socialists expressed disappointment over the restrictions imposed on the

---

du Charbon et de l'Acier," *Chronique de Politique Étrangère*, VI (1953), 12, hereafter cited as "La ratification du traité . . ."

[33]Belgium, Sénat, *Session 1951-52*, 344.

[34]Robert Als, "Le Plan Schuman dans la perspective luxembourgeoise," *Société Belge d'Études et d'Expansion, Bulletin Bimestriel*, LI (1952), 665-66; for Belgium see Sénat, *loc. cit.*, 60-68, which includes that portion of the committee report dealing with the constitutional aspects of the treaty.

Common Assembly and what they considered the inadequate representation of Germany, as the largest producer of the six, in both the executive and parliamentary sphere.[35] Although a court had been added to the Community's institutions on initial German insistence, hostile voices were now raised in Bonn warning that the judges would pass sentence according to national rather than supranational lights. In moments of truth, however, both Frenchmen and Germans had to admit that they feared each other more than the problems of the future. In this connection, some critics in Paris were appalled to learn that the treaty would bind them for the next fifty years.

Elder statesmen whose memories reached back to the beginning of the century recalled it as a time of Anglo-French rivalry, preceding the *Entente Cordiale*. This perspective highlighted the transformations wrought by one half-century and made the contemplated economic merger with an "unknown" Germany appear as a prohibitive risk. Would the next fifty years be equally cataclysmic? Would the school children of the '50's feel as out of place in the year 2000 as their grandparents did at mid-century? In more immediate and down-to-earth terms, would this new and unexpected association with another recent enemy draw France into an eventual conflict over the Oder-Neisse line? Could France effectively defend herself against possible future onslaughts from her eastern neighbor once her key resources and plants fell under supranational management? These political fears were supplemented by an abiding economic inferiority complex. The lowering of customs barriers among the six treaty partners, it was prophesied, would open the French market to Germany's vigorous steel industry. This would raise the steel production of the Ruhr and cut German exportable coal surplus, thus adding to the fuel shortage in other community countries. Gradually they would become economic satellites of the Federal Republic.[36] To many Frenchmen, Commu-

[35]Kurt Schumacher, *50 Jahre mit gebundenen Händen?* (Bonn, 1951), 14-15; an anonymous pamphlet *Was bringt der Schumanplan?* (n. l., 1951), rejected this viewpoint, holding that the Coal and Steel Community would only be effective if it included both producers and consumers.
[36]"La ratification du traité . . ." 12-16; the French viewpoint is also ably summarized by Frederick Sethur, "The Schuman Plan and Ruhr Coal," *Political Science Quarterly*, LXVII (1952), 515.

nist leader Jacques Duclos put it crudely, but by no means implausibly, when he said: "You have the choice of voting for Krupp or for France."[37]

No one really understood the common market. Its assumption that increased production in Germany would entail an upsurge which would, in one form or another, affect the entire unified area did not occur to these critics. If the production of steel reached levels sufficiently large to exhaust the coal supply, then the industries of the common market would be sufficiently prosperous to import fuel into the community. Besides, would German coal be more freely available to producers *without* a common market? The fact was, of course, that the national markets continued to dominate the outlook of conservative business and the radical Left. They could not conceive of conditions they had never experienced and whose impact they lacked the imagination to envisage.

In the French Council of the Republic General de Gaulle's supporters attacked Schuman's failure to safeguard possession of the Saar, rightly seeing in the treaty a tacit agreement to its eventual return to Germany.[38] Even after the expected government victory, the Senators instructed it to watch carefully over the execution of the common market plan and embark on a financial and economic course which would give French industry "the means of fighting successfully against foreign competition."

Some of these misgivings were unquestionably prompted by arguments advanced by supporters of the Schuman Plan on the German side. One plea sounded particularly ominous to French ears:

... for Germany we must ask whether the Schuman Plan will allow her to meet the competition of her treaty partners. She brings to the community fifty-one percent of West-European coal production. However, her hegemony is one of quality as well as quantity, because she has a virtual monopoly of the high grade coal which is needed for the production of steel. Prices of German coal add to her advantage, which is important, for price is the measurement applied in the judgement of a producer. Under the Schuman Plan the cheapest producer

[37]France, Assemblée Nationale, *Séance de 1951*, 8024.
[38]France, Conseil de la République, *Séance de 1952*, 725.

is the best. But the best producer will receive investment capital from the community, so that he may modernize and rationalize his installations and increase his output. Thus the Federal Republic should, as the best producer of coal, receive substantial investment aid which private sources so far have been unable to provide. . . . At the same time the inefficient mines in Belgium and France will be closed in the course of the next five years, so that their marginal production will cease to exercise an unfavorable effect on the coal prices of the European market.[39]

This was the national argument in reverse. It was as unsound as the fears of those who claimed that their own economies were making unique sacrifices which would benefit only foreign competitors.

Not all Germans looked at it that way. The socialists formulated some of the same objections which were encountered on the French side. They, too, protested against the length of the commitment. What would happen, asked their leader Kurt Schumacher, if the French elections of 1951 were to bring General de Gaulle to power? In view of the uncertain political future of France, could one responsibly conclude an economic alliance with her for the next fifty years?[40] Like the French opposition, he went on to ask: in what adventures will this embroil Germany? "In the final analysis the Schuman Plan is a treaty whose German contribution was made by . . . the High Commissioners of France and the United States."[41] This point of view pictured the Federal Republic, in turn, as the economically inferior member of the new partnership.[42] With increasing competition, the socialist critics expected Germany to fall further and further behind. Since the war, they argued, France had built a modern industrial apparatus while Germany had done no more than salvage a desperate marginal existence from ruins and dismantled installations. The deconcentration of cartels into smaller less efficient units of production was likewise

[39]Heinz Naupert, "Die Grundlagen des Schuman-Plans," *Der Betrieb*, V (1952), 41-42; see also H. W. von Dewall, "Schuman-Plan und Bergbau," *Bergfreiheit*, XVI (1951), 1-5.
[40]Schumacher, *50 Jahre mit gebundenen Händen?*, 18-20 [41]*Ibid.*, 6.
[42]Fritz Hellwig, "Die deutsche Eisen-und Stahlindustrie innerhalb der Europäischen Gemeinschaft für Kohle und Stahl," *Bergfreiheit*, XVI (1951), 9-10.

adduced as a serious handicap. Since the treaty only affected concentrations created after its coming into force, French industry would not have to follow Germany on the road of de-cartellization and could maintain its advantage. As French observers had worried that a growing German steel capacity might swallow up the Ruhr coal surplus, so Germans feared that the common market would drain her coal mines to such an extent that she could no longer supply such old and cherished clients as Sweden. If her economic relationship with the Scandinavian power should suffer, how would this affect the flow of Swedish iron ore to the steel mills on the Ruhr?[43] It was a strange debate, with socialists defending cartels, and opposing internationalization of the economy. But these arguments made no impression on the friends of the Schuman Plan. Return of economic sovereignty and the access to larger markets required no justification in their eyes, and these benefits were not called in question by the socialist attack.

Even the final charge on the Saar compromise, which placed the social-democratic opposition in the same posture as certain members of the French Right, did not stall passage of the treaty. Rather than see in the exchange between Schuman and Adenauer a prelude to the return of this small but vital region, Schumacher's acolytes were furious that the French instead of the German government signed the treaty on its behalf. It prompted them to reject ratification "equally as international socialists and as German patriots."[44]

Finally the parliaments approved the Paris compact one by one. In France, where opposition had been especially varied and determined, the inevitable nature of the event was demonstrated by the speed with which matters took their course. Was the debate really serious? Would the French Assembly refuse to ratify a French plan? On November 30, 1951, the Foreign Affairs Committee of the National Assembly approved ratification 26 to 18. On December 11, a motion on the floor to return the bill to committee was defeated 376 to 240, and two days later the measure itself passed by an almost identical vote. The bulk of the opposition came from 97

[43]A. Vosen, "Für und wider den Schuman-Plan: Ökonomische Argumente in der Debatte des Bundestages," *Mitteilungen des Westfälischen Instituts für Wirtschaftsforschung, Essen*, III (1952), 25-29.

[44]Schumacher, *50 Jahre mit gebundenen Händen?*, 22-23.

Communists and 116 members of the Rally of the French People.
The main supporters were 105 socialists, 87 catholics, 71 radicals,
and 65 independents and farm-bloc members. The Council of the
Republic followed suit after a week's debate, with a decisive margin: 182 to 32. This time the partisans of Charles de Gaulle abstained. The Communists cast the only hostile vote.

In Germany the SPD simply did not have the votes to defeat the
measure. Notwithstanding Schumacher's eloquence, his warning
of new barriers against east and north, notwithstanding his bitter
denunciation of "the presumption of those who misuse the European idea in the service of Greater France,"[45] his supporters could
do no more than go down fighting. The government's position was
fortified by the impending liquidation of the International Ruhr
Authority. German rights in the Saar had been explicitly recognized. The socialist concern for a "real" European union was questioned by Heinrich von Brentano, who asked Schumacher's successor, Erich Ollenhauer, why a support of European integration must
express itself in bitter opposition to the first major step in that direction. In the end, the socialists stood alone, and on January 11,
1952, the Bundestag ratified by a vote of 232 to 143.[46]

In Belgium the debate was prolonged and complicated by a split
within the socialist party. The moderate left in the Senate offered
to vote for the treaty if the government accepted a detailed reorganization plan. Without this plan, the socialists insisted, Belgium
could not meet the challenge of integration.[47] Failing to gain majority support for this compromise, they generated audible surprise
by meekly abstaining. In the Senate 102 ratified, 4 opposed, 58 sat
on their hands. In the Chamber the socialists were led by Paul-
Henri Spaak, and all but a few of their votes were cast with the
majority of 165 against 13. Among the few hold-outs, however,
were such prominent leftist leaders as Achille van Acker and
Edouard Anseele.

The socialists' dilemma in Belgium was real and profound. On
the one hand, they feared that the competition on the common market might result in extensive unemployment. That this nightmare

[45]Kurt Schumacher, *Macht Europa Stark!* (Hanover, 1951), 18.
[46]Anon., "Le débat sur le plan Schuman au Bundestag," *Réalités Allemandes*,
No. 37 (1952), 45-55.
[47]Belgium, Sénat, *Session de 1951-1952*, 78-82.

exercised a powerful sway can be appreciated if one recalls that the Great Depression at its height had idled a larger percentage of the labor force in Belgium than in Germany. On the other hand, as members of a party with an international tradition, they were naturally attracted to any scheme that promised to break down those barriers of nationality which Marx had taught them to deride as artificial. As in Germany, their stand was complicated by union pressure in favor of ratification. Organized labor apparently had more faith in the special safeguards of Belgian interest provided by the treaty than some socialist members of parliament. In any case, the lop-sided final vote did not reflect either the tight struggle or its critical nature. Belgian accession was important, and it was closely contested. Without the participation of this industrially saturated country, surrounded on all sides by the territory of other members of the community, the success of the Schuman Plan would have been jeopardized.

Following Luxembourg's ratification in May 1952, the treaty could go into operation. The capital of the Grand Duchy had been accepted as the temporary home of the European Coal and Steel Community. The time had come to go to work. Personnel had to be found to staff those institutions through which the Plan was expected to integrate the economies of six nations. Their powers and relationships are discussed in the chapters that follow.

PART THREE

THE INSTITUTIONS OF THE EUROPEAN COAL AND STEEL COMMUNITY

CHAPTER SIX

The High Authority: An Executive and Legislative Directory

THE TREATY THAT WAS SIGNED AND RATIFIED BY GERMANY, FRANCE, Italy, and the Benelux nations created a community whose goals were exclusively economic and social, with the latter aspect, according to some, running a poor second. The aims of the European Coal and Steel Community were economic expansion, increased employment, and the improvement of the standard of living. These goals were to be achieved by the most efficient distribution of goods and the highest possible levels of productivity and by the avoidance of basic and persistent economic disturbances. There must be no drastic lay-offs in the name of efficiency, no radical and precipitous experiments at the expense of any single interest. The treaty demanded transformation while eschewing revolution. The Community must provide a regular supply of coal and steel to the common market. All consumers "in comparable positions" must have equal access to all sources of supply. Prices were to be kept at the lowest possible level, consistent with the realizing of a reasonable profit and the maintenance of continuous production. The aim was a situation conducive to sound expansion. Finally, the Community must assure the improvement of the working and living conditions of its labor force. Thus the treaty required a balance between the three elemental economic interests of society: capital, labor, and consumer.

Parallel with the prohibition of economic and social preferment went measures forbidding practices designed to protect the national markets of old. Duties, or their equivalent, and publicly financed subsides—duties in reverse—were outlawed. It became equally unlawful for producers, consumers, and governments to resort to discriminatory or monopolistic practices in pursuit of goods, markets, or profits. A free economy must be restrained neither by national nor by private interests, neither by state nor by business action.[1]

To gain these ends, the framers of the treaty abandoned the approach of functional integration, practiced by the OEEC, in favor of institutional integration. At the base of the Schuman Plan was the conviction that integration could not be taken for granted until there existed ways of enforcing and preserving agreement. Dropping trade barriers was one thing, keeping them down another. Moreover, artificial stimulants might be needed to revive an initially sluggish free-trade area. "Permanent free trade," could not be "attained without the transfer of powers to supranational authorities."[2] The European Coal and Steel Community was to provide the first great test of this rule.

Policy-making roles in this process were assigned to the High Authority and the Council of Ministers; and though the former was not granted the sweeping and unique powers contemplated by the original Schuman Plan, its supranational complexion was sufficiently novel and striking to put it constantly in the limelight. Its leading position was spelled out in Article Eight of the treaty which specified that "the High Authority shall be responsible for assuring the fulfillment of the purpose stated in the present treaty under the terms thereof."

The High Authority, it will be recalled, was to consist of nine members appointed for a term of six years and eligible for re-election. Initially, eight seats on this college were to be filled by appointment through unanimous action of the Council of Ministers. The last member was chosen by simple majority vote of the High Authority itself. During the group's first term, all vacancies would be filled by unanimous agreement of the member states. Thereafter the first eight would be appointed by a five-sixths majority, the ninth coöptively. Subsequent to the beginning of the second term, three members would retire every two years, and later appointments would be made alternately by the governments and by High

[1] *Treaty Instituting the European Coal and Steel Community* (Luxembourg, 1952), Articles 2-4, hereafter cited as *Treaty*.

[2] Rolf E. Sannwald and Jacques Stohler, *Economic Integration, Theoretical Assumptions and Consequences of European Integration*, tr. by Herman F. Karreman (Princeton, 1959), 255.

Authority coöption.[3] The national veto power over reappointments was limited to two, and excess vetoes could be nullified by the Court.

If a member's service was terminated by resignation, he was required to stay on until the appointment of a successor. This provision was violated in 1957, when Vice-President Franz Etzel became German minister of finance, and vacated his post at once on the assumption that simultaneous holding of national and supranational office constituted an impropriety. A member could also be removed by the Court on petition of his colleagues or the Council of Ministers, for "gross error," or on the basis of the conflict of interest provisions of the treaty. A successor was appointed, provided the unexpired portion of the term exceeded three months.[4]

After naming the members of the High Authority, it became incumbent upon the Council of Ministers to designate a president and two vice-presidents for a two year term. Unless the designation coincided with the election of an entire new slate, the nomination of these officers was to follow consultation with the High Authority.[5] On the surface of the treaty their function was purely administrative and involved no additional power or responsibility; merely a higher salary.[6] In practice it developed, however, that the president, or one of the two vice-presidents in his absence, spoke for the High Authority both before the Assembly and in the Council of Ministers. Despite the provision of collective responsibility, an early tradition identified the officers of the High Authority as the primary spokesmen of executive policy.

The treaty further specified that membership in the High Authority was confined to member nationals. Not more than any two of these, it will be recalled, were to be citizens of the same country. In practice this meant that both France and Germany each claimed two seats while the other nations contented themselves with one. However, since membership in the Community remain-

---

[3]This leaves one question: Does 'alternate' mean that the first three will be filled by the governments and the next three by coöption, or will the process alternate with each individual? Institut Royal des Relations internationales, *La Communauté Europeénne du Charbon et de l'Acier* (Brussels, 1953), 29, 29n.

[4]*Treaty*, Arts. 10-12. [5]*Ibid.*, Art. 11.

[6]Communauté Europeénne du Charbon et de l'Acier, *Journal officiel*, March 24, 1954, hereafter cited *JO*.

ed open to any country disposed to subscribe to the treaty, the initial equilibrium need not be permanent. In addition, the Council of Ministers could by unanimous vote change the size of the High Authority.

Far more important than numbers, however, was the additional proviso that the oligarchs of the High Authority must "exercise their function in complete independence in the general interest of the Community." They must not accept or solicit instructions from private or official sources while the governments pledged "to make no effort to influence the members of the High Authority in the execution of their duties." Article Eleven of the supplementary *Protocol on the Privileges and Immunities of the Community* provided that members were to enjoy on the territory of member states "immunity from legal action for acts performed by them in their official capacity including their speeches and writings," and that "this immunity shall continue after their functions have ceased." The decisions of the High Authority, therefore, were expected to reflect well-considered, collective, and independent judgments, guided solely by the interests of the Community. They were not to search for compromises between six separate national interests, or between national interests on the one hand and Community interest on the other.[7] Their job was to execute the treaty, not arbitrate between its signatories. This independence was further safeguarded by outlawing any professional activity, paid or unpaid, or the holding of interests in the coal and/or steel industry during a member's term of office, "or for a period of three years thereafter."[8]

At the time the treaty was signed, many observers considered these provisions unrealistic. They did not believe that men born in an age of nationalistic hypertension and the adulation of material success would exercise political or economic judgments independent of these forces. What has been the experience? To begin with, the Europe of 1950 was no longer the Europe of 1939. Before the war, the installation of the Coal and Steel Community would have been unthinkable. A dozen years later, six nations that had been at

[7]Netherlands. Staaten-Generaal, *Zitting 1950-51, Document No. 2228, Goedkeuring van het op 18 april 1951 te Parijs ondertekende verdrag tot oprichting van de EGKS . . . ; Memorie van toelichting* (The Hague, 1951), 10 hereafter cited as *Memorie van toelichting*.

[8]*Treaty*, Art. 9.

war only recently agreed to relinquish substantial elements of their sovereignty. They had entered freely into this close collaboration; they had consented to abandon the pursuit of narrow national goals because of the overriding importance of naked survival. It was, therefore, not so much a question of whether the members of the High Authority might be capable of living up to the treaty, but rather of whether any of the signatories could afford to sabotage it. Who would want to risk the whole experiment for some temporary local advantage? In other words, conditions favored compliance with seemingly idealistic postulates. To some extent at least national and supranational interests had become identical. No one since then has been able to accuse the High Authority of violating its oath. Critics may fairly claim that it has been conservative in using its powers, but it has never been vulnerable to the charge of showing partiality to any given national or business interest. Nor have events confirmed a German socialist contention that it would always "listen to the American purveyors of capital, fronting for the United States government."[9]

The dilution of the national interest was accompanied by a change in the nature of economic pressure. The common market, though planned and initiated without extensive consultation of business, became a fact to which business had to adjust. One outward result was the formation of market-wide trade organizations by the coal, steel, and scrap industries. Once the Community existed, its subject industries found it neccessary and profitable to break down in turn the barriers between national economic pressure groups. This was true regardless of their original attitudes toward the Schuman Plan. In fact, "the groups most fearful of the consequences of a large common market," came to be "the ones most consistently look[ing] to supranational action for their future welfare."[10]

Nevertheless, it remains true that a member of the High Authority may continue to live in two spheres: national and supranational politics. An appointee may be a leading political figure in his country, gaining additional prestige from membership in the ECSC gov-

[9]Anon., *Der richtige Weg? Eine sachliche Würdigung des Schuman-Plans* (n. l., Soziale Arbeitsgemeinschaft der SPD, n. d.), 10.

[10]Ernst B. Haas, *The Uniting of Europe; Political, Social and Economic Forces, 1950-1957* (Stanford, 1959), 339.

erning board. At the same time, his appointment deprives him of vital grass-roots contacts and forces his prolonged absence from the deliberations of his government, his parliament, and his party. While he climbs new heights of international eminence, he runs the risk of losing at home the essential base from which his career was launched. To what extent might the approval and attitudes of his old constituents and associates affect his actions in Luxembourg? At what point would he prefer the safety of his established orbit at home to the continued risks of the untried and intangible benefits of his position in the Coal and Steel Community?

During the presidency of René Mayer (1955-1957), it was rumored that he would resign to seek a seat in the French Council of the Republic. Observers on the spot still insist that he left Luxembourg in 1957 as a result of having had to surrender his seat in the Chamber, when in fact he did so to accept a directorship in the SOFINA holding company.

The case of Franz Etzel affords another inconclusive illustration of the same problem. His political career had begun after 1945. The son of a farmer, he had saved money as a miner to finish *gymnasium* and study law. After a tremendously successful career in corporation practice, Etzel founded and led the Christian Democratic Union in Duisburg and was elected to the first Bundestag. He quickly rose to the chairmanship of the Committee on Economic Policy, and was sent to Luxembourg as a safe, sane Adenauer man. For five years he was Vice-President of the High Authority. A sober, systematic and able executive, he pulled more than his weight in the ECSC, and it was therefore all the more disappointing when he resigned at the end of 1957 to become minister of finance in the third Adenauer cabinet. Was this another case of pressure operating in reverse? In the course of the guessing game for Adenauer's successor, the name of Etzel cropped up occasionally, but hardly as more than a dark-horse prospect. As early as the summer of 1956, his imminent appointment as vice-chancellor was rumored. The king's demise or retirement moving inexorably closer—though not as rapidly as many anticipated—was it a case of every pretender wishing to abide as close to the throne as possible? In short, was Etzel surrendering the Vice-Presidency of the High Authority for a possible shot at the highest political office in the Federal Republic?

In actuality, Etzel's dilemma was not as simple as that. His return to Bonn might have been the move of ambition, but of an ambition as much European as German. It was designed to deepen the European complexion of the cabinet. Here the strongest figure, apart from the Chancellor, remained Ludwig Erhard, minister of economic affairs. This rotund, cigar-chewing Bavarian was prominently associated with the functional integrationists who saw the OEEC as a perfect instrument of economic unification. His influence faced substantial curtailment as Adenauer prepared to confine his jurisdiction to the domestic sphere while transferring international economic relations and the problems of integration to a new ministry of European affairs under Etzel. This maneuver would have reduced Erhard's position in the cabinet and his chances as Adenauer's successor. It pointed to the Chancellor's preference for a crown-prince of unequivocally "European" views. Erhard demurred and with success. He could not prevent his rival's return but managed to side-track him into the ministry of finance. Another supranational partisan had been added to the Adenauer coalition, but his effectiveness was limited from the outset. Not only was Etzel's move, therefore, for "Europe" as much as Germany; there is good reason to believe that had he known at the outset where he would land, he would have opted to remain in Luxembourg.

Equally baffling was the case of the first Italian appointee to the High Authority: Ezio Giacchero. A handsome man with the profile of a Roman emperor, he was a track star in his youth and a professor of engineering at the Polytechnic of Turin at the age of twenty-three. As a parachute captain, he lost one leg in North Africa and was discharged from the army in 1942. Despite this infirmity, he recruited a Resistance volunteer division in Piedmont during the following year and occupied the prefecture of Asti under the United States Military Government. Within four years of his election to Italy's first postwar parliament in 1948, he had risen to the vice-chairmanship of the Christian Democratic group. Scarcely forty, he was called to Luxembourg.

Again the observer will ask himself whether it was good politics for a rising young politician to leave the national scene at this stage in his career. Giacchero was a natural choice for the High Authority because he had been active on the European scene. Early in his parliamentary career, he met Coudenhove-Kalergi, of whose postwar inter-parliamentary organization he became a vice-president. He joined several other European groups and committees, notably associating with the European Federalists. His government dispatched him to the Consultative Assembly of the Council of Europe, where he chaired the Commission for Scientific and Cultural Affairs. His promotion to the High Authority gave to Italy a representative versed in the game of politics, technically qualified and suitably prominent in European affairs. Yet during his tenure of seven years he played a disappointingly inconspicuous part in the affairs of the Community. His replacement by Piero Malvestiti, another Christian Democrat, in 1959 did not, as in the case of Franz Etzel, result in a spectacular return to national politics. So far, Giacchero's service in Luxembourg has been an unrewarding cul-de-sac. Some Italians at the ECSC from time to time expressed a private feeling that it might be a considerable asset to have remained apart from and undefiled by the odoriferous atmosphere of recent Italian politics. But as that country's political crisis shows no sign of abating, there is no indication of his returning as savior to displace the current tarnished contingent of potential prime ministers.

Less evident and well-known is another factor which makes for national-supranational ambivalence. Whenever the High Authority confronts a decision that requires consent of the national governments, each member goes home to feel the pulse of his compatriots. Before the last word is spoken, an attempt is made to identify the possible sources of national resistance and to devise formulae by which resistance may be overcome. Besides functioning as Community spokesmen in their own country and with their own governments, High Authority members will frequently address industrial and labor groups in order to generate sympathy and understanding for their work. Thus their liaison role may serve to align Community action with national realities or to convince important sectors of public opinion that cooperation with the ECSC and its policies is in their own and the general public interest.

The relation between the national and the supranational theater of political operations is complex and opaque. Nor is this conflict of loyalties and ambitions exclusively political. In an economic policy group, a man's past business associations are bound to be equally, if not more, telling. René Mayer's unexpected return to business, rather than politics, has been mentioned. Other members of the High Authority were from the outset identified with well-defined economic interests. Léon Daum, a former mining engineer and steel executive, was appointed not only because of his obvious qualifications, but also to quiet industrial fears of a hostile supranational technocracy. Since he was sixty-five years old at the time of his appointment, there was little question of the repercussions which this new position might have on a future career. But there were doubts concerning his effectiveness. Although his services have been above moral reproach, he has been far less insistent on a rigorous application of treaty articles on discrimination and cartels than other members of the Community's executive. Without deviating from the High Authority's record of honest independence, his views and policies were predictably bound to reflect the convictions of a long and successful industrial career.

By the same token, Paul Finet's service to the Community has been affected by half a century of service to the labor movement. This ninth, coöptive, member was chosen precisely because his presence completed the portrait of a true community rather than a potential association of entrepreneurial interests. Born and reared in Belgium's industrial belt near Charleroi, Finet had served in the ranks of his country's unions before becoming Secretary-General of the Belgian Federation of Labor after the great general strike of 1936. Since 1949, he had been president of the International Conference of Free Trade Unions. On the High Authority he became the logical spokesman on social questions.

An entirely different case was the resignation of Jean Monnet. For two and a half years, the first President of the High Authority guided the Community's early crucial steps. Then in 1955 he packed his briefcase and left. He went back, not to home-front politics, where he had never played a public role, nor to the distilleries of his forebears. Rather he resumed the battle for Europe, endangered by the French National Assembly's refusal to ratify the Eu-

ropean Defense Community treaty. Visionary and planner rather
than administrator, he felt that the time had come to lead another
forward push, leaving the day-to-day conduct of Community affairs to others. He passed from one stage but not from the scene.

Former civil servants of ministerial rank seemed to be most im-
pervious to the outside pressures of former associations. Leaving
their places in the administrative hierarchies of their nations, they
surrendered old privileges and seniorities for advancement. Therefore even the most cynical observer could agree that they had every
reason to represent the Community with the greatest possible zeal.
This applied to Albert Wehrer, Luxembourg's former ambassador
to Germany, and Dirk Spierenburg, former Director-General of
Foreign Economic Relations in the Dutch Ministry of Economic
Affairs. The latter's superb bargaining talents produced a brilliant
blend of economist and diplomat. He became the chief negotiator
for the European Coal and Steel Community in its relations with
other international bodies and third countries and the most suave
and articulate defender of its policies. A member of the first High
Authority in 1952, he was reappointed by lot to another full six
year term in 1959. He may go down as the most significant servant
of this first of European communities.

The High Authority stands at the focal point of many interests
and pressures. So far no breath of scandal has touched it. No single
influence has unduly prevailed. Criticism has claimed now a soft-
ness toward capital or labor, now timidity in the face of national
pressure, and then again an unrealistic disregard of the political
realities that go into the making of a community of nation states.
What remains pertinent here is a final examination of the possible
collective significance of the changes which have taken place in the
High Authority during the first decade of its history.

Superficially, the original nine may be divided into five categories. Three members were recruited from top-level political circles,
holding either cabinet rank or a leading position in the government
party. This would include Franz Etzel, Ezio Giacchero, and Albert
Coppé, at the time of his appointment Belgian Minister of Reconstruction. Comparable business echelons were represented by the
two French members, Jean Monnet and Léon Daum. The top civil
service stratum, just below ministerial rank, entered the High Au-

thority in the persons of Dirk Spierenburg and Albert Wehrer. Paul Finet exemplified the fourth category, a labor leader who had presided over both national and international labor organizations. Only socialist Heinz Potthoff, the second German member, might be considered as having operated on a more modest eminence. Since 1951, he had been German chief delegate on the International Ruhr Authority, during a time when the liquidation of that organization was imminent and when a seat at its deliberations was no longer a choice appointment, assuming that it ever had been in German eyes.

There were still other ways by which the members of the executive, individually and collectively, might be labelled. Monnet was not chosen because of his business experience, but because he had headed the French delegation to the Schuman Plan parley. Spierenburg of Holland and Wehrer of Luxembourg had served in the same capacity. While one of the French members of the High Authority was thus recruited from among the "European" technocrats, the other—Léon Daum—was deliberately chosen to represent conservative steel interests who viewed the Community with unconcealed antipathy. Germany sent Franz Etzel, on the one hand, Europe-minded, prominent in the CDU, and a corporate lawyer with an extensive heavy-industrial clientele; on the other, Heinz Potthoff, a supporter of the opposition in the Bundestag, sharing its reservations vis-à-vis the ECSC, and, through union and career experience, identified with the coal industry. To go a step further, one might also point out that after the appointment of a lukewarm Social-Democrat from Germany, it seemed advisable to choose a more enthusiastic exponent of the European dream on the Left in the person of Paul Finet. Thus the entire membership was grouped around a hard core of "founding fathers," Monnet, Spierenburg, and Wehrer, but it also included pro- and anti-European spokesmen of industry (Etzel, Daum) as well as of labor (Potthoff, Finet).

Jean Monnet was the first of this original team to resign in the wake of France's rejection of the EDC treaty. There was quick agreement that his successor would have to fill his shoes in a double sense: as member and as president of the High Authority. The new *primus inter pares* would have to guide the Community through the storm unleashed by the French failure to endorse the second step toward a united Europe. He must be prominent as well as a dedicated proponent of the new order. Nothing was perhaps more ironical than to seek the savior of Europe in the country which had just dealt such a stern blow to the new utopia. But the assignment was ably completed with the appointment of René Mayer. Connected with the circles of high finance through maternal descent from the House of Rothschild, he had played an important role in the profitable nationalization of the railroads of Northern France. Moreover, since the war, he had held a variety of ministerial posts as well as the premiership on one occasion. From the prestige point of view, Mayer was certainly an equivalent replacement for Monnet, and in terms of administrative and political experience, he was probably an improvement.

In January 1958, Franz Blücher, Vice-Chancellor of the Federal Republic, became Franz Etzel's successor. While his previous rank certainly reflected luster on the group he was about to join, it was rumored that he went unwillingly and considered the appointment a distinct demotion, perhaps even a form of political burial.[11] Etzel's departure also coincided with the resignation of René Mayer, which constituted a much more marked prestige crisis in the history of the High Authority. With the impending installation of the Common Market and Euratom, Mayer had done his job. The ECSC had survived the EDC crisis, and Europe was about to take another step forward. In addition, his presidential term was about to expire, and the general question of whether or not a president of the executive would quietly step back into the ranks could assuredly be answered in the negative, where both Mayer and Monnet were concerned. The two men had started at the top. Unless they were appointed to new terms, they were bound to seek new fields of activity elsewhere. A former French premier, in particular, was inconceivable as a mere member of the High Authority, especially after it had ceased to be the only European executive.

Mayer's successor was chosen from a different category and from

[11]Blücher was probably disgruntled for not also succeeding Etzel as vice-president of the High Authority. By 1958 the Common Market and Euratom were beginning operations. To the one Germany furnished the president of the Commission (Walter Hallstein), to the other the vice-president (Heinz Krekeler). Hence the Federal Republic willingly, and to Blücher's detriment, gave up the vice-presidency in Luxembourg.

a different generation. Roger Reynaud had been a high civil servant in the ministry of finance, though not on the directoral level, and a member of the executive committee of the French Christian labor movement. At forty-two, he was the second-youngest man ever to be appointed. Whatever his qualifications and abilities, which appeared considerable, his nomination seemed to indicate that members of France's first political and economic team were unwilling at this point to accept a position in Luxembourg. In conjunction with the simultaneous elevation of Paul Finet to the presidency of the High Authority, there were also misgivings about Reynaud, a representative of labor, replacing a member who so palpably had come from a big business milieu.[12]

The most recent changes in the personnel of the High Authority have tended to redress the balance of eminence.[13] In 1959 Ezio Giacchero was replaced by Piero Malvestiti, equally prominent in the councils of the Italian Christian Democrats, a former member of several cabinets and, interestingly enough, transferred to Luxembourg from the Vice-Presidency of the European Economic Commission. He is the new President of the High Authority. The seat of Franz Blücher, who died on March 26, 1959, has been taken by Fritz Hellwig, whose background is the same as former Vice-President Etzel's. As past head of the German Industrial Institute he shares his predecessor's big-business associations while in the Bundestag he, too, has been chairman of the Committee on Economic Policy.[14] Léon Daum, finally, has been replaced by the French socialist, Pierre-Olivier Lapie, member of several French cabinets and past Vice-President of the National Assembly under the Fourth Republic. Inasmuch as his party was still playing a key role in the affairs of France at the time of his appointment, the shifts caused by the events of 1958 would not detract from his nomination. It highlights, however, a curious and unparalleled development: France, first represented by the two business magnates Monnet and Daum, then Mayer and Daum, now has on the High Authority both a socialist and a Christian labor leader.[15]

[12]See, for instance, *Frankfurter Allgemeine Zeitung*, January 9, 1958.
[13]These lines were written in February of 1962.
[14]Lindsay, *European Assemblies*, 185.
[15]Here, too, there is evidence of a certain amount of inter-agency horsetrading. The shift to the left on the High Authority has been counterbalanced by

On the whole, members of the High Authority have continued to be recruited from ministerial or equivalent positions. In terms of the distribution—politics, business, civil service, labor—the balance has shifted to the Left. The two original appointees from the civil service sphere are still on the job. The same is true of Paul Finet and Heinz Potthoff, both from socialist and labor backgrounds. Roger Reynaud is an addition to both categories, having been both civil servant and union official—though no socialist— and replacing a businessman-politician. Substituting a French socialist for Léon Daum constitutes a similar, even more radical change. The German and Italian newcomers, on the other hand, represent the same elements as their original predecessors. The important shift has come in the French membership of the High Authority. Lapie and Reynaud are further to the Left, and—if one may say so—less eminent than Daum, Mayer, and Monnet. This does not reflect on their persons, but on the importance assigned to their positions by the French government which nominated them.

High Authority decisions are made by simple majority vote. Five members constitute a quorum. In cases of exclusive jurisdiction, the nine issue decisions which are binding in all respects, or recommendations which prescribe objectives but allow every latitude, short of treaty violation, in the manner of accomplishment. Finally, they may render opinions which are purely advisory. Decisions and recommendations go into effect when they are received by the parties concerned or published in the *Journal officiel*.[16] The year's activities must be recapitulated in an annual report,[17] which is sent to the Common Assembly, the Council of Ministers, and the Consultative Assembly of the Council of Europe.[18] Since April 1956, the High Authority has also published quarterly estimates of prospects, activities, and policies regarding the common market.[19]

The members of the High Authority are jointly responsible for

a moderate to conservative preponderance on the EEC and Euratom commissions.

[16]Published in German, French, Italian, and Dutch.   [17]*Treaty*, Art. 17.

[18]*Ibid.*, Arts. 24, 77 and *Protocol on Relations with the Council of Europe*, Art. 3.

[19]*Treaty*, Art. 46, Sec. 2 and *JO*, April 30, 1956.

their actions. In an address before the Common Assembly, Jean Monnet provided the classic description of this aspect of its function: "In the work of the High Authority, everyone plays his part, in accordance with his [special] competence. . . . There is neither specialization nor delegation of powers. In its work and its decisions the High Authority preserves a collegiate aspect, just as its responsibility before you is a collective one."[20] The president, or either vice-president in his absence, occupies the chair during meetings, directs the administrative services, and assures the execution of all decisions. But in their drafting his voice counts no more, legally, than that of any member. This homogeneity of function notwithstanding, practically every one of the Community's *strategoi* has some special qualification which can be brought to bear on a particular problem. In such an eventuality *he* may formulate the decision, recommendation, or opinion, which—after majority assent, of course—goes to the public as a joint act.

From the very outset observers recognized a trend toward departmentalization[21] and debated its propriety.[22] As expert on problems of production and finance in the coal and steel industries and as arbiter of the common market, the High Authority cannot simply convene to dispose of every problem from beginning to end *in collegio*. Issues must be categorized and dealt with by smaller expert groups. Accordingly, the directorate of the ECSC agreed to divide into seven sub-committees of three to four members each. These sub-committees respectively prepare decisions in the following areas:

1) Market, cartels, and transport.
2) Investment and finance.
3) Social problems.
4) External relations.
5) General objectives and market research.
6) Administration.
7) Press and information.[23]

[20]Communauté Europeénne du Charbon et de l'Acier, Assemblée Commune, *Débats*, II, 214, hereafter cited as *Débats*.
[21]Institut Royal des relations internationales, 37.
[22]*Memorie van Toelichting*, 13.
[23]*JO*, November 24, 1954; also Henry J. Merry, "The European Coal and

Every member of the High Authority, therefore, belongs to two or more of these sections, whose chairman, however, may be regarded as the executive's expert in each particular jurisdiction. For example, Dirk Spierenburg has long headed the working group on foreign relations, and Paul Finet still presides over the preliminary deliberations on social problems. During his incumbence, Léon Daum guided the sector of investment and finance while Franz Etzel was responsible for common market, cartels, and transport. The external reflection of this procedure can be seen before the Common Assembly, where the working group chairmen generally report on High Authority activity in their sector and reply to questions from the floor.

Specialization does not end at this point. Nine men, no matter how they divide their work, cannot single-handedly collect information and make valid decisions in regard to a multinational industrial complex which produces, very roughly, 250 million tons of coal and 60 million tons of steel per year. The High Authority's decision-making force is, therefore, based on the labor of a number of administrative departments whose tasks parallel the working committee structure. Department heads serve the executive as a whole. They are responsible to the nine, not to the individual members in their capacity of working committee chairmen. These departments represent problem areas (Economics, Social Questions, Cartels and Concentrations, and External Relations), specific treaty functions (Common Market, Investments, Finance, and Transport), and services (which include the legal staff, the statistical division, interpreting and translating, press and information, and the secretariat).[24]

The secretariat operates the administrative machine, and is responsible for the coördination of work by the High Authority, working committees, and the departments. The secretary's task

---

Steel Community, Operations of the High Authority," *The Western Political Science Quarterly*, VIII (1955), 169n.

[24]Daniel Henri-Vignes, "Notes sur l'évolution institutionelle de la Communauté Europeénne du Charbon et de l'Acier," *Les Cahiers de Bruges*, IV (1954), 42-43. During 1959-60, this departmental organization was streamlined and simplified, the secretariat expanded to a secretariat-general. See Europäische Gemeinschaft für Kohle und Stahl, Hohe Behörde, *Achter Gesamtbericht über die Tätigkeit der Gemeinschaft* (Luxembourg, 1960), 22-23, hereafter cited as *Gesamtbericht* with preceding numerical identification.

transcends the customary routine of preparing the agenda and keeping the minutes of the meetings of the executive college. He keeps track of the work of each department and working committee, issuing a weekly report on the accomplishments of both. If a pending matter is not making reasonable progress, he prods the department concerned. If this produces no results, he brings the lag to the attention of the responsible working committee. On the basis of a weekly balance sheet, the secretariat compiles a bi-annual list of closed and pending questions. Furthermore, it maintains official day-by-day contact with the other institutions, such as the Assembly and the Council of Ministers. In 1952 the secretary was also the Community's press officer. From 1953 to 1959 this task was shouldered by a director for press and information. More recently, the secretary, now secretary-general, has resumed the task of being official spokesman of the High Authority.[25]

A policy question is first taken up by the High Authority at its weekly meeting, which generally takes place on Friday morning. It is then passed to the working committee or department under whose jurisdiction it falls. On the Saturday before each weekly gathering, the secretariat begins compiling the agenda on the basis of successive progress checks with the departmental secretaries. Wednesday is reserved for meetings of the working committees, at which time it is decided which of the pending issues are ready to be presented to the plenum. At the Friday conference of the High Authority, which is also attended by the Secretary and the divisional heads immediately concerned with a given item on the agenda, the decisions, recommendations, and opinions which the treaty exacts are formulated. Following their acceptance, they are published and communicated to the governments, firms, and individuals affected.[26] Finally, the High Authority may decide against final action in a specific case and return the matter to a working committee, with or without specific instructions for their guidance.

This summary describes routine procedures of the High Authority up to the reorganization of 1959. Even within these limits it is

[25]*Ibid.*, 22.
[26]Excepting those covered in *Treaty*, Art. 47, Sec. 2: "The High Authority shall not divulge information which is by its nature considered a professional secret and in particular information pertaining to the commercial relations or the breakdown of costs of production of enterprises."

far from exhaustive. Frequent and direct contacts among departments, between departments, individual members, working committees and the High Authority as a whole occur daily and hourly. Since the executive establishment is far from Pentagon-sized, direct and frequent personal meetings on all levels, and between all levels, take place constantly. The following schematic presentation (see Chart I) attempts merely to identify the main channels of activity and the areas of responsibility, without tracing the countless human exchanges characterizing any large enterprise, and which happily elude generalization.

Thus far the emphasis has been on the High Authority as the executive of the European Coal and Steel Community. Here its functions are quickly described: it carries out the treaty, through decisions, opinions, and recommendations. In this microcosm the former takes the place of a constitution, and the latter are the laws of the Community. The High Authority, therefore, makes and executes the laws, within a strictly circumscribed orbit.

The nine men at 2, Place de Metz in Luxembourg frame operational legislation. To carry out their mission, they levy a tax on gross coal and steel production. The maximum limit to which they may go is set by the treaty, but the specific rate is determined by them. In times of shortage or depression, the executive may regulate the volume of production and distribution. Again, its decisions are legislative acts to meet specific situations, which the treaty merely covers in general. In the controversial realm of cartels and concentrations, the treaty outlines its powers, but the Community executive rules on specific cases. Finally, the treaty gives it authority to levy fines against enterprises which fail to execute decisions that the High Authority is entitled to render under its provisions. Here it sits in judgment, though its "sentences," like all other decisions, may be appealed to the Court of the European Coal and Steel Community.

The powers concentrated in the hands of the High Authority make that body easily the most determinant in the Community. Since it executes, legislates, and even adjudicates, there can be no question of a well-defined separation of powers. There is no sphere

CHART I
ECSC—Organization of Executive Responsibility, 1952-59

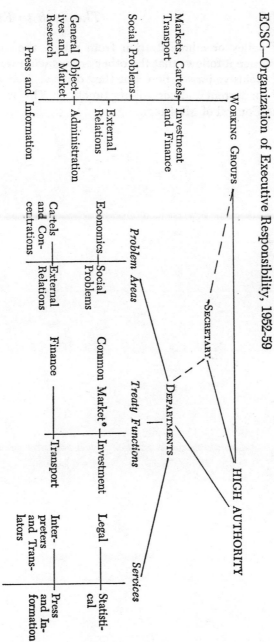

WORKING GROUPS

Markets, Cartels, Transport —— Investment and Finance

Social Problems

General Objectives and Market Research —— External Relations —— Administration

Press and Information

Problem Areas

Cartels and Concentrations —— Economics —— Social Problems —— External Relations

Treaty Functions

Common Market* —— Investment —— Finance —— Transport

Services

Legal —— Statistical —— Interpreters and Translators —— Press and Information

"SECRETARY"

DEPARTMENTS

HIGH AUTHORITY

*Unlike the other departments this has two members of directoral rank—one for coal, one for steel.

————— Channels of Authority

— — — — — Channels of Supervision

of policy or administration from which the nine are excluded. Whence it follows that the other organs will exercise little by way of exclusive jurisdiction. But they do have a considerable number of concurrent and controlling functions. This is true, above all, of the Council of Ministers.

CHAPTER SEVEN

Political and Corporate Liaison:
The Council of Ministers and
The Consultative Committee

THE ORIGINAL SCHUMAN PLAN DID NOT PROPOSE A COUNCIL OF MINIS-
ters. Its authors hoped to avoid any compromise with national interests. Before 1950, experience, notably in the Council of Europe,
had shown that the veto of sovereignty paralyzed international institutions and that specific national representation would, therefore, conflict with the supranational aspirations of the future European Coal and Steel Community.

Two circumstances abetted compromise. First, the Benelux countries feared their own economic absorption by the industrial giants,
Germany and France, and demanded a Council of Ministers in
order to protect their economic integrity. In addition, a more thorough analysis of the Monnet blueprint revealed that in a project of
sector integration the supranational community could not function
unless continuous liaison with member governments was provided.
This second argument was most frequently advanced in the successful attempt to make the Council palatable to the more enthusiastic advocates of European union.

At the outset of the Community's history, the Council, directly
representing the participating governments, played an indispensable constituent role. It was identical with the foreign ministers
who, in April 1951, put the finishing touches to the treaty, agreed
on the first eight members of the High Authority, and finally determined such technical details as salaries and emoluments of the
governing body.

Under the provisions of the treaty after adoption, the Council of
Ministers was endowed with the general function of "coördinating

107

the activities of the High Authority and of the governments who {remained} responsible for the general economic policies of their countries." To this end, the two were to "consult together and exchange information," and the Council could ask the High Authority "to examine all proposals and measures which it {might} deem necessary or appropriate for the realization of the common objective."[1]

These provisions reveal two relationships. Whenever the High Authority adopts policies that can be expected to affect national industries outside its immediate jurisdiction, it must consult the Council of Ministers. On the other hand, the Council may prod the governing board to take measures which it considers essential for the welfare of the Community and which the executive has for some reason failed to initiate.

When the High Authority approaches the Council, it may be for consultative purposes only. Such rapport is prescribed, for instance, when the Community is about to act against a state whose policies interfere with free competition in the coal or steel industries.[2] Retaliative action against members or enterprises which pay abnormally low wages must be preceded by ministerial *pourparlers*.[3]

Other steps of the High Authority require concurrence from the Council by simple majority vote. Financing of industrial research,[4] and the promotion of new enterprises to increase employment fall into this category.[5]

Another type of proceedings demands a consonant two-thirds majority. Unless it is obtained, the tax levied on production, the Community's chief source of revenue, may not be raised above 1 per cent of the value of the gross [6] A fairly intricate course of mutual counsel must be followed in connection with the training and resettlement of surplus labor. Ordinarily the Community may grant financial aid if the government concerned will provide matching funds. Under special circumstances, however, the entire burden may be assumed by the High Authority, provided two-thirds of the Council back the project.[7]

Unanimous consent of the Council is mandatory before the ex-

[1]*Treaty*, Art. 26.   [2]*Ibid.*, Art. 67.   [3]*Ibid.*, Art. 68.   [4]*Ibid.*, Art. 55, Sec. 2. [5]*Ibid.*, Art. 56b.   [6]*Ibid.*, Art. 50, Sec. 2.
[7]*Ibid.*, Art. 56c. Article 56 was amended on February 10, 1960. See *Bulletin der Europäischen Gemeinschaft für Kohle und Stahl*, IV, No. 2 (1960), 41-42.

ecutive can institute special financial mechanisms to safeguard the smooth operations of the common market,[8] or before it can respond to Community needs in ways not specifically enumerated in the treaty.[9]

In these instances, and the list is illustrative rather than complete, the policies of the Community affect the entire national economy and are of obvious concern to the governments and their representatives on the Council.

In other sectors of High Authority-Council collaboration, the first step may be taken by either side. During times of depression, the executive may establish production quotas to assure a maximum distribution of demand throughout industry. Once the crisis has passed, these quotas must be withdrawn. In either case a concurrent majority in the Council is prescribed. The process is analogous when the excess of demand over supply results in a critical shortage of goods or raw materials. But should the Council of Ministers under both circumstances feel that the time for such action has come, while the High Authority holds the contrary view, it may by unanimous vote force the executive to establish quotas. Should the High Authority decide to abolish them, the Council may reverse that decision in the same manner.[10] The identical regimen governs inauguration and termination of price controls.

The treaty, therefore, provides a number of instances in which the High Authority must consult or obtain the consent of the Council in order to act. The initiative rests with the executive, except in three major instances where the Council may initiate policies only if the High Authority fails to recognize or respond to an emergency. On the whole, the treaty establishes the Council as the conservative force in the supranational constellation. Its basic purpose is to see that integration remains partial and that the Community does not usurp powers of economic control at the expense of the governments.

While the treaty sets forth in some detail the duties and prerogatives of the Council of Ministers, its actual work goes on behind closed doors. It is by far the most secretive of all Community agen-

[8]*Treaty*, Art. 53b. [9]*Ibid.*, Art. 95. [10]*Ibid.*, Arts. 58-59.

cies, confining public relations to the issuance of a sparse communiqué after every meeting. Each member has one seat and one vote.[11] So far it resembles all such councils currently in operation. But in the European Coal and Steel Community, the ministers' work follows new and different paths. In cases requiring mere consultation, it need not vote at all, but merely forward a copy of its minutes to the High Authority. Unanimous action is required only in a specific minority of instances. Concurrence by simple and qualified majority is both new and intricate.

With the present membership of the Community, a simple majority, four votes out of six, is identical with a two-thirds majority. Until the pool expands, therefore, a distinction between the two is meaningless. But the treaty mentions other qualifications that go beyond the counting of heads. Germany and France cannot be outvoted by the other four countries. Though unanimous agreement may not be required in many cases, the assenting votes must always include at least one country producing a minimum of 16⅔ per cent "of the total value of coal and steel produced in the Community."[12] There can be no valid majority without one of the two great powers. When a High Authority petitions for simple or qualified concurrence and the Council vote results in a tie, the request will be deemed carried after a second reading whenever the three affirmative votes include those of Germany and France.[13] These two expedients avoid the alternative of granting two votes to the two major producers, a solution which, it was feared, would permanently deadlock the Council whenever the Big Two opposed the Little Four of the Community.

The Council represents the governments specifically and individually, but without allowing them the unlimited enjoyment of their sovereign status. For it, too, is an autonomous institution of the Coal and Steel Community, one of several charged by Article Three of the treaty with the operation of the common market for coal and steel. The proviso that "the Council shall communicate with the member states through . . . its president," underscores the fact that the total is more than the sum of its parts.[14] A report from an individual member to his government does not have the force of an

---

[11]*Ibid.*, Art. 27.   [12]*Ibid.*, Art. 28, as amended on January 1, 1957.
[13]*Ibid.*, *loc. cit.*   [14]*Ibid.*, *loc. cit.*

official act of the group. Additional confirmation of this can be derived from those provisions of the pact which allow the High Authority to challenge individual states for failure to live up to their obligations, but which give the executive no right anywhere to act against the Council as a whole.[15]

The membership of the Council, furthermore, is far more fluid than that of comparable organizations. The treaty does not say *which* minister shall represent a government. At the outset, a few gatherings convened under the traditional diplomatic aegis. With a rotating chairmanship, changing alphabetically by country every three months, Chancellor Adenauer as German Foreign Minister became the first President of record. Since then, Council seats have more often than not been occupied by policymakers in economic affairs. The attendance at a conference depends on the agenda. Some sessions have brought together six ministers of labor. Others were held by the heads of transport. The forty-first meeting on February 7, 1957, for instance, boasted a roll of sixteen ministers and secretaries of state, and an agenda including general economic, social, and transport problems. Gatherings of this size may break up into two or three work sessions before the plenum convenes to give its final verdict. As far as one can determine from the outside, the ministers of economic affairs occupy a senior position at these high-level mass meetings even when other departments are represented by men of full cabinet rank. Other colleagues follow their lead and defer to their dispositions and do not seem to determine policy on their own. (See Chart II.) Under different circumstances a country might be represented only by a top-level, but non-voting, civil servant, deputizing for his superior. In such cases another minister is empowered to vote by proxy for not more than one absent Council member.

The meetings of the Council of Ministers take place at irregular intervals approximately once a month. In the interim, a secretariat headed by a secretary-general and a fluctuating variety of committees, similar to the expert commissions of the OEEC, carries on. This sub-structure functions in accordance with the Council's rules of procedure, which the treaty consigns to its discretion.

[15]*Ibid.*, Art. 88. Art. 33 gives the Council the right to sue "for the annulment of decisions and recommendations of the High Authority."

In this picture the Coördinating Committee, COCOR for short, is of overriding importance. Chaired by the Secretary-General, and composed of high-ranking civil servants from the national ministries of economic affairs,[16] it brings continuity to the Council's activities. Ministers come and go with the tide of parliamentary politics. With two exceptions, however, the personnel of COCOR has remained strikingly constant. These men prepare for final disposition all matters taken up at the monthly sessions, and take from the Council questions on which no final decision has been reached. In such cases the ministers have been known to empower COCOR to complete action in accordance with ministerial instructions, and upon final agreement, their work is published as a Council decision. This key committee, furthermore, exercises great power by establishing precedence among matters that are brought to the Council's attention, although it is not a policy-making group under the law and its members as such are not subject to the directives and orders of the respective national cabinets. When in February 1957, for instance, a joint decision of the High Authority and the Council initiated a general study of national incomes and markets, COCOR was entrusted with planning the nature and extent of the inquiry. The Coördinating Committee is the Council's informal fact-finding and spade-working organ, through which it can initiate investigations without having to depend on either the High Authority or other Community organs for its information. It represents one of the most provocative implementations of the treaty, and it deserves detailed and continuous study.

Since it initiates, supplements, and sometimes completes ministerial action and since it controls the entire fact-gathering mechanism of the Council of Ministers, the Coördinating Committee regulates the composition and activity of numerous standing and *ad hoc* committees. The coördinators nominate the members of the two standing groups for tariff and foreign trade, as well as the many expert bodies convened for specific one-shot purposes. Such technical advisory groups need not represent every country. If a given issue is of no concern to a member, he is obviously free to remain unrep-

---

[16]*E. g.*, a *Ministerialdirektor* in the case of Germany, Director-General for Holland and Belgium, while Italy has generally been represented by her ambassador to Luxembourg.

resented. The decision, again, lies with the representative on CO-COR.

In conclusion, then, the Council of Ministers, which has included as many as three ministers from each country when the occasion warranted, usually meets once a month. Between sessions a permanent coördinating committee carries on its work. This committee prepares business for the Council meetings, completes unfinished items in the Council's name, and appoints and controls the work of the other standing and *ad hoc* committees. It is the animator of a system of national checks on the supranational authority.

While the Council of Ministers was clearly intended to limit the powers of the High Authority, it does not follow that the two are rivals. Both groups have no choice but to exercise their prerogatives and to discharge their duties. They have usually done this without excessive friction or antagonism. There is no evidence that the ministers have persistently whittled at the powers of the High Authority, either by advocating an unduly strict construction of the treaty or by seeking amendments to the Community's disadvantage. Ever since the treaty went into effect, the Council has met with reasonable regularity to consider those questions which were consigned to its jurisdiction. It has run true to form, however, in a disappointing lack of initiative. It has responded to requests for consultation and has rendered opinions and decisions as required by the treaty. But rarely, it seems, has it tackled problems without prior High Authority prodding. The 1957 decision to study and survey the common market, taken at the request of the Luxembourg member, whose country produces no coal and is particularly vulnerable to fuel shortages, may constitute the only exception to this rule. Even here, however, action was taken jointly with the executive, and at the conclusion of the session Luxembourg's problem was dumped into the lap of the executive. In a deadlock the governments not only refuse to stand on the prerogatives of sovereignty, but (like the states in the American federal system) are only too happy to take an aspirin and leave the headaches to the federal agencies. A similarly generous viewpoint prevailed at a later meeting dealing with coal shortages at the retail level. Although the treaty might

Chart II

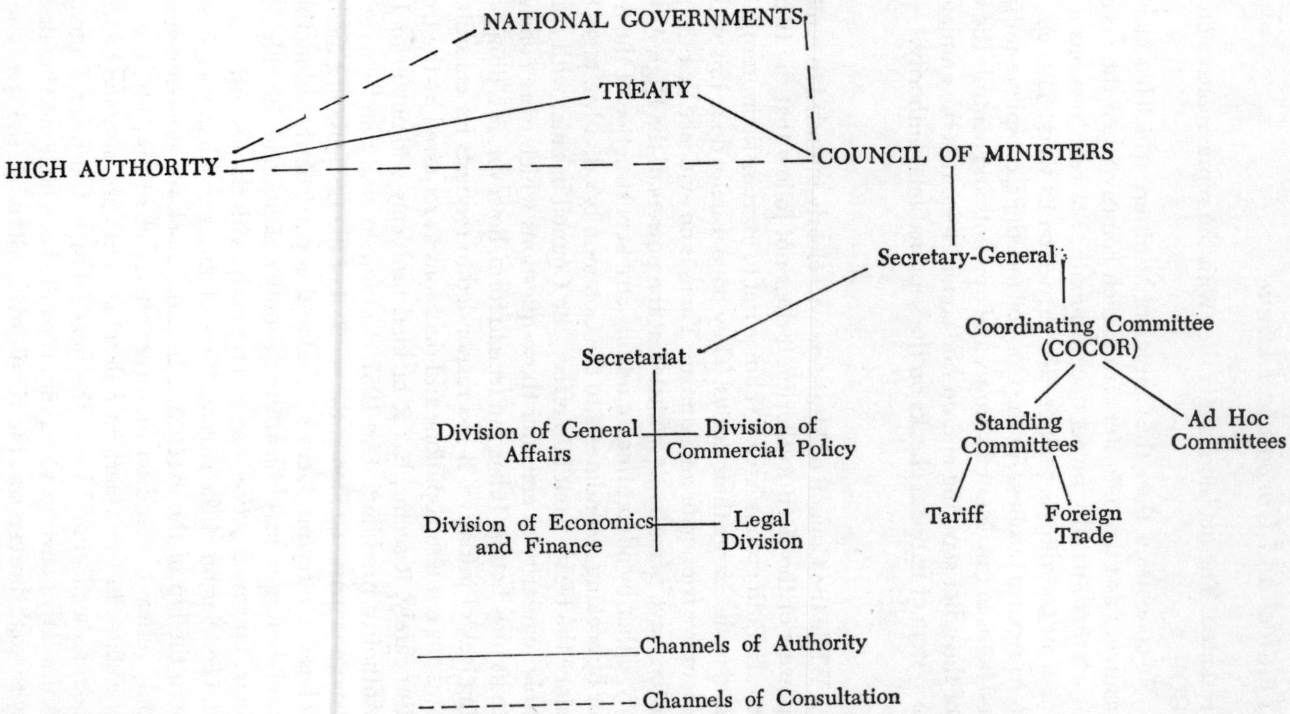

HIGH AUTHORITY

NATIONAL GOVERNMENTS

TREATY

COUNCIL OF MINISTERS

Secretary-General

Coordinating Committee (COCOR)

Standing Committees

Tariff

Foreign Trade

Ad Hoc Committees

Secretariat

Division of General Affairs

Division of Commercial Policy

Division of Economics and Finance

Legal Division

Channels of Authority

--- Channels of Consultation

be so construed as to bar the High Authority from jurisdiction on this level,[17] the ministers delegated the quantitatively small but politically explosive issue of fuel supplies for homes and families to the ECSC. One would like to accept the Minister's explanation of this step, which emphasized that problems should be solved by action and not be dragged on through jurisdictional wrangles. Unfortunately, they have since failed to live up to their pious maxims.

In 1959, when the fuel market had turned tail, and mines were short of storage space for their surplus coal, the High Authority promptly came forward with a number of solutions. These fell generally under Article 95, which allows expansion of the treaty framework, and Article 58-1, which deals with a "manifest crisis" as the result of declining demand. Each provides that the remedies receive the unanimous approval of the Council. On this occasion some governments, France in particular, showed no gratitude for Community good offices. They refused to sanction any of the curative proposals.[18]

This deadlock, which continues, is no institutional conflict. The coal recession struck Belgium and Germany, by-passed the nationalized mines of France, and had little occasion to affect Italy, Holland, and Luxembourg whose production was negligible or nil. France, therefore, refused to concede that the Community was faced with a crisis under the treaty. Bluntly, the French argued that German industry had continued a high pace of production even after the recession was well under way and declined to shackle its own coal output to compensate for such imprudence. One could have wished for a more generous attitude in Paris, but the point was not without validity. The treaty did not spell out at what point economic difficulties in one or more countries did, in fact, become a "Community crisis," and it failed, more specifically, to provide for a means of action in emergencies that resulted not merely from the ebb and flow of demand but also from defects in the economic structure of member states.

Despite this recent difficulty, however, it cannot be said that the Council's policies have been guided by a petty and jealous regard for national prerogatives. Its actions have been those of an institution whose task is to help in the accomplishment of the Commu-

[17]*Treaty*, Art. 80. [18]*Achter Gesamtbericht*, 127.

nity's mission. Its relationship with the nine has been characterized by coöperation rather than competition. Even a conservative in integration, like Ludwig Erhard, has confirmed that neither side has narrowly held to its position under the treaty, but that both have shown "understanding for each other's tasks and duties."[19] An even more forthright appreciation of the High Authority came from Belgium's minister of economics, Jean Rey: he regretted the failures of the OEEC and the frustrations of Benelux, which were due, he stated, to the absence of a supranational board. Ministers, he went on, cannot represent their economies and integrate them at the same time.[20]

In the constituent phase of the European Coal and Steel Community, the Council of Ministers was not only responsible for the initial organization of the High Authority; it was also called upon to establish the Consultative Committee, which plays a modest part in the executive and legislative sphere of the coal and steel pool. It consists of fifty-one members representing in equal parts labor, producers, and consumers of coal and steel. Theoretically, the Committee adds another representative dimension to the Community. If the High Authority exemplifies the "union," the Council of Ministers the states, and the Common Assembly the political forces, then this gathering of three times seventeen gives a voice to the producers and consumers of material wealth.[21] It is the replica of a corporative system in which occupational and economic representation supplements political delegation. Without the utopian pretensions of Mussolini's era, it provides a forum in which the class struggles of the coal and steel pool may be harmonized and where the conflicting interests of its major economic forces may seek expression and compromise.[22] Lest this unsavory parallel be misunderstood, one should point to a more recent antecedent in the

[19]*Débats (édition provisoire)*, November 8, 1957, 322.   [20]See above, 28-30.
[21]Though one must keep in mind the language of the *Treaty*, Art. 18: "There shall be created a Consultative Committee attached to the High Authority . . ."
[22]No parallel with the corporate state should be attempted without consulting G. Lowell Field, *The Syndical and Corporative Institutions of Italian Fascism* (New York, 1938), particularly 14-15, and, still invaluable for English and American readers, Carl T. Schmidt, *The Corporate State in Action* (London, 1939).

Economic Council of France, first established in the 1920's, restored by the Popular Front government in 1936, and incorporated into the constitution of 1946. Its structure is more complex, representing all instead of part of the economy, and gives no voice to the consumers as such. But as a consultative body with all its limitations and problems, the French experiment foreshadows the Consultative Committee in both positive and negative respects.[23]

The organization of the Committee proceeds in three stages. First, the Council of Ministers designates the organizations, trade associations, and unions which shall be represented. These next submit a list of their candidates, proposing two for each seat at their disposal. At last, the Council makes the final selection on the basis of the aspirant's personal qualifications. Once appointed, the members of the Committee "shall not be bound by any mandate or instruction from the organization which proposed them as candidates."[24]

Under various provisions of the treaty, a host of activities by the High Authority require prior consultation of the Committee. The periodic assessments of Community objectives and accomplishments may be published only after they have been submitted to the three "corporations." The support of industrial research programs must be preceded by a consultation. Preparations for the readaptation or redeployment of surplus labor will be initiated after an exchange of views with the Committee.[25]

Whenever the High Authority requests an opinion, whether it be in response to a treaty requirement or not, it may ask the Committee to render it within ten days. These views shall be transmitted with the minutes of the meeting to both the executive and the Council of Ministers. The same distribution is required after the Committee has met and deliberated at the request of a statutory majority of its members.[26]

---

[23]For good summaries of the Economic Council's structure, functions, and activities, see O. R. Taylor, *The Fourth Republic of France, Constitution and Political Parties* (London, 1951), 61-62, and Maurice Duverger, *The French Political System*, tr. by Barbara and Robert North (Chicago, 1958), 73-76.

[24]*Treaty*, Art. 18.

[25]For a complete list of all provisions bearing on the role of the Consultative Committee, see Institut Royal des Relations Internationales, 45-47.

[26]*Treaty*, Art. 19.

The Committee's workings are in some respects simpler, in others more complex, than either treaty or organization reflect. The distribution of membership among economic interest groups indicates the basic purpose of acquainting the High Authority with the divergent viewpoints of industry, business, and labor on a given issue. At the same time, through regular contacts with its governing body, the Community would, it was anticipated, cease to be an ominous mystery to employer and employee. Moreover, the two would learn to deal with one another on a routine and coöperative basis. These expectations have born some fruit, for neither has the Committee fought the High Authority, nor have its component elements been invariably at odds with each other. Thus it may have spelled harmony between elements of the Community and reconciled otherwise antagonistic forces.

On the other hand, the Committee is not as plain a gathering of economic and individual capacities as the treaty would lead one to believe. The determination of its membership alone is a Chinese puzzle. Except in the case of labor, and there only perfunctorily, the components of the group were not internationally or supranationally organized. Accordingly, the first division of seats occured along national lines, taking into account the weight that ought to be assigned to each of the three interests within each national delegation. This resulted in the following distribution:

Country	Producers	Workers	Consumers	Total by nation
Germany	5	5	6	16
Belgium	3	2	2	7
France	5	5	4	14
Italy	2	2	2	6
Luxembourg	1	1	1	3
Netherlands	1	2	2	5
Total	17	17	17	51*

*See Footnote 27

Selection of organizations and enterprises followed (Chart III). The tendency towards large concentrations among producers—there is no "small business" in coal and steel—made this compara-

[27]Communauté Europeénne du Charbon et de l'Acier, Haute Autorité, Comité Consultataif, *Manuel*, 3. ed. (Luxembourg, 1956), 13. For the original decision *cf.*, *JO*, February 10, 1953, and *Echo des Mines et de la Métallurgie*, LXXXXI (1952), 777.

tively easy. Identification of the major consumer interests in the Community was likewise not difficult. But the appointment of labor representatives offered problems. In the early '50's at any rate, the largest unions in France and Italy were dominated by Communist leaders. To allow them a voice in the endeavor which they had so bitterly opposed would have seemed to stretch tolerance beyond reasonable limits.[28] The inevitable, but not wholly satisfactory outcome, was that the labor delegation on the Committee from these two countries was chosen from Socialist and Christian unions. Thus its members speak for only a part, even a minority, of their organized comrades.

Far more serious is the general preponderance of producer interests. Here looms the most decisive cleavage between theory and practice. In accordance with the treaty, one third of the membership openly represents producing industries. In addition, the labor membership of the committee is exclusively recruited from coal and steel, the same sector that furnishes the producer representatives. Finally, these can be found even among consumer spokesmen. Here a majority represents energy industries (notably electricity), transport, and chemical manufacture, but a minority again represents the steel and iron industry, which after all is a leading consumer of coal. One Italian member, Carlo Tomatis, is president of his country's Committee of Coke Producers.[29] (See Chart III.) This imbalance does not spring from a premeditated producer conspiracy but from the weakness of partial integration. There is no way in which the workers of many consumer industries can be drawn into ECSC activities. As long as the Community controls only one major source of energy, a comprehensive representation of consumers of energy is out of the question. In the sense that this narrows the scope of the Committee, it inevitably makes of it the meeting ground of limited special interests rather than an objective and representative gathering of experts. Its evolution as a Community organ substantiates most apprehensions on this score.

Under its current rules of procedure,[30] the work of the Consultative Committee is directed by an executive committee of six,

[28]This problem arose once more during the selecting of the members of the Common Assembly. See below, 141-42.
[29]*Manuel*, 16, 19, 21-24. [30]*JO*, January 31, 1955.

Chart III.

ORGANIZATIONS AND INTERESTS ON THE CONSULTATIVE COMMITTEE

Country	Sector	Organization or Interest	Number of Seats
A. Employers			
Germany	Coal	Unternehmensverband Ruhrbergbau, Essen	2
		Unternehmensverband des Aachener Stein-kohlenbergbaus, Aachen	1
	Steel	Wirtschaftsvereinigung Eisen- und Stahl-industrie, Düsseldorf	2
Belgium	Coal	Fédération des Associations Charbonnières de Belgique, Brussels	2
	Steel	Comité de la Sidérurgie, Brussels	1
France	Coal	Les Charbonnages de France, Paris	1
		La Régie des Mines de la Sarre, Saarbrücken	1
	Steel	La Chambre Syndicale de la Sidérurgie Française	1
		La Chambre Syndicale des Mines de Fer de France	1
		La Chambre Syndicale de la Sidérurgie de la Sarre	1
Italy	Steel	Associazione Industrie Siderurgiche Italiane Assider, Rome	1
Luxembourg	Steel	Groupement des Industries Sidérurgiques Luxembourgeoises, Luxembourg.	1
Netherlands	Coal	Gezamenlijke Steenkolenmijnen in Limburg, Heerlen	1
	Steel	Vereeniging van de Nederlandse IJzer-en Staalproducerende Industrie, IJmuiden	1
			17
B. Employees			
Germany	Coal	Industriegewerkschaft Bergbau, Bochum	2
	Steel	Industriegewerkschaft Metall, Frankfurt/M.	2
	Both	Deutscher Gewerkschaftsbund, Düsseldorf	1
Belgium	Both	Centrale Nationale des Employés de Belgique, Brussels	1
	Steel	Centrale des Métallurgistes de Belgique, Brussels	1
	Steel	Centrale Chrétienne des Métallurgistes de Belgique, Brussels	1
France	Coal	Fédération Nationale Force Ouvrière des Mineurs, Paris	1
	Coal	Fédération Nationale des Syndicats Chrétiens des Mineurs, Paris	1
	Steel	Fédération des Métaux, Paris	1
	Steel	Confédération Générale des Cadres, Paris	1
	Steel	Industrieverband Metall in der Einheitsge-werkschaft der Arbeiter und Angestellten des Saarlandes, Saarbrücken	1

Chart III (Continued)

ORGANIZATIONS AND INTERESTS ON THE CONSULTATIVE COMMITTEE

Country	Sector	Organization or Interest	Number of Seats
B. Employees (Continued)			
Italy	Steel	Federazione Italiana Metalmeccanici (Socialist)	1
	Steel	Federazione Italiana Metalmeccanici (Christian)	1
Luxembourg	Steel	Fédération Nationale des Ouvriers de Luxembourg, Esch s/Alzette	1
Netherlands	Both	Christelijk Nationaal Vakverbond and Katholieke Arbeidersbeweging alternate	1
			17
C. Consumers			
Germany	Coal	Chemical, energy and cement industries each 1	3
	Steel	Machine and metal industries (2), domestic trade (1)	3
Belgium	Coal	Chemical industry and coal retailers to homes	1
	Steel	Machine and metal industry	1
France	Coal	Railways (1), Import-Export (1)	2
	Steel	Machine and metal industry (1) Domestic trade including scrap dealers (1)	2
Italy	Coal	Cokeries	1
	Steel	Machine and metal industry	1
Luxembourg	Coal	Railways	1
Netherlands	Coal	Domestic dealers	1
	Steel	Shipbuilding industry	1
			°17

°Source: *JO*, February 10, 1953.

headed in accordance with the tri-partite division of interests by a president and two vice-presidents, and a number of standing committees. The executive prepares the agenda whose contents will be drawn from requests for consultation on the part of the High Authority, and any question presented over the signature of at least three members. In regard to the latter, the inner circle enjoys considerable discretion and may reject for consideration any query which in its opinion concerns matters not falling under the Committee's jurisdiction.

As in the case of France's Economic Council, the complexities of structure and operation have prompted the complaint that the results were not worth the administrative and mathematical effort.

During the first year of its history, the Committee was consulted on the establishment of rules governing the common market, the fixing of maximum and minimum prices, and various secondary questions growing out of these principal matters. The High Authority solicited advice on such problems as the maintenance of a steady flow of iron ore to Community mills and the prospects of competition between coal and oil on the energy market. There were twenty-three committee meetings in all, and seven plenary sessions.[31]

What was accomplished by this activity? Did the Consultative Committee furnish workable answers? Was its advice adopted? Certainly, the nine for whose benefit this advisory group was organized never denied its potential usefulness. The High Authority sent a representative to all plenary meetings. In 1953 it inaugurated the practice of a trimestrial report to the Committee, following which members were free to ask questions on current and pending problems. After a fairly vigorous beginning, however, the number of questions asked at these meetings has declined steadily. While this fact alone is not sufficient to pass judgment on the effectiveness of the Consultative Committee, it is not encouraging.

Like the Ministers, the advisory group excludes the public from its meetings. It does not follow parliamentary procedure. This results from the nature of its work, but deprives the outsider of the evidence necessary to judge its accomplishments. The Committee must be consulted under specific conditions. It may propose freely, but obviously has no power of disposition. It makes no decisions. With its opinions, it transmits a copy of its minutes which reveal internal differences and divergent views on a given problem. The High Authority may adopt from these whatever it pleases. It may prefer the verdict of a minority over that of the majority. It may disregard all recommendations. As a result, formal votes have become less and less frequent, and the tone of the meetings more informal with the passing of time.

Nevertheless, the Consultative Committee is not without direction or without centers of gravity. These are provided by the inevitable ties between the individual members and the interests

[31]A. R. Métral, "Le Comité Consultatif, cheville ouvrière de la CECA," *Annales des Mines*, CXLIV (June, 1955), 37.

they represent. The problem of effective independence in the High Authority was discussed at some length in the preceding chapter. The answer had to be cautious. In the Consultative Committee independence is fiction pure and simple. There are sound reasons for this. The members of the Committee serve the Community on a part-time basis. They continue in their other professions and, like some American state legislators, they are paid only when meeting. Their deliberations constitute an additional, not a main occupation. The enterprises and organizations involved tend to nominate two types of emissaries. One may be the executive who directs and shapes policy in his private sphere and who cannot be reasonably expected to detach himself from the interest to which he has consecrated the efforts and ambitions of a lifetime. The second type is the chief-technician, professionally qualified to provide expert opinions, but unaccustomed to policy and decision making. In the latter case, experience in the Consultative Committee has shown that views are rarely expressed without prior telephonic consultation with superiors. Neither case promises independence "from the organization which proposed them as candidates." There is equally little likelihood of consensus among producers and consumers unless the delegates are instructed to arrive at an agreement.

This points toward a function of the Consultative Committee neither intended nor anticipated by the treaty. Just as the Consultative Assembly of the Council of Europe provided a regular meeting place for parliamentarians of many lands, revealed extensive identities of interest, and produced a potentially revolutionary basis for international party formation, so the Consultative Committee could contribute to the burgeoning international organizations of economic interests within the Community. In the sphere of labor such fusion preceded the Committee's birth, and this experience has led to greater unity among labor's seventeen than can be found among the remaining two-thirds of the Committee's membership. A recent and exceptionally perspicacious student of the Community has pointed to the growth of market-wide association among producers and consumers. He has seen the Committee increasingly as a "lobbying arena." As opinions are rendered less and less formally, votes have ceased to be recorded on the one hand, and the veil of secrecy surrounding meetings has thickened. Only members of the High Authority and the Ministers are admitted. Members of the Common Assembly have been explicitly barred and denied copies of the minutes. "As if unwilling to attract attention to their increasingly peripheral discussions, the business members of the Committee invoke the 'club atmosphere' . . . of their national trade associations."[32]

Secrecy and informality have been supplemented by outright passivity. In a growing number of cases, the Consultative Committee has returned requests for advice with a lazy shrug and the suggestion that the High Authority appoint an *ad hoc* committee of experts.[33] As a result, there has grown at the outskirts of the executive a large number of such committees, some of which have become virtually permanent, such as the Research Advisory Group. Particularly in the case of the group on industrial nomenclature, considerations of appointment follow the same complex pattern that was observed in the organization of the Consultative Committee. The latter has displayed some jealousy in the face of this competition, without generating the burst of activity which alone would dam this tide of proliferating constellations. One reason for this lack of competitive spirit must not be overlooked. It lies in the other avenues through which the interests represented are able to exert pressure. Collectively, the group is "attached to the High Authority." Individually, the members can influence their governments and through those governments the Council of Ministers. If one traces this channel of effectiveness, remembering that the narrow scope of partial integration has brought together in the Committee largely persons interested in the production of coal and steel, then it becomes clear once again that the temptation to lobby will win over a tepid desire and a limited competence to advise.

As a Community organ, therefore, the Consultative Committee has been a disappointment. Its history once more casts doubt on the usefulness of consultative organs. In addition, observers feel that even under prevailing conditions it has not made the most of its opportunities. What these opportunities might be has, however, not been explained. Governments everywhere must on innumerable

[32]Haas, 340.
[33]See the inconclusive consultations on maximum coal prices, *Dritter Gesamtbericht,* 91-92.

occasions consult private authorities to obtain special assistance which they cannot afford to employ permanently. Attempts to put such intermittent consultation on a continuous institutional footing promises little success. In the ECSC the High Authority's special expert committees illustrate the same need, the Consultative Committee's frequent inability or disinterest to fill the bill reflects the seemingly inevitable failure.

The problem arises from a confusion of purpose. If it is a matter of advice pure and simple, that can be best obtained on a private *ad hoc* basis. If it is a matter of representation by economic sector, then the consultative pattern must be abandoned and such corporate bodies given real, if limited, authority to legislate. In that case, a reappraisal of the representative framework is in order, and a decision or compromise between geographic and interest representation cannot be avoided. Perhaps it is time to take up the challenge formulated by General de Gaulle in 1948, when he described the dilemma of France's political institutions and her quest for economic recovery as hinging on a resolution of the "problems of association" of interests, few of whom were geographic.[34] As it stands, advisory corporate councils will continue to disappoint members and clients alike.

Whether a committee endowed with real powers would make its weight felt, develop administrative strength, and infuse the Community with vigor from a new direction may be left to speculation. What is certain is that those institutions which *review* the work of the High Authority,—the Common Assembly, and the Court—have implemented their tasks and responsibilities with creative and often unexpected vigor. How the Assembly in particular grew from limited beginnings is to be the subject of the next chapter.

[34]Matthew H. Elbow, *French Corporative Theory, 1789-1948, a Chapter in the History of Ideas* (New York, 1953), 202-03.

CHAPTER EIGHT

Organs of Review:
The Common Assembly

THE COMMON ASSEMBLY REPRESENTS BOTH EUROPE'S PARLIAMENTARY
tradition and the fear of a potentially absolute technocracy. Early
in the negotiations of the Schuman Plan, an interministerial committee of the French cabinet instructed its delegation to demand
the inclusion of a parliament in the treaty.[1] The proposal met no
opposition and resulted in a gathering composed of "representatives of the people of the member states of the Community,"[2] later
acclaimed by Jean Monnet as "the first European assembly invested with powers of decision."[3] For more than five years it served the
European Coal and Steel Community alone. In 1958 it was merged
with the European Parliamentary Assembly, which also constitutes
the representative body of the European Economic Community
and Euratom.

The powers of the Assembly were specific but limited. In open
session at its regular meeting it discussed the annual report of the
High Authority. If the work of the executive failed to win its approval, it had the option to express its displeasure through a motion
of censure, which could be put to a vote after a three day cooling-
off period. In order to pass, this proposition had to carry by a two-
thirds majority, following which the High Authority was compelled
to resign. Appointment of a new board was the province of the
Council of Ministers.[4]

While the Assembly could not amend the treaty—this right was
reserved to the national governments and their legislatures—it was

[1]Paul Reuter, *La Communauté Europeénne du Charbon et de l'Acier* (Paris,
1953), 52-53.
[2]*Treaty*, Art. 20   [3]*Débats*, II, 10.   [4]*Treaty*, Art. 24.

given a small share in this process. Article 95 of the treaty provided that changes in the functions of the High Authority, proposed after it had been in force for five years, must be approved in the last instance in the Assembly "by a majority of three quarters of the votes cast."[5]

Members could also present resolutions to the High Authority bearing on Community problems, but not necessarily covered by the annual report, and address written questions to the governing body. These, together with the answers, were to be published in the *Journal officiel*.

The Assembly had the right, therefore, to dismiss the High Authority, but it lacked the power to regenerate. It could object to the policies of the incumbents without assurance that the motion of censure would result in a new course under their successors. Some members demanded, therefore, that major changes in the executive —including new appointments at the expiration of the term of all or part of the governing body—be followed by a formal investiture, accompanied by a vote of confidence. Pressure in this direction met with some success. While the treaty was not amended, resignations by High Authority presidents have frequently been followed by consultations between the Assembly leadership and the national governments, and the new chief has invariably begun his term with an address before the parliamentarians, whose contents might be viewed as a formal policy declaration.[6] Never has this act, however, been followed by a vote of any kind.

The Assembly, then, was a parliament, not a legislature. Its limited role met the approval of governments and parliaments alike. The cabinets wished to protect the powers of the Council and preserve the limits of supranational integration. The national representative organs were determined to maintain their control over ratification. They feared a European assembly invested with legislative prerogatives. If the feeble Consultative Assembly had not confined itself to the limits set by its statutes, how much less likely was the Common Assembly to accept any circumscription of its powers once it had been endowed with the right to make laws? As time

[5]At the same time the *Treaty*, Art. 96 clearly reserved outright amendment to the states, acting upon the recommendation of two-thirds of the Council.

[6]Lindsay, *European Assemblies*, 222; Hans Furler, "Europäisches Parlament und europäische Politik," *Aussenpolitik*, XI (1960), 789-92.

went on, of course, the parliamentarians *in the Assembly* viewed the question from a different aspect. Legislation, amendment, and ratification were their meat and drink. A role that permitted none of these was bound to nettle and frustrate them. But under prevailing conditions the earnestness of their desire to expand the work of the Community's parliament was not likely to be put to the test.

Members of the Common Assembly were to be designated annually by each national parliament from its membership, or elected directly by universal suffrage "according to the procedure determined" by member nations. Germany, France, and Italy had eighteen seats each, Belgium and the Netherlands ten a piece, and Luxembourg four.[7] None of the members chose general election as the mode of selection, but there have been variations in the manner of appointment. Germany's delegation, for instance, was picked by the Bundestag for the entire legislative period.[8] In the Netherlands they were appointed by the presidents of both chambers upon nomination of the parties.[9] Belgian and Italian representatives were drawn in equal parts from both houses. The French and Dutch constituted a ratio of two-to-one in favor of the lower chamber while the Germans all came from the Bundestag and none from the Bundesrat.[10]

Direct elections have been widely advocated, but the European vote is still in the debating stage. The chief argument in its favor seems to be that European integration—as practiced so far—has captivated only imperfectly the imagination of the average citizen. If the voter in the Community were called upon at regular intervals to elect his representatives in a European parliament, it is argued, he might feel a greater concern for "Europe." After the first years of successful operation by the European Coal and Steel Community were not followed by an expected expansion of the supranational framework, the call for grass-roots support grew insistent. Perhaps a directly elected gathering, fortified with a popular European mandate, would give more vigorous support to the High Authority, especially in times of conflict with one or more of the governments. Passage of time has added some practical considera-

[7]*Treaty*, Art. 21.   [8]Lindsay, *European Assemblies*, 176.
[9]*Ibid.*, 117, 120-21.   [10]*Ibid.*, 118-19, 163, 171-72, 229.

tions which favor direct elections. The proliferation of international assemblies in Europe has made it next to impossible for some members to carry on simultaneously at home and abroad. In a tabulation covering the period from October 10, 1958 to January 22, 1959, Kenneth Lindsay has shown that different European assemblies met a total of thirteen days in October, fifteen days in November, eleven days in December—Christmas notwithstanding—and fifteen days in January.[11] A large number of national parliamentarians, therefore, must be abroad some days every month. The more active Europeans among them will be gone so much that their constituents at home may feel increasingly under-represented.

Advocacy of direct elections, however, has been far from unanimous. Considering the Common Assembly's limited powers, some observers have refused to recognize the need for a direct mandate. How can the electorate gauge a man's ability to support or correct the High Authority on issues with which he can become familiar only as a result of considerable reading and study over a long period of time? Persistent crises in France and Italy have lent substance to the fear that direct elections might enable substantial numbers of extremists from both sides to gain a seat in the Assembly and wreck the Community from within.[12] These are not the only objections. Would members of national parliaments be allowed to run for a European Assembly? Though experience would qualify them, another election campaign might detract from their usefulness as national legislators. The problems of a crowded calendar would persist. If members of parliament were to be disqualified, would the supranational body become a gathering of political amateurs, whose lack of skill and experience might harm its prestige? Finally, if members of parliament could stand, yet have to resign their seats upon election to a federal parliament, would the prospect be attractive? Would international deputies be able to exert further pressure on the national government if dual membership were no longer legal? A study group which considered the whole complex of European assemblies in 1959 drafted a number of compromise suggestions: these include election of members by the national parliaments from outside their ranks, and the election

[11]*Ibid.*, 3-4.

[12]For a summary of pros and cons see "Faut-il élire l'Assembleé de la CECA au suffrage universel?" *France-Europe*, VIII, No. 32 (1955), 27.

to the national parliaments of alternates who would sit while the member was away on European business.[13] They revealed that the question cannot be settled by preference alone. Meanwhile, the original procedures have survived for lack of an alternative.

The regular session of the Common Assembly convened on the second Tuesday in May and adjourned on June 30, the last day of the fiscal year. In addition, it could hold extraordinary sessions at the request of the Council, of the High Authority, or of a majority of its membership.[14] Its meetings were open to members of the executive and to the ministers, both of whom could demand the floor.

As Luxembourg provided no adequate meeting hall, all sessions usually convened in Strasbourg on the premises of the Consultative Assembly of the Council of Europe. On one occasion the Assembly met in the Senate of the Belgian parliament. In November 1957 it gathered in Rome. These arrangements, regardless of the specific meeting locale, caused a formidable exodus of an army of translators, interpreters, secretaries, file clerks, and trucks piled high with impedimenta of all kinds. Three to four times a year the Assembly's offices in Luxembourg were swept of inhabitants and equipment and spread over the high roads of Alsace-Lorraine. Despite the housekeeping problems raised by this ambulatory procedure, the Community sensibly refused the even greater expense of building a permanent home for its Assembly as long as it did not have a permanent capital. Since the opening of the European Parliamentary Assembly, serving agencies both in Luxembourg and Brussels, the problem has become susceptible of a permanent solution, but none has been found at this writing (February 1962).

The operations of the Common Assembly were further complicated by the use of four official languages: Dutch, French, German, and Italian. This required whole platoons of interpreters who provide simultaneous translation of debates, and their subsequent publication in each Community tongue. Of the Assembly's ninety-two administrative employees in 1956, for instance, more than half were linguists. On the floor, happily, the confusion of speech is less

---

[13]Lindsay, *European Assemblies*, 83.   [14]*Treaty*, Art. 22.

evident. A great majority of members speak and understand French. Italians, Belgian, and Dutch often as not address their colleagues in that persistent *lingua franca* of Western Europe. Nevertheless, a variety of reasons militated against the adoption of *one* official language. Prestige undoubtedly stood high on the list. Multilinguality symbolized that nations may relinquish their political sovereignty without yielding cultural independence. Besides, the parliamentarians had an obvious interest in the accurate reporting of their speeches to their constituents. They wanted to deliver them in their mother tongues. Translation at the source would only increase dangers of misquotation and misinterpretation, both ever-present nightmares of political life even under normal circumstances.

Technical obstacles, moreover, did not interfere with a smooth session. On the morning after each debate, members were furnished printed copies—the "preliminary edition"—of the previous day's proceedings, in which all remarks were reproduced in the original language. Authoritative translations followed a few weeks later. All documents were promptly distributed, and the other amenities of parliamentary life not neglected. The sessions themselves were conducted in a dignified tone. Oratorical flourishes and digressions were wanting, and few addressed the gathering without good reason, or spoke without a sufficient fund of concrete information. No hot wind of demagoguery was apt to deflect the members from their purpose, or drive weary listeners from the galleries into the cobblestone streets of Strasbourg. Regard for decorum prevailed at all times.

The Assembly, in common with the other institutions of the Community, devised its own procedure.[15] All the treaty revealed on that score was that it should elect a president and other officers from the membership.[16] The rest was silence. Stability and caliber of membership, political organization, the committee structure, and relations with the other branches of the Community developed in varied and interesting ways from a brief and curt basic text.

The national parliaments quickly relinquished the right of appointing new Assembly members every year. Thus the fear that unduly short terms would result in an unwholesome lack of conti-

[15]*Ibid.*, Art. 25.   [16]*Ibid.*, Art. 23.

nuity turned out to be unfounded. A study of the Assembly's membership from September 1952 until its merger with the European Parliamentary Assembly in March 1958 showed the exact opposite, as reflected in the following table:

Length of service	Number of Members	Remarks
Less than twelve months	9	Incl. two deaths
Twelve months	3	
Twelve to twenty-three months	27	" three "
Twenty-four to thirty-five months	19	" one "
Thirty-five to forty-seven months	9	" " "
Forty-eight to fifty-nine months	6	
For the entire life of the Assembly	29	
Total	102	

More than one third of the seventy-eight members enjoyed a permanent pass to this chartered company of European representatives. The annual term, stipulated in the treaty, applied to only three parliamentarians. A minority of nine served a shorter time. They were removed by death or by the call to higher office, as in the case of René Mayer, who became French premier in 1953. Among the replacements since 1952 the average has been just a fraction of a month less than two years.[17]

The Assembly has had other assets besides the willingness of its members to retain their mandates. By and large, the national parliaments defied pessimists on another score by sending to Strasbourg their leaders rather than colleagues whose absence might not be noticed. A catalog of members included such luminaries as Heinrich von Brentano, who left in 1955 to become German foreign minister; former French foreign minister Yvon Delbos; Amintore Fanfani, who resigned from the Assembly to succeed Alcide de Gasperi at the head of the Italian government; and de Gasperi himself, who became the Assembly's second president. Both René Mayer and Guy Mollet were members until they returned to Paris in 1953 and 1956 respectively to be invested with the responsibility

[17]The calculations are the writer's own, drawn from Europäische Gemeinschaft für Kohle und Stahl, Gemeinsame Versammlung, *Jahrbuch-Handbuch, 1956* (Luxembourg, 1956), 13-64; *Jahrbuch-Handbuch, 1957* (Luxembourg, 1957), 17-62; *Jahrbuch-Handbuch, 1958* (Luxembourg, 1958), 17-69.

of leading their nation. Paul-Henri Spaak, the Assembly's first president, and then Secretary-General of NATO, has been another distinguished alumnus, as was F. J. Strauss, currently Germany's dynamic and controversial minister of defense.

Unlike the High Authority, the Common Assembly went through no crisis of prestige. Among the pillars of the Belgian delegation were Senator Fernand Dehousse, president of the Consultative Assembly; Paul Struye, long-time president of the Senate; and Pierre Wigny, until recently foreign minister. Germany's last contingent in 1958 included Kurt Kiesinger, long-time chairman of the foreign relations committee of the Bundestag; Erich Ollenhauer Schumacher's immediate successor as leader of the opposition; and Hans Joachim von Merkatz, head of the German Party and its representative on the third Adenauer cabinet. Outstanding Frenchmen embraced the present prime minister, Michel Debré; the former delegate to the Nuremberg trials and former minister of justice, François de Menthon; and René Pleven, ex-premier and father of the aborted plan for a European Defense Community. The rosters of the Common Assembly read very much like a Who's Who of Western European politics. It was always composed of able and ambitious men, whose presence lent weight to the Community parliament in particular and to the ECSC in general, men who were not content with membership in a rubber-stamp organization. Their presence reflected the importance which the national parliaments attributed to the Community and its activities, and the extent to which it quickly became good politics to translate that concern into action.

In the realm of organization the Common Assembly began where the Consultative Assembly had left off. It, too, seated its members in alphabetical order rather than by national delegation. In the selection of a presiding college, however, it timidly persisted in appointing one president and five vice-presidents so that each nation might be represented at the top. It was reported, furthermore, that Paul-Henri Spaak was the first to wield the gavel because his supporters constituted a majority more intent on defeating his German competitor, Heinrich von Brentano, than in electing a socialist. This attitude was supplemented by the vote of the German SPD contingent, which backed a Catholic compatriot rather than a left-wing foreigner.[18]

In time the ascendancy of national vanities declined. Spaak's successors—Alcide de Gasperi, Guiseppe Pella, and Hans Furler—owed their elevation to membership in a Christian Democratic party, whose partisans held almost half of the Assembly's seats. In Furler's case, both party and national politics went into play. As of 1956, a Frenchmen headed the High Authority, and an Italian presided over the Court. It seemed only proper that the chairmanship of the third major organ should fall to a German. The same compromise came to be reflected in the selection of the presiding college, which contained not only one member from each country, but at the same time three Christian Democrats, two Socialists, and one Liberal.[19]

In small matters at least, nationalism has had to compete with this intangible "new spirit'" abroad in Europe since mid-century. In the Common Assembly it has won its most signal victory in the organization of the membership along party lines. While the Consultative Assembly produced no consistent pattern of development on this score, and provided meeting and office facilities for national delegations, the Common Assembly almost at once broke new ground. Its rules, adopted in 1953, provided for the forming of political groups with a minimum membership of nine.[20] The budget allocated ten thousand dollars a year to each group plus two hundred additional dollars per member.[21] These funds were intended to defray the expenses of a permanent secretariat, which each party maintains in Luxembourg.

Thanks to the stipulation of a minimum membership, only three

[18]A recent student of the Common Assembly, while noting Spaak's non-socialist support "from the French speaking areas," asserts that "all Socialists, including the Germans," voted for him. This is at variance with the version of the event I received from officials whom I interviewed at the Assembly. See P. J. G. Kapteyn, "The Common Assembly of the European Coal and Steel Community as a Representative Institution," in Lindsay, *European Assemblies*, 231.

[19]Lindsay, *European Assemblies*, 236.

[20]ECSC, CA, *Règlement de l'Assemblée Commune* (Luxembourg, 1956), 35.

[21]*Débats*, IV, 62.

party groups organized, and all but three members affiliated.[22] The largest section, the Christian Democrats, had thirty-eight members. Although one might anticipate that in the realm of international party organization the Socialists would lead in experience, tradition, and adeptness, the Christian element did not start from scratch. A confessional party was playing a major role in each of the six countries. Germany's CDU/CSU and Italy's Christian Democrats had been the government party since shortly after the end of World War II. In Belgium and Luxembourg the Christian Social parties frequently participated in the formation of governments and were in each case the largest single political group. France's MRP, despite a marked decline, still basked in the glory of leaders like Schuman, Bidault, and Pierre-Henri Teitgen. In Holland, the Christian element was equally predominant, though split between a Catholic and two Protestant parties—orthodox and reformed Calvinists.[23] Internationally, these Christians had fought in the forefront of the European movement through the *Nouvelles Équipes Internationales,* headed by Georges Bidault. There was a Christian International, not as old but as vigorous as that of the Socialists.

Although these party groups were not officially organized until June 23, 1953, the Christian Democrats held their first meeting on the eve of the initial gathering of the Common Assembly. Largely Catholic, they also included three Dutch and three German Protestants. Apart from its basic Christian orientation, an admittedly broad base, the group represented a considerable range of views from moderate Right to moderate Left. Again, the guidance was provided by an executive committee of six members, one from each country, but its president throughout the Common Assembly's history was E.M.J.A. Sassen of the Netherlands;[24] the secretary,

[22]For the original organization and membership of the groups, see *JO,* April 28, 1954.

[23]Out of a total membership of 150 in the Second Chamber, the Christian parties held seats as follows:

	1956	1959
Catholics	49	49
Anti-Revolutionaries	15	14
Chr. Hist. Union	13	12
	78	75

H. Daalder, "The Netherlands," in Lindsay, *European Assemblies,* 115.

[24]In the European Parliamentary Assembly Pierre Wigny of Belgium succeeded after Sassen was appointed to Euratom.

Nicolas Margue of Luxembourg. Selecting a presiding officer from the Benelux area avoided wrangles among the powerful members while a secretary from the Grand-Duchy offered the advantage of being always close to the seat of administration.

The Christian Democrats have made much of the liaison between the international group and the constituent parties. Mr. Sassen was much in evidence at the congresses of the German CDU and the French MRP and was invited to attend strategy meetings of the CDU group of the Bundestag when European questions were on the agenda. On the other hand, Chancellor Adenauer's attempts to unite the three Dutch professional parties have been unsuccessful. Equally feeble at present are the prospects of an international Christian party.

The Socialists built their organization around a tradition of international coöperation that extended back into the nineteenth century. The original twenty-three members of their group came from Germany's S.P.D., France's SFIO, the Socialist parties of Belgium and Luxembourg, and the Dutch Labor party. Italy not only failed to nominate Communists to the Assembly, but also refused a mandate to members from Pietro Nenni's left-wing Socialist group. Instead the non-Christian Left was recruited from the moderate Saragat Socialists and from the Republican party. (Chart IV.) During the 1956/57 sessions, when considerable efforts were underwritten by the Socialist International to bring the Montagues and Capulets of Italian socialism under one roof, it seemed momentarily as if the Nenni wing might also come to Strasbourg. But the failure of this effort left everything as it had been.

The Left in the Common Assembly followed the orthodox procedure of a six-man executive. Its presidency, moreover, was regularly struck by the lightning of promotion. Guy Mollet became French prime minister. Henri Fayat resigned in 1957 to accept the portfolio of foreign trade in Belgium while Pierre-Olivier Lapie was elevated to a seat on the High Authority. The incumbent, Willy Birkelbach of Germany, so far has defied precedent. Perhaps his colleagues were counting on his party's inability to win elections. This succession shows, however, that the Socialists tend to elect a member who has acted as a spokesman in the Assembly for some time, with little concern over his country of origin. Their secretariat is also in the hands of a Luxembourger, Jean Fohrman, Lord-Mayor of Esch.

Unlike the Christian Democrats, who held briefing sessions before committee and plenary meetings, the Socialists devised an autonomous committee system. The group divided into two committees of apparently disparate importance. The legal committee appears to have been fairly insignificant. The work group for economic affairs, on the other hand, was sub-divided into different *ad hoc* sections dealing with the burning issues of the moment. During the Assembly's time, these were most often concerned with coal supply, cartels, and transport. They prepared members for committee work and laid down the party policy on a given issue. Each committee verdict had to be ratified by the twenty-three members meeting in plenary session before being taken to the committee or Assembly floor.

The Socialists also maintained extensive liaison with kindred organizations, such as the International Federation of Free Trade Unions, the labor members of the Consultative Committee, and the Socialist group at the Consultative Assembly of the Council of Europe. On October 20, 1956, at the annual joint meeting of these two assemblies, a coördinating committee of four members from each was organized to maintain policy liaison on questions debated in both gatherings. Finally, the Socialist group established permanent contact with the parties of the member countries in an attempt to maintain its own line of communication with the national parliaments, and because its members felt that the Socialist parties of the Six were not pulling together in the field of European policy. The Common Assembly group and representatives from the six national parties held their first congress in 1957.

The Liberal group was the third and most heterogeneous party organization in the Common Assembly. Its full name was "the group of liberal and kindred factions," and its secretary, the French Independent André Mutter, led the fight in 1953 against the formal recognition of political groups.[25] Only two of the group's original fifteen members belonged to parties bearing the liberal label. One came from Belgium, the other from Italy. The rest included at least one "left wing liberal" from the French Radical-Socialists, and

[25]*Débats*, I, 63.

moderates like the German Free Democrats (2), Luxembourg's *Groupement démocratique*, and France's UDSR and *Gauche Républicaine*. The conservative wing was composed of an Italian monarchist, the German Party, and five French Independents. (Chart IV.) Because of its size, this diversified aggregation only named a president, two vice-presidents and a secretary. The first and last of these posts were continuously occupied by René Pleven (UDSR) and Adreé Mutter (Independent). To a considerable extent, this group was a monument to France's political division. In the last Assembly ten of its seventeen members came from the parliament on the Seine.[26]

At the time of its merger with the European Parliamentary Assembly, the ECSC parliament had two unaffiliated members. One was a Dutch Liberal, H. A. Korthals, who considered the Liberals in the Assembly too conservative for his taste and too anti-clerical to suit his own pious constitutents. The other was Michel Debré, defected French Social Republican and subsequent prime minister (1959-1962). In 1957 he was joined by the Gaullist deputy, Raymond Triboulet, who initiated a new and surprising trend by joining the Liberals. These two partisans of the French war hero, one affiliated, the other not, provided the only semblance of opposition on the Assembly floor. They argued that European union was a political problem and insisted that decisions affecting the continental future could only be made at the national level. Hence they viewed the ECSC and the hustle and bustle of the Common Assembly as peripheral activities, not constructive but sinister since they seemed to prepare a large scale usurpation of national sovereignty. Debré advocated the establishment of a council of European prime ministers, who would elect a chairman responsible for carrying out European policies. It was hard to tell whether this advocacy of a political OEEC was intended to be taken seriously. Its chief purpose was undoubtedly to hold back Europe until France was once more strong and united.[27]

The presence of these dissident voices served to draw attention

[26]In the European Parliamentary Assembly the Liberal group has greatly increased and maintains a secretariat of its own. This is partly due to the events of 1958 in France, whose numerous UNR delegates have likewise expressed a Liberal preference.

[27]Cf., Michel Debré, *Ces princes qui nous gouvernent* (Paris, 1957), 114-19.

CHART IV.

Composition of the Political Groups in the Common Assembly (1958)

Country	Christian Democrats	Socialists	Liberals	Unaff.	Total
Germany	CDU/CSU 9	SPD 7	FDP 1		18
			DP 1		
France	MRP 3	SFIO 4	Inds. 3		18
			Rad.		
			Soc. 1		
			Ind.		
			Rep. 1		
			Gauche		
			Rep. 1		
			Soc.		
			Rep. 1	Soc. 1	
			UDSR 1	Rep.	
			Gauche		
			Dem. 1		
			ASR 1		
Italy	Christian Democrats 12	Republicans 1	Lib. 2		18
		Soc.	Monarchists 1		
		Dems 2			
Belgium	CSP 5	Soc. 4	Lib. 1		10
Netherlands	CPP 3	Labor 3		Lib. 1	10
	Anti. Revolutionary Party 2				
	Christian Hist. Union 1				
Luxembourg	CSP 2	Soc. 1	GD 1		4
Total	37	22	17	2	78

Source: *Jahrbuch-Handbuch der Gemeinsamen Versammlung, 1958* (Luxembourg, 1958), pp. 56-57.

to the general absence of representatives from the European opposition. Although France, Italy, and Luxembourg had sizeable Communist contingents in their parliaments, none of them were ever successfully nominated for a seat in the Assembly.[28] The same difficulty kept Italian neo-Fascists from attending the Strasbourg conclaves. In a sense the Assembly constituted one large West European district in which the pro-Europeans received practically all seats on the basis of a mandate from about 70 per cent of the voters. A recent survey indicated that the success of European institutions and efforts did not reduce the strength of the anti-democratic forces hostile to integration.[29] The De Gaullists on the contrary experienced a spectacular upsurge in their fortunes but, having assumed the responsibilities of power, began to look at Europe with a much less jaundiced eye.

Party organization on an international level was certainly one of the more signal contributions of the Common Assembly. Whether it will serve to bring forth a European nation is decided by wishful thinking rather than evidence. Since the opposition has remained on the outside, it is likely to remain unaffected. It has been rumored, however, that Italian Communists have attempted to infiltrate other unions, hoping to get closer to the benefits associated with the ECSC. In France they have supported measures of social readaptation sponsored by the Community, taken credit for them on the local level, and collected as much as 50 per cent for their war chest from member beneficiaries. De Gaullists in turn were never entirely consistent in their opposition. On September 12, 1952, Michel Debré said to the Common Assembly: "I favor a European political authority. I even favor a jurisdiction smaller than that encompassed by the countries belonging to the Council of Europe, if the members of that Council do not wish to join us. But I must make two capital reservations. The first is that this authority must be confederate in character. The second is even more important: France must enter it together with the French Union."[30] Five years

[28]Forming an Italian component without Communists, Nenni-Socialists, and neo-Fascists has not always been easy, and has resulted in delays that have accounted for the eventual inclusion of Monarchists and—regrettably—a considerable amount of Italian absenteeism from the Assembly.

[29]Lise Pfannenschmidt, "Anti-Democratic Parties in European Politics," *Les Cahiers de Bruges*, VIII, No. 1 (1958), 42-50.

[30]*Débats*, I, 78.

later, however, he warned his compatriots that united Europe "will result not in the restoration but in the abasement of France."[31] In Italy, Fascists have advocated a social Europe based on Mussolini's phantom social republic of 1943, just as a neo-Nazi group in Germany, which publishes the periodical *Nation Europa,* has refused to concede that Hitler was not a European.[32]

Among the friends of integration, there have been no defections. The Christian Democrats continued to march in the van. International Liberalism has, if anything, became more devoted to the European vision. The tone was set by an editorial in *World Liberalism* in 1952: "Whereas the Socialists enjoy a common dogma, the Christian Democrats a common religion, and the members of the European movement a common political aim, the Liberals of the world enjoy a common detestation of nationalism."[33] Outstanding leaders of the movement, like René Mayer and Senator Roger Motz of Belgium have loomed large in the history of the ECSC. At the same time, it must be recognized that not all Liberals, by Common Assembly terms of reference, are connected with "World Liberalism."

The Socialists, divided on the Schuman Plan, have quite obviously not obstructed the European Coal and Steel Community. While they continue to advocate that the proletariat of the world unite, they find it harder to take a precise stand on the less visionary matters of economic integration. Above all, it seems that national parties continue to press for "socialism in one country." Only the Dutch Labor Party has made a strong statement for integration as part of its platform. The Italian and Luxembourg party programs disregard the European problem. In 1955 Belgian Socialists merely "welcomed" further integration.[34] The German SPD advocated "reconstruction of Europe as a community of equals" only, while a recent French statement was obviously the fruit of long and agonizing compromise: ". . . the party reaffirms its loyalty to the policy

[31]Debré, 117.

[32]Raffaele Patitucci, *Partito Socialisto Europeo—Unità Socialista—Unità Europea* (Rovigo, 1953); Kurt P. Tauber, "German Nationalists [sic] and European Union," *Political Science Quarterly,* LXXIV (1959), 564-89.

[33]"Fifth Liberal International Congress, Strasbourg, 25-28 September, 1952," *World Liberalism,* II (1952), 24.

[34]Julius Braunthal (ed.), *Yearbook of the International Socialist Labor Movement, 1956-57* (London, 1956), 387, 160.

... aimed at the economic integration of Europe by the extension of economic institutions with limited competences and real powers under democratic control, and the progressive organization of a market with Socialist principles."[35] As late as 1957, the meeting of Socialist parties from the Community countries recognized that contact between the twenty-three men in the Common Assembly and the national parties was wholly inadequate and that the local Socialist press showed lamentable indifference to European institutions and problems.

The party groups in the Common Assembly developed no new and comprehensive dogma of their own.[36] They put little into their national platforms that was not already there. On the other hand, they gave a distinctive form and quality to life and work in the Assembly. Their permanence was acknowledged when the new European Parliamentary Assembly ruled that members would sit by party affiliation. The practice of having party spokesmen take the floor for an entire group has gained ground, curtailed repetitive speech-making, and increased the tempo and caliber of parliamentary procedure in Strasbourg. Financial support of the groups has furnished them with essential staff and helped research and preparation of debates. The level of the Assembly's proceedings would have been significantly lowered without the pioneering in international party organization. Their importance on the floor had its parallel in the committee chambers. This involved another aspect of Assembly activity on which the treaty was silent.

At the very beginning the Assembly decided that the frequency of its meetings should not be left to the chance desire of either members, the High Authority, or the Council of Ministers. In 1954 its rules provided for two extraordinary sessions per year. The first, in November, was designated as an organizational meeting, which would also deal with the headaches of the coal industry. The second, in February, would pass the budget and discuss High Authority policies and long-range Community objectives before the publi-

---

[35]*Ibid.*, 231, 211.

[36]Th. E. Westerterp, "Europese fractievorming, een eerste experiment," *Internationale Spectator*, XII (1958), 374-75.

cation of the annual report. Finally, an agreement was reached with the Consultative Assembly for a joint session in October.[37]

These meetings, added to the regular sessions in May and June, provided an adequate calendar for the Assembly's workload and eliminated additional meetings. Between each plenary gathering, a variety of committees, created by resolution on January 10, 1953, provided further continuity.[38] Four large committees, consisting of twenty-three members dealt with the common market, political questions and external relations, finance and social problems. Three small committees, nine men strong, were assigned transport, the budget, and administrative matters. In May 1955 the Assembly created the so-called "working group" to discuss questions of organization and jurisdiction within the Community, and projected extensions of its radius and effectiveness, including the expansion of the common market and the direct election to Assembly seats. Other permanent or temporary committees may be organized according to need. Assignments are made at the annual *session constitutive* in fall and are distributed by party and nationality. Vacancies are filled by the president in accordance with these same considerations.[39]

The pattern of national distribution, agreed on at the time the Committees were created, resulted in the table shown on page 145. With the exception of Luxembourg, the number of committee seats per country exceeded the national representation by approximately 50 percent. The four delegates from the Grand-Duchy, however, shared no less than eleven assignments. In providing for this disproportionate representation, the Assembly accepted Nicolas Margue's argument that his nation, while numbering only 300,000 souls, produced three times as much steel as the Netherlands.[40] Yet this same member was the first to complain that he belonged to two committees meeting at the same time.[41]

Assignment of committee chairmanships, vice-chairmanships and the key post of *rapporteur* indicated no consistent adherence to a set pattern of national distribution. (Chart V.) Belgians headed more than one fourth of all committees, a ratio far above her membership. Holland's share was somewhat above the representative

[37]*Règlement*, 13.   [38]*Jahrbuch-Handbuch, 1958*, 60-65.   [39]*Règlement*, 35-36.
[40]*Débats, Session d'ouverture*, 64.   [41]*Ibid.*, II, 183.

Type of Committee	France	Ger- many	Italy	Bel- gium	Hol- land	Luxem- bourg	Total
Large (4)	5	5	5	3	3	2	23
Small (3)	2	2	2	1	1	1	9
Total assignments per country excl. of "working group."	26	26	26	15	15	11	

level, that of France a shade below. Of tho vice-chairmanships the Netherlands' number was most conspicuously out of proportion on the plus, Italy's on the minus side. While Germany and France furnished *rapporteurs* approximately in proportion to their total membership, here, too, the Low Countries were over-represented, whereas Italy once more contributed the least. The members from Holland and Belgium shouldered the largest load in the committees, so much so, that some wits declared Dutch to be the *lingua franca* of the Assembly. This distribution reflected a wholesome absence of petty national jealousies, though one might perhaps have seen more of it if one of the three large nations had monopolized key assignments. Clearly, the Assembly was more intent on doing its work than on playing a nation-by-nation numbers game.

This pragmatism was all the more indispensable when one considered that committee assignments also had to take into account party affiliations. When the committees were first put together, adequate representation had to be provided for thirty-eight Christian Democrats, twenty-three Socialists, eleven Liberals and two independents. (Chart VI.) To the American, accustomed to a two-party system in which the majority claims all committee chairmanships and a majority of all seats, the distribution in the Common Assembly might have appeared curious. The Socialists actually chaired more committees than the Christian Democrats. Of the vice-chairmanships, purely nominal in significance, the largest party also received less than its proportional share. How was this apparent modesty suitably compensated? First, three out of four As-

Chart V

Distribution of Committee Posts by Nations

Year	France	Germany	Italy	Belgium	Netherlands	Luxembourg	Total
			Chairmanships				
1953	no published data available	no published data available					
1954	no published data available	no published data available					
1955[1]	1	3	1	2	1	0	
1956[5]	1	2	1	2	2	0	
1957[7]	2	1	2	3	1	0	
Total	4	6	4	7	4	0	25
% of membership	23.1	23.1	23.1	12.8	12.8	5.1	100
% of Chairmanships	16	24	16	28	16	0.0	100
			Vice-Chairmanships				
1953	no published data available	no published data available					
1954	no published data available	no published data available					
1955[3]	1	4	2	1	3	1	
1956[5]	3	4	0	2	2	1	
1957[7]	5	3	1	1	3	1	
Total	9	11	3	4	8	3	38
% of membership	23.1	23.1	23.1	12.8	12.8	5.1	100
% of Chairmanships	23.7	28.93	7.9	10.52	21.05	7.9	100

Chart V (Continued)

Distribution of Committee Posts by Nations

Year	France	Germany	Italy	Belgium	Netherlands	Luxembourg	Total
			Rapporteurs				
(*Note*: A given committee may submit more than one report at a session. If the same person functioned at several sessions in one year, he was counted only once.)							
1953	1	2	0	3	1	1	
1954[2]	2	3	1	1	5	0	
1955[1,3]	3	7	1	2	2	2	
1956[4,5]	5	7	0	3	3	1	
1957[6]	5	3	2	3	5	0	
1958[8]	3	1	0	1	2	0	
Total	19	22	4	13	18	4	81
% of Rapporteurs	23.5	27.0	5.0	16.0	23.5	5.0	100

[1] *Jahrbuch-Handbuch, 1956*, pp. 55-59. May 14, 1955 an eighth committee was added.

[2] *JO*, June 9, 1954; December 11, 1954.

[3] *Ibid.*, April 19, 1955; June 10, 1955.

[4] *Ibid.*, March 5, 1956; June 5, 1956; November 16, 1956.

[5] *Ibid.*, December 12, 1956, henceforth *JO* publishes names of committee members and officers annually.

[6] *Ibid.*, January 28, 1957; March 11, 1957; June 8, 1957; July 19, 1957.

[7] Includes new Committee on Mine Safety, *Ibid.*, December 9, 1957.

[8] *Ibid.*, March 7, 1958. The extraordinary session, February 25-28, 1958 was the last of the Common Assembly. It merged with the European Parliamentary Assembly the following month.

sembly presidents were Christian Democrats. Next, forty-three out of eighty-one *rapporteurs* belonged to the center. Thus the largest group presented more than half of all committee reports to the plenum, exercising a preponderance for which they were willing to sacrifice other privileges.

Yet, distribution of assignments along party lines also remained fluid. In 1956 the Socialists provided as many *rapporteurs* as the Christians. At the last session four out of seven reports were presented by the left-wing minority. In 1957 the center chaired a larger number of committees than either competitor. The Assembly simply refused to have its work obstructed by rigid regulations. One of its great contributions resides in the realm of administrative common sense.[42] As much as the High Authority, and to a far greater degree than the Council of Ministers, it succeeded in obliterating traditional barriers between members and creating a palpable *esprit de corps*. In the life of future European parliaments it will always have to be acknowledged as the great pioneering institution.

What did this admirable apparatus accomplish? The Common Assembly never overthrew the High Authority. At no time did a majority of its membership voice open and unqualified disapproval of Community policies. From time to time, observers asked whether it would really require the statutory two-thirds majority to bring about an executive crisis. Could the High Authority have remained in office even if only faced by a simple, but hostile, majority? A test case would have been an interesting contest of power, but none arose. The only crisis approaching censure grew out of a Socialist declaration submitted on June 22, 1956 and including three complaints: (1) that the High Authority had developed no social policies, (2) that it was not curbing cartels to the extent demanded by the Treaty, and (3) that it was not keeping the Assembly abreast of market conditions. "As a result," the document concluded, "the Socialist group makes a most formal point of the concern with

[42]For an analysis of similar developments under the aegis of the European Parliamentary Assembly, see Eric Stein, "The European Parliamentary Assembly: Techniques of Emerging Political Control," *International Organization,* XIII (1959), 233-54.

Chart VI

Distribution of Key Committee Assignments by Parties

Year	Christian Democrats	Socialists	Liberals	Unaffiliated
		Chairmanships		
1953	no published information available			
1954	no published information available			
1955[1]	3	3	2	0
1956[5]	2	4	2	0
1957[7]	4	3	2	0
Total	9	10	6	0
		Vice-Chairmanships		
1953	no published information available			
1954	no published information available			
1955[1]	5	4	2	1
1956[5]	5	2	4	1
1957[7]	4	5	4	1
Total	14	11	10	
		Rapporteurs		
1953	5	1	1	0
1954[2]	7	4	0	2
1955[1,3]	9	5	3	1
1956[4,5]	9	9	1	0
1957[6]	10	4	4	0
1958[8]	3	4	0	0
Total	43	27	9	3

(*Note:* A given committee may submit more than one report at a session. If the same person functioned at several sittings in one year, he was counted only once.)

[1] *Jahrbuch-Handbuch,* 1956, pp. 55-59. 1955 saw the addition of another committee. The "groupe de travail."

[2] *JO,* June 9, 1954; December 11, 1954.

[3] *Ibid.,* April 19, 1955; June 10, 1955.

[4] *Ibid.,* March 5, 1956; June 5, 1956; November 16, 1956.

[5] *Ibid.,* December 12, 1956. Henceforth *JO,* annually publishes committee assignments.

[6] *Ibid.,* January 28, 1957; March 11, 1957; June 5, 1957; July 19, 1957.

[7] Includes new Committee on Mine Safety, *Ibid.,* December 9, 1957.

[8] *Ibid.,* March 7, 1958, following last session of Common Assembly.

which it views the policies of the High Authority."[43] This elicited
a sharp retort from René Mayer, a quick and experienced veteran
hardened in the endless battles of the French parliament, who protested that the declaration conflicted with accepted practice. Sure
of his ground, he demanded that it be withdrawn and replaced by
a proper motion of censure. Both Christian Democrats and Liberals left no doubt that they would defeat such a move. The Socialists therefore dropped the matter and allowed their attack to be
turned into a significant demonstration of support.

This incident remained unique. There continued to be individual
criticism of individual High Authority action. But the Common
Assembly was far too impressed by the part which the High Authority played in European integration to provide the national governments through the Ministers with an opportunity to replace
some good Europeans with less enthusiastic ones. A motion of censure would have endangered the work in which both the governing
body and the Assembly were the dynamic elements.

The relationship between executive and parliament was surrounded by an aura of mutual understanding. Many avenues of
contact were quickly opened. Members made full use of the right to
ask questions on the floor and in writing, and responses were invariably prompt and courteous. Committee *rapporteurs* called on the
High Authority's departments for factual and statistical information. There was no indication that they ran into iron curtains of secrecy, and the substance of many debates in Strasbourg came from
the expert coöperation of High Authority officials at the other end
of the line in Luxembourg. Committee meetings were frequently
attended by members of the nine and their staff, so that information and exchange could be provided on the spot. In this manner,
members of the two branches of supranational government met at
180 out of 402 conclaves during the Assembly's life, and these figures leave out of account others attended by non-policy making
members of the executive.[44] This was not pure kindness on the
High Authority's part. When the committee on the common market
foregathered on November 13, 1953, Vice-President Etzel urged
the parliamentarians to come away from these deliberations with
the determination to "arouse understanding for the problems of the

[43]*Débats*, XIII, 791.   [44]Lindsay, *European Assemblies*, 219.

European Coal and Steel Community" among their colleagues and governments. Jean Monnet added that he was looking for help from the national parliaments in those areas where the High Authority could not act without ministerial concurrence.[45] In short, the High Authority attempted to complement the liaison function of the Council with inter-parliamentary contacts, through whom effective pressure could be brought to bear on reluctant ministers on the national level. Whatever the powers of the Council in the supranational setting might be, Monnet—certainly no friend of the Assembly as such—recognized that its members were responsible to the parliaments at home. Therefore, the deputies from six nations had to be converted to the European cause. The fact that the Assembly contained the cream of six national parliaments made this approach both promising and on the whole rewarding.

This partnership did not blind observers to certain jurisdictional jealousies between Assembly and executives. The parliamentarians smarted notably under the treaty's failure to give them any direct control over the budget of the Community.

Each institution draws up an estimate of its fiscal needs, but the draft budget is written "by a commission composed of the president of the Court, the president of the High Authority, the president of the Assembly, and the president of the Council of Ministers."[46] Once this committee of presidents adopts the financial commitment, the executive is both authorized and obligated to collect the necessary revenue and to provide the amounts required by each branch. The use of these funds is audited annually, and reported to the Assembly. The institutions may appear as partners in budget-making, but the High Authority is clearly in the driver's seat. It prescribes and collects the taxes.[47] It alone determines and knows, therefore, what sums will be available. Only part of these may be used for administrative expenses. A large portion goes into a re-

[45]These remarks can be found in the Committees' minutes which at the time of their examination by the writer were not open for citation. They provide a far more accurate view of the partnership between High Authority and Assembly than does the analysis by Claude Lasalle, "Aspects institutionnels de la Communauté Charbon-Acier," *RDP*, LXXIV (1958), 412-13, which credits the French origin of the High Authority presidents wth their felicitous entente. While Mayer "was steeped in French parliamentary traditions," Monnet certainly was not.

[46]*Treaty*, Art. 78, Sec. 3.　　[47]*Ibid.*, Art. 49.

serve fund and into investment and readaptation budgets.[48] Their management involves decisions which are the High Authority's to make, in conjunction with the Council whenever it involves non-integrated sectors.[49] By process of elimination, therefore, the governing body raises the money for every whisk broom and every paper clip. To be sure, it *must* do this under the treaty, and the Presidents, chaired by the Chief-Justice, keep it from making arbitrary use of Community funds. But in case of a deficit, an emergency which has so far never arisen, the presumable control by the individual institutions of their budget would certainly turn out to be illusory, despite the fact that the distribution and use of Community monies forms part of the annual report and may be subject to Assembly censure. For a vote of non-confidence, whatever else might be accomplished in its wake, would not of itself increase the Community's operating capital.

It is apparent, of course, that the Assembly has never used the budget to engineer a motion of censure. There never has been a shortage of administrative funds. But there have been minor clashes over money as well as over principle. During deliberations on the 1954/55 budget, President Monnet questioned certain increases in the Assembly's administrative staff. The Assembly committee on administration objected to this infringement of its status as a "sovereign institution" of the Community. Monnet finally withdrew the specific complaint, but did not yield on principle. He promised the money, provided that detailed justification for the addition be forthcoming, and awaiting the completion of the Assembly's personnel statute, then pending.[50] On the other hand, though the committee lost the substance of the case, its chairman nevertheless requested the presidents to send him future preliminary budgets, with the cautiously negative justification "that the committee could not view such a procedure as violating the treaty."[51] The request was substantially granted. The Assembly had neither a treaty right to this information, nor was there legal ground for refusal. The power of the purse was not affected by a

[48]*Ibid.*, Art. 50.   [49]*Ibid.*, Art. 54, Sec. 1 and Art. 56.

[50]The statute was not adopted until January 28, 1956. See *Vierter Gesamtbericht, 1956*, 24; Claude Lasalle, "Contribution à une théorie de la fonction publique supranationale," *RDP*, LXXIII (1956), 475-76.

[51]See note 43.

more generous sharing of fiscal data. The incident, therefore, illustrates once more a refreshing lack of ceremony in the adjustment of intra-community conflict, and it serves to emphasize that the basic powers of the institutions, once spelled out by the treaty, could not be subject to much subsequent adjustment.

In 1955 the Assembly established the Working Group which was to investigate ways and means of increasing range and effectiveness of the Community. This committee demanded for the parliament a share in the formulation of long-term and emergency policies.[52] Most of the questions raised by it made up much of the heritage of unsolved problems which were passed on to the European Parliamentary Assembly.

The relations between the Common Assembly and other institutions showed less growth. In 1956 it unsuccessfully demanded to receive a copy of the minutes of the Consultative Committee. The request was denied on the grounds that it violated the treaty provisions concerning "information which by its nature is considered a trade secret"[53] and that it would deprive the Committee members of their freedom of expression.[54] Pierre Wigny, in his report on the first five years of the Community, recalled the fear among his colleagues that the Committee might behind closed doors turn itself into a "corporate parliament" and usurp some of the Assembly's functions. While he agreed that these fears turned out to be groundless,[55] effective liaison between the two bodies was never established.

Little more can be said of the Assembly's rapport with the Council of Ministers. The treaty permitted the latter to convoke the former, but this never happened. If both Council and High Authority agreed on modifications of the basic instrument rendered necessary by circumstances, and permitted under the provisions of Article 95, these amendments must be ratified by the Common Assembly before enactment. This provision did not go into effect until late in 1957, shortly before the Assembly's demise. Finally, Article 23 allowed members of the Council to attend meetings of the Common Assembly, where they might "be heard at their request." But

---

[52]*Débats*, IX, 10.   [53]*Treaty*, Art. 47.   [54]*Débats*, XIII, 796.
[55]Pierre Wigny, *Rechenschaft über die Gemeinschaft der Sechs* (Luxembourg, 1957), 45-46.

the ministerial benches were usually empty, or at best occupied by one lonely visitor, who merely came to bring his colleagues' greetings and good wishes.

The Assembly felt neglected and averred that poor attendance on the part of the ministers indicated their coolness toward integration. To soothe ruffled feelings and put the position of the Council into a fairer perspective, Belgium's minister of economic affairs spoke to the Assembly on June 25, 1957, in his capacity as Council president. He explained that the growth of European institutions had vastly increased the task of parliamentarians and ministers alike. Taking his own example, Rey pointed out that he was in the midst of guiding crucial bills through the Belgian parliament, leading debate before the chambers on the Common Market and Euratom treaties, and simultaneously attending to his duties as member of the Council of Ministers of the ECSC, the OEEC, and Benelux, to say nothing of the work as the head-administrator of Belgium's economy. He besought the members' help on the national plain. If the ministers were subject to less domestic harassment, they might devote more time to Community affairs.[56]

These remarks coming from a man whose European convictions, as it happened, were above suspicion, did not fail to impress. They further elucidated certain obscure aspects in Council-Assembly relations. In Strasbourg, the same ministers, provided they were present, faced some of the deputies to whom they were responsible at home. Only the circumstances differed. At home the cabinet member approached the tribunes of his nation more humbly since they often held over him the power of political life and death. In Strasbourg, he was free to attend or stay away, but must be heard when he rose to speak. His actions as a servant of the Community were beyond the reach of Assembly censure. If the Assembly, therefore, wished to exert pressure on the ministers, its members must bring together the national and supranational spheres of parliamentary life.

To test the Assembly's spirit on this score, the ministers appeared in force at the Rome gathering in November 1957. Each member of the Council made a report, pointing out meanwhile that this was a voluntary act and did not imply a shift in the institutional balance

[56]*Débats*, XXIII, 534-35.

of power.[57] They likewise defended themselves ably against the accusation of being the narrow representatives of national interests. Belgium's Jean Rey once more rose to point out that local economic interests, rather than national governments, had been the main obstacle in the path of continental fusion. Business was afraid to lose tariff protection; labor feared competition from low-wage areas; agriculture trembled at the prospect of losing century-old economic privileges. Despite these pressures, whose political meaning they could ill afford to overlook, the governments had instituted the European Coal and Steel Community. They had appointed and endowed the High Authority.[58]

The Council's case was strengthened by the inconsistencies in Assembly complaints. On the one hand, hope was expressed at Rome that some day the Council would function as a European senate.[59] Yet, at the same session, René Pleven exclaimed: "A day will come when the Council of Ministers will undoubtedly be responsible to the European Assembly."[60] There was greater unanimity on grievances than on cures. The ministers could not be an upper chamber and responsible to the Assembly at the same time.

Still, throughout the Assembly's history, many have seen the Council as its companion piece, representing the states and occupying a position comparable to the American Senate in this supranational federation. The analogy is, however, unsound. Assembly and Council have in common the inability to legislate in the orthodox sense of the term. Otherwise the two "chambers" exercise completely different functions and nowhere share responsibility and power. The Common Assembly can overthrow the High Authority. The Council has a limited power of appointment. There is no overlap there. The Assembly has the power of post-facto interpellation, the Council the prerogative of prior consultation. In short, the two institutions play definite roles, but in complementary rather than identical spheres.

From the very outset, the Common Assembly objected to the modest part assigned it by the treaty. While the parliamentarians devised no sweeping cures, substantial progress was made in overcoming some of the more formal restrictions. The High Authority

[57]*Ibid.*, 9 *novembre, 1957, édition provisoire,* 284-85.
[58]*Ibid., loc. cit.,* 430-33.   [59]*Ibid., loc. cit.,* 346.   [60] *Ibid., loc. cit.,* 388.

found it opportune to meet some ambitions more than half-way. The party and committee structure made the Assembly an impressive pioneering effort in international collaboration. New instruments of operation encouraged liaison and exchange of information with the executive. A distinguished membership avoided barren feuds while establishing a dynamic, progressive partnership.

The Common Assembly, one completed chapter in the history of European integration, broke much new ground on the road to union.

CHAPTER NINE

Organs of Review: The Court

"THE FUNCTION OF THE COURT IS TO ENSURE THE RULE OF LAW IN THE
interpretation or application of the present Treaty and of its im-
plementing regulations."[1]

This statement (Article 31) embodied another addition to the
original Schuman Plan, credited to a German desire for an independent check on the power of the High Authority.[2] Like that of the
Common Assembly, the history of the judicial branch of the European Coal and Steel Community came to a formal end in 1958,
when it became the "Court of the European Communities." Meanwhile, it had been composed of seven judges whose salaries, privileges, immunities, and modes of appointment corresponded to
those of the members of the High Authority.[3] The guardians of the
law were not, however, required to be nationals of a member country, although no one from outside the Community was ever appointed. The treaty merely specified that the tribunal must be
composed of persons both independent and competent.[4]

Independence in the judiciary had the same meaning as in the
executive sphere. It required prior resignation from all other political and administrative offices, cessation of business and professional activities, and the disposal of direct or indirect "interests in any
business related to coal or steel, during their terms of office and
during a period of three years thereafter."[5]

---

[1]*Treaty*, Art. 31.
[2]Carl H. Hahn, *Der Schuman-Plan* (Munich, 1953), 55; Berthold Moser,
Die überstaatliche Gerichtsbarkeit der Montanunion (Vienna, 1955), 10.
[3]*JO*, July 6, 1954. [4]*Treaty*, Art. 32.
[5]*Treaty, Protocol on the Code of the Court of Justice*, Art. 4, hereafter cited
as *Protocol*.

Competence, on the other hand, was nowhere defined. Formed in 1952, the Court included members without prior judicial experience or specific legal training. Professor Jacques Rueff of France was a well-known economist while P. J. S. Serrarens of the Netherlands had for many years held the post of Secretary-General to the International Federation of Christian Labor Unions.[6] As the seventh member, his position paralleled that of the ninth coöptee of the High Authority, for like Paul Finet, he represented organized labor.[7] In addition he broke the rigid pattern of one appointment from each member country. Theoretically, his spot might some day be filled by a judge from a "third" country. In any case, these two appointments illustrated that competence could be found outside the legal profession and among men who provided expertise concerning the structural, economic, and social problems of the Community.

Judges could be removed by the unanimous decision of their colleagues, provided that such a verdict was based on doubts concerning their independence and competence. Once this consensus had been reached and communicated to the presidents of the other institutions, the seat was legally vacant.[8] At no point in the procedings was there mention of contact with the government of the national involved. At no point in the Court's history did such an emergency ever arise.

Unlike the High Authority, the tribunal elected its own president for a term of three years, and could divide into two separate chambers in order to speed up preliminary examination of cases. When assembling as one body, at least five judges had to be present, and it could only "validly sit with an uneven number of members."[9]

In addition to the seven judges, the Court's staff included two

---

[6]Mason, *The European Coal and Steel Community*, 41n.

[7]On October 7, 1958, Judge Serrarens retired, to be replaced by Professor A. M. Donner, a Dutch specialist in administrative law, who has since become President of the Court. Italy at present has two judges, both of whom have had careers in international jurisprudence. Labor is thus no longer specifically represented, and with the additional resignation of Judge Rueff on December 21, 1959, the last non-jurist has left the Community bench.

[8]Jean de Richemont, *Communauté Europeénne du Charbon et de l'Acier: La Cour de Justice, code annoté, guide pratique* (Paris, 1954), 14-16.

[9]*Protocol*, Art. 18.

advocates and a clerk. The former had the task to "... present publicly and with complete impartiality and independence oral reasoned arguments on the cases submitted to the Court, in order to assist the Court in the performance of its duties."[10] After each party had stated its case, the advocate rose as a kind of *amicus curiae* to contribute an objective third point of view. This process was derived from an identical practice followed in French administrative justice, notably in cases before the Council of State.[11] The two advocates were also appointed by agreement among the governments for a term of six years. They could be, and were, reappointed. The practice has been to select a French and a German national for these posts. Their removal, however, rested not solely with the Court, but required a unanimous vote of confirmation by the Council of Ministers.[12]

The clerk, known as *greffier* in France and as chancellor in Germany, occupied a position roughly analogous to the secretary-general in the other institutions, directing the administrative machinery and the personnel attached to the judicial branch. Also trained in the law, he was responsible for the smooth and proper functioning of the sessions and the staff. His tenure was identical with that of the advocates, except that he was invariably appointed for six years, even when filling the unexpired term of a predecessor.[13]

The secretaries-general and the clerk merit a brief digression. With the exception of a change early in the history of the Community, in which Edmond Wellenstein of the Netherlands replaced his compatriot Max Kohnstamm as secretary of the High Authority, these men have had uninterrupted tenure since 1952. They have invariably been chosen from the smaller nations. Two secretaries were Dutch—Wellenstein (High Authority) and de Nerée tot Babberich (Common Assembly)—the clerkship of the Court has been in the hands of A. van Houtte of Belgium; the secretariat of the Council was occupied by a Luxembourger, Christian Calmes. This policy was another product of national arithmetic. Hierarchically, these men stood at approximately the same eminence as the directors of the departments of the High Authority. But the major opera-

[10] *Ibid.*, Art. 11.
[11] Louis Delvaux, *La Cour de Justice de la Communauté Europeénne du Charbon et de l'Acier* (Paris, 1956), 2.
[12] Richemont, *Communauté Europeénne du Charbon*, 49.   [13] *Ibid.*, 79.

tional divisions of the executive—Common Market, Production, Investment, and Finance—were headed either by a German or a Frenchman. Only Foreign Affairs (Balladore-Pallieri of Italy), and Cartels and Concentrations (Hamburger of the Netherlands) had been conferred on citizens of other members. To avoid excessive inequities, therefore, the secretariats were doled out to the "little four." In the long run, this had the additional advantage of eliminating potential Franco-German rivalry over so conspicuous an assignment as the secretaryship of the High Authority, for instance. At the outset, it probably indicated that the importance of these administrators was underrated. Certainly the extent to which they have brought continuous influence to bear on both administration and policy, and to which degree this may or may not have modified big-power preponderance, is a question deserving of a full study. Particularly in the High Authority, where the secretary general maintains the tempo of efficiency, and in the Council, where he presides over the Coördinating Committee, these officials are in a position to exercise substantial powers.

On December 10, 1952, the judges and their staff took their oath of office and opened shop in the lovely Villa Vauban, surrounded by one of Luxembourg's most exquisite small parks. It had been planned that the tribunal would not only serve the ECSC but also other European institutions, whose organization—it was anticipated—would take place more speedily than turned out to be the case. With the disappointing rejection of the European Defense Treaty by the French National Assembly and the subsequent still-birth of the European Political Community, the Court's case load until 1958 was much lighter than expected. This did not affect the statutory importance of its work, however.

As the guardians of the rule of law in the Community, the judges exercised powers that were not subject to review within or without the Community. There was no consultation with the Council of Ministers, no contact with or appeal to the national courts. It was maintained in theory, though never tested in practice, that a decision of the Community tribunal could be appealed to the International Court of Justice. Yet it is hard to see how such a step could have been entertained. In case of a litigation between an enterprise and the High Authority, the former would plainly not come under the jurisdiction of an international court. When the Court was called upon to settle a dispute between two member nations, on the other hand, two possibilities emerged. If the case concerned matters outside the scope of the European Coal and Steel Community, the Luxembourg Court must refuse consideration. If it concerned an issue affecting the Community, it was an intra-Community matter, which once more eliminated the international jurisdiction of the Hague Tribunal. There remained the possibility of an outside power going to The Hague to sue the Community. This never occurred, but it would have ruled out the Community's court altogether. Thus an appeal from Luxembourg to the World Court never took place and was not likely to in the future. Another confirmation of the Court's status in this connection could be derived from the fact that its decisions were based on the *droit interne* of the Community, which included the legal traditions of the member states but no precedents of international law.[14]

As far as the ECSC is concerned, the seven judges are the focus of ultimate review. The only practical check on them is the power of the Council of Ministers over reappointments. Since there were no changes of personnel while the tribunal served only the ECSC, the efficacy of this weapon was never tested. The Court is, however, additionally restricted. All it can do is annul High Authority decisions. It is not authorized to recommend alternatives. Legislation is not one of its functions except, perhaps, in two instances. The degree of zeal with which it watches over the observance of the treaty exercises a direct effect on High Authority policies. Each decision of the executive is carefully previewed before enactment in order to reduce the likelihood of a successful challenge at the bar of justice. Secondly, it may in those instances in which the Council of Ministers can force the High Authority to act be the recipient of an appeal for action *(recours contre l'inaction)*. Then the Court must decide whether or not an emergency calling for executive measures actually prevails.[15] Finally, amendments proposed under

[14]Maurice Lagrange, "L'ordre juridique de la CECA vu à travers la jurisprudence de sa Cour de Justice," *RDP*, LXXIV (1958), 862-63.
[15]Delvaux, *La Cour de Justice*, 26-27.

Article 95 must be submitted to an opinion of the Court after they have been accepted by the Council. All in all, the position of the Court credits an attempt of the original negotiators to establish a judicial agency strong enough to assure the rule of law under the treaty but not strong enough to usurp the powers and functions of the other institutions of the Community.

Within this general framework the Court served a variety of purposes. Insofar as member states remained sovereign outside the Community, it became an international tribunal, competent to handle cases between members and between the High Authority on the one hand and the governments on the other.[16] It could hear complaints of a state against the High Authority, or disputes between two states at the request of one. Nowhere, however, did the treaty give the executive the privilege of citing a government before the judiciary.[17] The Court was the exclusive organ of constitutional review. The judges interpreted the treaty whenever they were called upon to pass on the legality of an act attributed to one of the Community's institutions. If the controversy was within the Community, Article 38 prescribed that a member state or the High Authority might request invalidation of acts by the Common Assembly or the Council on grounds of incompetence or substantial procedural violations.[18] When the validity of an act of the executive was contested before a national tribunal, the case must be certified to the ECSC Court which was to "have exclusive jurisdiction thereon."[19] Thirdly, the seven judges sat as the Community's administrative arbiters in litigations between organs of the Community on one hand, and individuals or member states on the other. In practice this has always involved challenges of High Authority decisions which could be attacked on grounds of non-competence, violation of forms—such as failure to go through the consultative process required in a given action—and abuse of power (*i.e.*, using a legitimate function under the treaty to gain improper ends). Enterprises were permitted to file such suits only when the decision or

[16]For this and the following, see Albert van Houtte, "La Cour de Justice de la Communauté Europeénne du Charbon et de l'Acier," *European Yearbook*, II (1956), 183-222, the most lucid and penetrating summary of the Court's functions.

[17]*Treaty*, Arts. 88-89.   [18]*Memorie van toelichting*, 18-19.   [19]*Treaty*, Art. 41.

recommendation attacked concerned them directly.[20] Lastly, the Court had a disciplinary jurisdiction in cases involving the impeachment of its own members or the members of the High Authority.

The procedure of the Court is relatively simple. It begins with a written request from the plaintiff setting forth the nature of the charge. If the High Authority is the defendant, the Court asks for the submission of all relevant Community documents. Following the plea of the defense, the Court may dismiss the case, otherwise it holds a preliminary hearing before one of the chambers or a *Juge-rapporteur*. At the end of the oral hearing, the advocate presents his own neutral estimate of the case. The Court then deliberates *in camera*, but the decision by majority vote is made public before the parties, and the names of the participating judges are made part of the record, though not the way in which each voted. A case may be reviewed only if the plaintiff can show decisive new evidence that was not available at the time judgement was rendered.[21]

Considering the facts of partial integration and the limited scope and power of the Community, potential plaintiffs before the Court constitute a definitely circumscribed group. They include, above all, coal and steel enterprises, their associations, and the governments of member states. Some enterprises and/or persons, not under the jurisdiction of the ECSC, may nevertheless come before the Luxembourg Court, provided they can show that a decision of the High Authority affects them directly. In the case of a deconcentration order, for instance, a large complex of coal and steel production, judged to be operating contrary to the treaty and ordered to dissolve, may include branches in other industries who would share the right to contest the executive order. An enterprise subjected to discriminatory practices by a Community enterprise could likewise lodge a complaint before the Court.[22] All cases must refer, however, to an "external act" of the Community. Instructions from

[20]Fritz Muench, "Die Gerichtsbarkeit im Schuman-Plan," *Gegenwartsprobleme des internationalen Rechts und der Rechtsphilosophie. Festschrift für Rudolf Laun* . . . (Hamburg, 1953), 128-31; Eric Stein, "The European Coal and Steel Community: The Beginning of Its Juridical Process," *Columbia Law Review*, LV (1955), 989; Delvaux, 21-26; Richemont, 372-404.

[21]R. C. Valentine, *The Court of Justice of the European Coal and Steel Community* (The Hague, 1955), 151-67.

[22]*Treaty*, Art. 63, Sec. 2b; Gerhard Bebr, "The European Coal and Steel

the High Authority to its employees or agents and the concurrent opinions of the Council of Ministers as such cannot be contested at the bar, unless they lead to a decision whose import may be alleged to conflict with the treaty. In such an instance it is the decision, however, and not the preceding instruction, which will be challenged.[23]

As is so often the case, practice turned out to be simpler than theory. Only two defendants have appeared before the Court: the High Authority and the Common Assembly. The latter was involved in three suits involving alleged breaches of employment contracts. It lost two of these cases, but was exonerated in a third because it had already provided the plaintiff with adequate indemnification. The fourth litigation of this nature involved the High Authority and likewise resulted in the Court's finding for the plaintiff.[24]

All other cases to come before the Court of the European Coal and Steel Community between 1952 and 1958 contested decisions of the High Authority. Their course justified three conclusions:

1) That the Court adhered to a strict construction of the provisions of the treaty.[25]

2) That the legal staff of the High Authority worked conscientiously and efficiently, since executive decisions were rarely challenged, and then as a rule without success.

3) And, less ascertainably, that a considerable number of potential cases were adjusted out of court.

In support of the first view, three illustrations may be cited. The first involved one of the rare instances in which the Court found against the High Authority. Early in 1954, the executive rendered two decisions designed to encourage competition in the common market. One allowed enterprises to depart from charging published prices if a transaction was unique, and the price paid could not,

---

Community, A Political and Legal Innovation," *Yale Law Journal*, LII (1953), 883-85.

[23]*Ibid.*, 911.

[24]ECSC, Court of Justice, *Recueil de la jurisprudence* . . . (Luxembourg, 1955-   ), II, 29; III, 122, hereafter cited as *RJ*.

[25]For a contrary view, see Lagrange, 846-47.

therefore, be considered to discriminate against another client. The other permitted steel producers to allow discounts averaging as much as 2½ per cent from their published price lists without issuance of a new scale. These decisions became the subject of suits by both the French and the Italian governments, and the Court decided that Article 60, Section 2, of the treaty prescribed prior publication of *exact* prices, for which reason the decision of the nine was a clear violation and must be annulled forthwith. At the same time, it held that the High Authority was responsible for the enforcement of published prices at all times.[26] A second example involved an Italian enterprise which had been pressed by the High Authority to make specific overdue payments to a scrap equalization fund, (about which more shall be said in the next chapter). Here the Court ruled that the High Authority had sanctioned the arrangement under which this agency operated, but it went on to say that by this act the nine had delegated the collecting of monies to it. Hence they could not dun an enterprise on the fund's behalf.[27] Finally, the Court was approached by a number of firms complaining against a High Authority decision which attempted to meet the growing scrap shortage on the common market by prescribing penalty payments for enterprises increasing their consumption of that scarce commodity above a mutually agreed base level. Several steel mills in southern France complained that they were almost exclusively equipped with electric furnaces and that any increase in their production must result in an increased intake of scrap with the ensuing penalties.[28] On this occasion, the Court, while recognizing the hardship, nevertheless insisted that the executive decision had been in exercise of legitimate functions.[29]

The second conclusion follows from the evidence regarding the first. The overwhelming majority of complaints against the High Authority were dismissed. Only when the executive itself ventured into a more generous interpretation of the treaty did the Court call it back to order. In one instance, the Court counseled with the governing body to learn whether a decision could not be suspended while it was under fire. With executive agreement, this was done.

---

[26]For a very able discussion of this case, see Stein, "The European Coal and Steel Community," *loc. cit.*, 989-94.

[27]*RJ*, IV, 45-48. [28]*Ibid.*, IV, 407-08; 443-44. [29]*Ibid.*, IV, 432, 468, 507.

The case itself was not settled until after the Court's jurisdiction was enlarged by the inauguration of the European Economic Community and Euratom.[30]

As far as the operation of the judicial branch in the European Coal and Steel Community was concerned, its presence guaranteed observance of the treaty. The fact that recourse existed caused the executive to step warily before issuing decisions. At the same time, the practice of strict construction prevented a multiplicity of trivial litigations and saved the Community from becoming enmeshed in the intrigues of the supranational ambulance chaser. Because of the clear language of the treaty, there was comparatively little earnest controversy over what was legal and what was not. Because of the Court, there was no disposition on any side to file suits just to see whether or not the executive could "get away" with abusing enterprises or governments, or whether enterprises might with impunity disregard the decisions of the Community's governing board.

[30]*Ibid.*, III, 243.

PART FOUR

"WE HAVE CLEARED THE PATH FOR EUROPEAN UNION"

CHAPTER TEN

ECSC at Work

To assure a regular supply of basic goods to all customers in comparable positions at the lowest possible price and to encourage expanded production, technological progress, and improved living and working conditions—these were the sweeping, ambitious goals of the treaty establishing the European Coal and Steel Community. Import and export taxes within the common market were outlawed at once, together with state subsidies and various other discriminating practices. "Normal conditions of competition" were "to be established, maintained and observed." Financial means and technical information were to be put at the disposal of enterprises.[1]

What did this mean? Not a European millennium to be sure, but it did represent the first energetic attempt to transfer from the individual European states to a new federation economic controls over a limited industrial sector in an area of 449,000 square miles with a population of 160 million. Industrially, it involved in 1952 41.8 million tons of steel, and 238.9 million tons of coal, in each case about half the output of the United States. As the treaty's provisions revealed, this amalgamation was expected to have a variety of exciting consequences, many of which were anticipated on the basis of false assumptions or on a misreading of existing conditions. It was fashionable to compare Europe's energy consumption with that of the United States and predict that the common market would close some major gaps. That a continental power, in order to bridge vast distances, would always consume more energy than a fraction of a far smaller landmass, regardless of population, was overlooked. Much was made of the interdependence of the Franco-German markets which were to constitute the hard core of the new

[1] *Treaty*, Arts. 3-5.

venture. French ore would find its way into German blast furnaces, and German coal would travel in quantity to the mills of Lorraine. Nothing of the sort happened. The hope of a growing interpenetration of French and German markets failed to materialize.

German coal exports to France stood at 5.7 million tons before the signing of the treaty. In 1952 they had risen to 6.2 million without benefit of the Schuman Plan. At the end of 1958 they had gone up another modest .7 million. The growth was not spectacular and lagged behind corresponding increases in domestic consumption. French coal exports to Germany remained negligible throughout the period.[2] By the same token, French ore sales in Germany, while tripling in volume, remained unimpressive. German demand continued to concentrate on high-grade Swedish ore while her overseas investment developed new resources in Canada and Brazil. In 1954, for instance, she imported more ore from these American properties than from France.[3] At the same time, the chief community market for the Lorraine mines obviously remained the Lorraine mills. These figures proved nothing, of course, either for or against integration, except that the mere removal of economic barriers between two neighbors did not of itself increase exchange or create a new demand.

A broader question could be posed in reverse: even if it did not justify all expectations, did the common market increase production? Statistically, the answer came easily. Between 1951 and 1957 coal output increased, though not spectacularly.[4] Intra-Community trade over the same period rose by some 15 per cent, and coal imports into the common market almost doubled.[5] The volume of iron ore mined during these years expanded by one-third.[6] Steel output during 1951-52 alone climbed from 38 million to 42 million tons, despite receding exports to third countries.[7] During 1954-55 the rate of production in community steel mills was twice that of

[2]K. K. F. Zawadzki, "The Economics of the Schuman Plan," *Oxford Economic Papers* (new series), V (1953), 176-79.

[3]*Siebenter Gesamtbericht,* 392; *Achter Gesamtbericht,* 416

[4]ECSC, HA, *Statistisches Bulletin,* VII, No. 6 (1959), 4-5.

[5]*Ibid.,* 67.   [6]*Ibid.,* 155.

[7]*Besonderer Bericht über die Errichtung des gemeinsamen Marktes für Stahl* (Luxembourg, 1953), 17-21; *Exposé über die Lage der Gemeinschaft* (Luxembourg, 1953), 49-50.

the USSR.[8] In 1959 these enterprises turned out 63 million tons, a 50 per cent increase over 1952.[9] This meant continuous self-sufficiency. Except for special steels imported from Austria, the region continued to supply its own needs. Exports to third countries, on the other hand, rose parallel with production to a very commanding 11.5 million tons in 1959. Trade within the common market rose by about one-third.[10]

How much of this was due to the elimination of tariffs and the unification of six national markets? There can be no unqualified answer. When reviewing the results of a course of action over a given period of time, any assesssment of the results has to recognize that it is impossible to relive the same period and to pass once more through the same circumstances while following different policies. Foolproof means of comparison are lacking, therefore.

For this reason, economists in Luxembourg refused to credit the ECSC with the growth of the market after 1952, just as they would not lay the recession, which began in 1957, at the Community's door. Even in the rigorously circumscribed setting of sector integration, generalization—pro and con—was next to impossible. Problems and conditions in the coal industry were unique. Circumstances in the steel sector were radically different.

Coal production had never risen spectacularly since World War I, since a variety of developments had supervened during the past half century. The efficiency of consumption had skyrocketed. Centralized heating systems and steam plants for the production of electricity had raised the output of energy per unit of raw material. The production of a ton of pig iron required 3,500 lbs. of coal in 1917; 2,901 twenty years later; and about 1,900 in 1946.[11] More recently, a British survey had shown that the amount of solid fuel required to produce four tons of steel in 1925 would presently result in an output of seven tons.[12] Even with expanding industrial

[8]*Vierter Gesamtbericht,* 50.
[9]Compare the figures in *Sechster Gesamtbericht,* 167; *Siebenter Gesamtbericht,* 118; *Achter Gesamtbericht,* 424-25.
[10]*Statistisches Bulletin,* VII, No. 6 (1959), 268-78.
[11]Elwood S. Moore, *Coal, its Properties, Analysis, Classification, Geology, Extraction, Uses and Distribution,* 2nd ed. (New York, 1940), 315; Philip J. Wilson and Joseph H. Wells, *Coal, Coke, and Coal Chemicals* (New York, 1950), 455.
[12]Fifth Plenary Meeting of the World Power Conference, *Power Today,* 3 v.

capacity, no significant increase in the demand for coal could be reasonably predicted. In a way, this was all to the good. Nature had not been kind to the European mine entrepreneur. The seams he exploited were thin and deep when compared to the riches of the Pennsylvania fields. Work at 3,000 feet below the surface was not uncommon. At these levels, temperatures were high, operations laborious, output low, and mechanization next to impossible.[13] Sinking long shafts, furthermore, required a tremendous initial investment, producing either scarcity or heavy concentrations of capital. In the Ruhr, two wars had enabled established enterprises to liquidate their capital debts, through inflation in one instance and currency reform in another. They could make the most of the relatively modest returns of their industry. The newcomer, in debt to government and banks, could not stay in a race with debt-free competition. Furthermore, the hazards of extraction made mining unattractive to labor and produced high wage-levels.[14] Controlled prices kept returns in all member countries unnaturally low when compared to the market-at-large.

To such basic and chronic problems must be added the rivalry from other sources of energy. Oil had long replaced coal with such formidable customers as the British Navy. Countries like Austria and Italy, poor in mining resources and far removed from major centers of production, had increasingly replaced the coal furnace with hydro-electric power. Over the horizon loomed the "ultimate weapon"—the nuclear reactor.

This amounted to a depressing catalog of hardships. How much could, and did, the European Coal and Steel Community do to assist a sick industry? The common market unquestionably opened new supply routes. A High Authority survey in 1956 asserted that the Ruhr, Lower Saxony, and Aachen shipped more coal to Holland and Belgium while supplying less to Southern Germany. Dutch Limburg and Belgium increased deliveries to France, which, together with the Saar, assumed to an increasing degree the responsibility for the small consumer needs of the southern Ger-

---

(Vienna, 1956), II, 237.
[13]Zawadzki, "The Economics of the Schuman Plan," *loc. cit.*, 158-62.
[14]André Dubosq, *Le conflit contemporain des houillières europeénnes* (Paris, 1930), 15-18.

man market.[15] But after Community production had reached a maximum level of roughly 250 million in 1956, it began to dip, and declined almost 6 per cent over the next three years. Since German coal producers did not at once cut back production but allowed stocks to rise from 176,000 tons in 1956 to over 7,000,000 million in 1959, one may possibly infer that the decline in demand may have been even greater.[16] This recession was confined to coal. Other sources of energy forged ahead. Whereas coal had accounted for 72.5 per cent of the community's energy consumption in 1950, that share had declined to 57.7 per cent by 1958.[17] Partially as a result of continuing prosperity, the ECSC enterprises were again able to increase their imports of liquid fuels and hydroelectric power. Another consequence of this upturn was a reduction in the cost of these imported resources. If these developments are added to the trend of increased efficiency in the employment of basic sources of energy, it is not surprising that the iron and steel industries of the common market continued to expand even between 1957 and 1959 while reducing their intake of coal.[18]

Steel, it has been pointed out, involved a larger number of diverse operations and, therefore, a more diversified jurisdiction. It included mining of ore, distribution of scrap, the manufacture of pig iron, ferro-alloys, and crude and semi-finished steel as well as finished wares of iron, ordinary and special steel.[19]

Besides coal, the industry needed ore. Here only France approached self-sufficiency. In Italy, Luxembourg, and Germany about half of domestic consumption came from abroad, and Holland and Belgium were almost completely dependent on imports.[20] Demand and production encountered none of the decay symptoms attending coal mining, and output in the common market increased markedly and unflaggingly. This was predominantly due to a 50 per cent increase in French extractions during the first seven years

[15]ECSC, HA, "Aufzeichnung über das Funktionieren des Gemeinsamen Marktes," *Doc. 7403/1/56, passim.*

[16]*Achter Gesamtbericht*, 382. It must also be remembered that West Germany was still importing U. S. coal under some long term delivery contracts.

[17]"Entwicklung der Kohlenpreise in den Hauptrevieren der Montanunion," *Statistische Informationen*, IV, No. 5 (1957), 319-29.

[18]*Achter Gesamtbericht*, 102-07.   [19]*Treaty*, Annex V.

[20]*Exposé*, 54; *Gesamtbericht 1952/53*, 38.

of the Community's history.[21] An unpublished High Authority survey in 1956 was only cautiously optimistic on this score and granted modestly that in view of an abiding prosperity it was difficult to separate the symptoms attending the fat years from the results of international planification. Yet there could be little doubt that the treaty had wrought some visible changes on the ore market. Before the opening of Community operations French iron ore had been subject to export restrictions. After their removal, outbound trade rose sharply, some 10 per cent between 1952 and 1953 alone. The result was an increase in domestic production despite a temporary decline in local consumption. Before 1953, French iron ore had been sold on a double standard. Domestic prices were fixed at 854 ffr. per ton, almost 150 ffr. below cost, while foreign customers were charged 1,325 ffr. There was no profit in domestic sales, and exports were subject to quota restrictions. The ECSC abolished double pricing, and the uniform charge was balanced at 1,240 ffr. throughout the community. It encouraged the increase of domestic sales and stimulated foreign demand. Sales from French mines to common market customers between 1952 and 1958 climbed by more than 65 per cent. The lesson seemed clear: removal of barriers and discriminatory practices raised domestic prices and incentives, reduced export charges, and therefore stimulated Community demand.

The common market's impact on steel production, on the other hand, was a different matter. Subject to intermittent "breathers," the rate of output in Western Europe had mounted steadily since 1947. All the Coal and Steel Community could visibly contribute was an increase in exchange between its members. Evidence shows that intra-Community trade in 1952 was about one-third of the total export to third countries, whereas it amounted to about 50 per cent six years later.[22] This may well have been due in part to the common market, but the contributions from generally increased demand and world prosperity must not be overlooked.

It is not the purpose of these pages to belittle the achievement of this first experiment in supranational management. The point is

[21]*Statistisches Bulletin*, VII, No. 6 (1959), 155; *Achter Gesamtbericht*, 414.
[22]*Dritter Gesamtbericht*, 54-55; *Achter Gesamtbericht*, 428-29.

that its "facts and figures" do not speak the clear language which the acolyte of European union would like to hear. More important, the European Coal and Steel Community had a variety of objectives which were, by no means, all economic. Above all it must not be understood as constituting an end in itself. Of the many stories that have grown around the almost legendary figure of Jean Monnet, none is more significant and characteristic, apocryphal though it may be, than the one that credits to him the remark: "I don't give a damn about coal and steel, what I am after is European union." The Luxembourg venture was the sputnik of integration. It did not signify the conquest of supranational outer space. In the long run, the endeavor would justify itself only if it broke new ground politically by wielding its powers effectively, imposing its will, and demonstrating enough dynamic, compelling energy to force from the governments and nations of Europe a growing acceptance of the vaster objectives which it merely foreshadowed.

This is how the power grant to the Community must be viewed. If progress in industry and society followed the signing of the 1951 treaty, it was really immaterial to what extent one could prove that it was the result of the agreement. To put it differently, if the Community prospered, that was one way of launching "Europe." But the larger battle could only succeed if economic power in turn gave rise to political strength. Granted that the decade of the fifties was a period of affluence. Granted that the Six flourished to a conspicuous degree. But one must investigate at the same time whether the Treaty gave the Community the stamina to realize all goals freely. Did it justify the hope that economic integration by sectors would advance to economic integration pure and simple and, ultimately, from economic to political union?

No amount of statistically generated excitement can conceal the restricted scope and impact of the Schuman Plan in many areas of economic activity. To begin with, partial integration set inevitable limits to the effectiveness of the European Coal and Steel Community. Ordinarily in a federation, there is an attempt at a clear division between the powers exercised by the federation and those reserved to the component parts. That such a distinction was impossible under the Paris agreement was exemplified by the institut-tion of the Council of Ministers. Even when carrying out duties as-signed to it by the treaty, the Community impinged on sectors of state activity. The alignment of national and supranational spheres was a constant necessity. Thus the task "to assure a regular supply of basic goods to all customers in comparable positions at the low-est possible price" was not only a cumbersome sentence, but an as-signment on which the Community was really in no position to utter the last word.

What it could do was illustrated by its handling of the scrap problem.

"It is characteristic of scrap . . . that supplies are readily available only when demand is low, and that these same supplies tend to dis-appear mysteriously in a high period of economic activity, reap-pearing on the market only at a substantially higher price."[23] To-day's scrap is yesterday's steel. Today's steel will be scrap ten or fifteen years from now. Europe in 1952, on the threshold of sector integration, was at the end of a period of frantic scrap consumption. It was one commodity of which there was an ample supply at war's end. Germany, producing little else, exported it to Great Britain until 1950. Blast furnaces, handicapped by a steady, though lessen-ing, shortage of coking coal, used more scrap to reduce their re-quirements for hard fuel. As a result, the war-bred surplus dwin-dled, and by 1952 scrap was in short supply.[24]

The critical area was Italy. At the outset of the ECSC, France, Germany, and the Netherlands were still meeting their own needs while Belgium was apparently able to cover her deficit within the Community. Italy, however, imported 637,000 tons in 1952 alone, two-thirds from third countries. Because of her negligible ore and coal reserves, she had very little choice in the matter, and her needs could be expected to rise with progressive recovery. What would happen to prices if Italian buyers suddenly shifted their operations from overseas sources to the common market? The High Authority did not propose to find out. Since the provisions available to Italy in Europe after integration obviously would cost less than scrap imported from overseas, ways had to be found to close the price

[23]*Gesamtbericht 1952/53*, 40-41.   [24]*Fünfter Gesamtbericht*, II, 16.

gap, so that she could become competitive without abandoning her traditional sources of supply.

Here was a problem posed by the common market. The High Authority had the means of tackling it, and it did. To avoid extensive disturbances, it decreed the imposition of price controls on scrap effective March 1953.[25] Yet unless this step was supplemented by other measures, it would encourage Italian consumers to buy in such quantities from Germany and France that shortage would result where hitherto none had existed. The Italian burden would merely be shifted to other shoulders. Someone would always end up paying higher import prices and producing a more expensive and less competitive product. As a second measure, therefore, the High Authority instituted an equalization fund. Each consumer of scrap was asked to contribute $2 per ton of his intake. Proceeds of the levy went to importing mills at the rate of $20-$25 per ton on the average, in order to reduce their raw material overhead to the levels at which it would have stood had they been able to supply themselves on the common market. The subsidy reconciled community and import prices.

The two measures in conjunction braked untoward and spectacular price fluctuations. They did not create an adequate supply. On the contrary, the availability of third country scrap at Community prices induced steel producers to ride the gravy train of equalization instead of finding ways and means to reduce scrap consumption. For this reason the executive decided on steps three and four: premiums for steel producers who reduced their scrap demands, on the one hand; a sliding scale of penalty payments for every ton over and above the amount used at a mutually acceptable base date, on the other.[26]

Seen together, these four edicts staved off disaster long enough to allow pig iron production to catch up with demand. In 1958 a balance had been reached and scrap prices declined to levels of 1954.[27] The equalization fund became superfluous and collections ended on December 1, 1958. A specific crisis had been mastered.

While the case of scrap provided a splendid illustration of the powers which the Community could exercise over the commodities

[25]*JO*, March 15, 1953. [26]*Ibid.*, January 28, 1957.
[27]*Siebenter Gesamtbericht*, 98-101.

entrusted to its care, it might also be used to serve the opposite case. Since scrap was scarce during the first six years of the Community's life, the policy was to reduce its use in the production of steel. Equalization as such did not accomplish this purpose, but penalties did.[28] Their imposition clearly demonstrated that firms could be forced to pay fines. Yet the needs posed by the crisis were larger. They highlighted the imperative need for increased blast furnace capacity, and an augmented supply of coking coal through a direction of investment activities into these essential channels of expansion. They led the observer back from the contemplation of one success to a broader analysis of the Community's basic effectiveness as a power.

Certain conventional bases of authority existed. The European Coal and Steel Community possessed from the outset one right for which federal organs have had to put up a determined fight (witness the United States and Bismarck's Germany): to levy taxes and to borrow money.[29] The former was exercised through assessments on coal and steel, based on the average value of the year's production and at a rate not to exceed one per cent of the total.[30] Beginning February 15, 1953, every enterprise was to report its total production for the previous month and make payment in accordance with that report by the 25th. The amount due was to be forwarded to a collection office of the High Authority manned by a staff of four and a battery of adding machines. Inasmuch as the treaty forbade the High Authority to act as banker, the enterprises were given a list of banks "preferrably of a public character" which would act as depositories for the Community.[31]

Although the treaty permitted a tax as high as one per cent of the average value of total production, the assessment has fluctuated between .9 and .35 per cent. Each year has produced a considerable surplus. For the year 1958-59, for instance, the cost of running the agencies of the ECSC consumed only one third of the total revenue.[32] Hence it had at its disposal capital which it was permitted to employ to counteract capital shortage, to mitigate temporary dis-

[28]See above, 165.
[29]*Treaty*, Art. 49. This did not include provisions for a common currency.
[30]*Ibid.*, Article 50, Sec. 2.   [31]*Gesamtbericht 52/53*, 114.
[32]*Achter Gesamtbericht*, 366.

locations as a result of the introduction of new processes and equipments, and to encourage technical and economic research.[33]

At the same time, the High Authority did not hesitate to use its right to borrow. To establish a basis for its lending activities, it used most of its surplus up to 1956 to create a reserve fund of $100 million. The objective was to establish ECSC credit as quickly as possible so that it might attract capital from the American market into an area anxious and willing to roll up its sleeves, but handicapped by a shortage of financial resources.[34] Against this solid beginning the High Authority floated a series of loans which by 1959 had reached a total of $215 million.[35] Before 1956 these were contracted at relatively low interest; thereafter they took the form of bond issues, notably on the American market, which were generally subscribed in full on the day of issue.

The establishment of this reserve and the negotiation of loans constituted the most substantial of the Community's financial activities. Two aspects stood out. One was the desire to meet the problem of capital shortage, an obvious hindrance to the development of the industrial resources of Western Europe. The other was to direct investment of these sums into areas that promised the most constructive returns in the long run.

In 1953 a review of investment in Community industries disclosed that 37 per cent of new capital in the coal industry had been provided by the enterprises themselves, 12 per cent had been furnished by local lenders, and 51 per cent had come from the governments whose funds were largely of Marshall Plan provenance. In steel these same providers accounted for 30, 40 and 30 per cent respectively, half of the latter amount deriving from United States aid. In view of the slow and uncertain returns of mining, financiers on the spot were obviously reluctant to commit a substantial share of their strained resources to the coal industry. With the Korean war and the increased allocation of aid for military purposes, self-financing had to assume a larger share of the burden, encour-

[33]*Treaty*, Art. 50, Sec. 1.
[34]ECSC, HA, Finance Division, *Financial Report for the Years 1953-1954-1955* (Luxembourg, n. d.), 10.
[35]*Financial Report for the Year 1956* (Luxembourg, 1957), 17; *Sechster Gesamtbericht*, 372-73; *Siebenter Gesamtbericht*, 357; *Achter Gesamtbericht*, 371.

aged by "fiscal provisions allowing account adjustments of large amortization items for tax purposes."[36] The immediate problem was a declining supply of aid funds coupled to a persistent shortage of local capital.

The treaty gave to the High Authority the means of stepping into the breach either by granting credits directly or by guaranteeing credits furnished by third parties. Capital aid was to be confined to Community industries as a rule, but it could also be made available to others if the results would "directly contribute to an increase of production, to a decrease of production costs," and to the expansion of coal and steel sales. Nor did the ECSC look exclusively to the American capital market. Rather it hoped that its own solid credit position would attract European investors and induce them gradually to lower interest charges.[37]

The balance sheet of these efforts must be viewed from two angles: How much additional capital did it provide, and to what extent did it help "assure an adequate supply and expand production"? From the High Authority's financial report of 1956 one gathers that the Community's industries had invested $3.8 billion during the preceding three years. During that same period, the ECSC had guaranteed loans in the amount of $111.66 million, very roughly 2½ per cent of the total.[38] At the end of 1959, the respective totals remained no less divergent. Industrial investment totals for the 1952-59 period stood at $7.44 billion, and the Community contribution fell just short of $200 million.[39] Despite the fact that the High Authority had at its disposal more than $300 million from surpluses and loans, despite the fact that it was willing to guarantee, among others, five times the amount of its $100 mil-

[36]*Exposé 1953*, 133-36.
[37]*Financial Report 1953-1954-1955*, 7-8. This last consideration was far from negligible. In 1953, for instance, Community coal mines had borrowed $350 million. The liquidation of this debt constituted an annual obligation—principal and interest—of ca. $45 million. Since capital needs and borrowing activity continued, an impasse was in the offing in which the industry could no longer meet its current commitments and be forced to abandon further capital expansion. *Zweiter Gesamtbericht*, 162-63; Jean Salmon, *Le rôle des organisations internationales en matière de prêts et d'emprunts* . . . (New York, 1958), 273-305.
[38]*Financial Report for 1956*, 18-20.
[39]*Achter Gesamtbericht*, 218-37 contains a detailed report on investment activity in the Community.

lion reserve fund,[40] the total contribution was modest, if not negligible. Whatever the evolution of the capital market of the Six since 1952, it was hard to identify the High Authority as a major source of capital procurement. Even if one considers that it was not expected to pour in capital everywhere, but to use it in sectors where it was particularly hard to obtain,[41] the total result after an initial experience of five years was described as "very modest" by the Director of the Finance Division of the High Authority. He estimated at the time that five to six times the amount actually expended would have to be mobilized before a significant impact on then existing credit and capital shortages could be expected.[42]

One must add that the High Authority, after all, stood on the periphery of the whole question, for it had no control of national finances. During the period under review, the common market for coal and steel was bracketed by the conspicuous absence of fiscal integration. The treaty went even so far as to warn "that no member which applies exchange controls shall be obliged to assure . . . transfer" of funds "resulting from the . . . financial operations of the High Authority."[43] To the extent that "it *might* facilitate" investment by granting loans,[44] to the extent that it "*must* encourage technical and economic research,"[45] the High Authority had done what it could. To the assertion that the ECSC would have to do five to six times more to make a dent, one could reply that here was no evidence that it ever refused a loan on the basis of insufficient funds. Financial policy was not its province, and after an enterprise had exhausted all banking resources, it would go to the government before calling on the Community.

Investment policy and direction pointed to the same conclusion: limited power produced limited impact.[46] The Community as such had no jurisdiction over investments. The High Authority could

[40]Writer's interview with M. Paul Delouvrier, August 5, 1957. At the same time the Community's rate of interest was very low, Salmon, *Le rôle des organisations*, 310-12.

[41]For an outline of credit policies following the U. S. loans, see *JO*, July 31, 1954.

[42]See note 40.   [43]*Treaty*, Art. 52, Par. 2.   [44]*Ibid.*, Art. 54. Italics supplied.

[45]*Ibid.*, Art. 55. Italics supplied.

[46]For a good survey, see Franco Reco, "La politica di investimenti dell'Alta Autorità Carbosiderurgica," *Rivista di politica economica*, XLIV (1954), 1-16.

require enterprises "to submit individual projects in advance."
After each submission, it would "issue a reasoned opinion on such
projects." This opinion would be communicated to the firm and to
the national government concerned. That was all. The process involved neither a decision nor a recommendation, but merely a *prise
de position* that was not binding on the recipient.[47]

This placed the ECSC in a frustrating position. It wished to direct investment in various ways. In 1956, for instance, it was estimated that steel production would increase 21 per cent during the
next two years. However, the prospect for pig iron and coke was
considerably less impressive. Coal output was expected to increase
5 per cent at most. The message was clear: progress was so uneven
that the most advanced sector was apt to be retarded due to stagnation elsewhere. One solution was to build electro-ovens and replace coke with scrap. But then the same disheartening race would
begin all over again, and the scrap deficit would soar in turn. One
penury would be succeeded by another. Rather than fall into a
maze of complications where shortage crowded shortage, the High
Authority decided to give investment priority to the expansion of
coal mines, coke ovens, and blast furnaces.[48] Yet it could proffer
little more than advice. It was able to punish increased scrap consumption. It could certainly refuse to employ its own funds in ventures that would increase the threatening imbalance in production.
When a project submitted for evaluation could be shown to "require subsidies, assistance, protection, or discrimination contrary
to the treaty," the executive could block it then and there.[49] Beyond that, it could merely hope that its opinions would be respect-
ed, either by the enterprises themselves, or by the governments and
the banks who might be called upon to finance a given expansion.
If the firms chose to disregard the High Authority's verdict, then in
most cases only pressure from government or potential backers
could assure its effectiveness. Even then the increasing amount of

[47]*Treaty,* Art. 54, Pars. 3-4. For High Authority decision concerning procedures and conditions under which enterprises are to submit requests for an
opinion, see *JO,* July 20, 1955 and *Vierter Gesamtbericht,* 189-92.

[48]Wilhelm Salewski, "Investitionssorgen der Hohen Behörde," *Der Volkswirt,* No. 44 (1956), 19-22; Heinz Potthoff, "Europäische Investitionspolitik
im Kohlenbergbau und in der Stahlindustrie," *Bergbau und Wirtschaft,* X
(1957), 5-6; *Fünfter Gesamtbericht,* 326-28.

[49]*Treaty,* Art. 54, Par. 5.

self-financing prompted by persistent prosperity might enable some concerns to go ahead with their plans, all opposition notwithstanding.[50]

It cannot be denied that the treaty's feeble devices in the investment field could be used with effect. A steel enterprise in the Benelux area received a large government loan following a positive opinion from Luxembourg. An enterprise in France was known to have lost official backing as a result of High Authority opposition to its expansion plans. By the same token, a Saar firm contemplating the construction of an electro-oven was denied a loan. But in this last instance, triumph was tempered with frustration. The firm, *Société des Usines à Tubes de la Sarre*, stymied at first, sued the High Authority. Subsequently, it appears to have found the necessary capital and was able to carry out its plans. When the case came to court, therefore, the plaintiff surprisingly asked the Court to refuse jurisdiction since the Community's opinion had had no result whatsoever. The advocate-general concurred by emphasizing that in conflicts of this nature the ECSC could neither enforce its views nor retaliate against violators.[51] In the final analysis, the role assigned to the High Authority in the direction of investments was no more than a walk-on part.

If the Community could only contribute modestly to the direction and expansion of production, what could it undertake to provide equitable distribution? Discrimination was a phenomenon of many facets. A variety of obstacles, both natural and artificial, could intervene between producer and buyer.

Not all clients are equidistant from the source. Costs of shipment and transport vary. Prices and rates can be manipulated to compensate for the difference in distance, and such compensation may even be carried to the point of discriminating against a producer next door in order to satisfy demand at a more distant point. Double pricing which generally distinguished between domestic and foreign consumers was certainly practised throughout the Community area before 1952. France, as has been seen, had pegged the domestic price of iron ore at a forbiddingly low rate so that French

[50]Samwald and Stohler, *Economic Integration, Theoretical Assumptions and Consequences,* 101.

[51]*JO,* February 20, 1957; *Frankfurter Allgemeine Zeitung,* November 19, 1957.

customers in the south, several hundred miles from the mines of Lorraine, could buy it more cheaply than a German rolling mill in the Saar some fifty miles away. Transport rates, on the railroads in particular, were based on the assumption that a trip ended at the border. The total cost was computed as several short trips, depriving the shipper of the benefits of degressivity (*i.e.*, decreasing cost per mile in proportion to the length of the total journey). Added to that were charges of loading and unloading from one national railway system to another, even when the freight continued through customs in the same box car.

These constituted discriminations in terms of prices and rates, often based on national law and national policy. There was more to come. Coal and steel production was often dominated by producer's cartels and sales organizations, attempting to control national and international markets. These groups monopolized output, fixed prices, conditions of sale and distribution, and thus directed their product toward whatever customer they happened to prefer.

The Community intended to hurdle these obstacles, and the treaty gave it powers to deal with them—up to a point. In every instance, general policies remained under national jurisdiction. In the case of the provisions dealing with cartels and concentrations, one may ask, moreover, whether the action envisaged by the pact would be relevant, effective, or necessary.

To prevent price discrimination, it was determined that consumers in comparable positions would pay comparable prices on comparable transactions. It ruled out all price manipulations designed to destroy competition or favor specific customers. Enterprises must publish price lists and conditions of sale.[52] The High Authority could prescribe minimum and maximum prices if this was considered necessary to attain the objectives of the treaty. Under certain circumstances, it could be forced to do so by a unanimous vote of the Council.[53] Enterprises were fined for violations, repeaters twice as heavily as first offenders.[54]

[52]*Treaty*, Art. 60.   [53]See above, 139-41.

[54]*Treaty*, Art. 64. For a general summary of these controls, see Fritz-Ulrich Fack, "Wirtschaftsordnung zwischen Freiheit und Bindung," *Die öffentliche Wirtschaft*, I (1956), 10-16.

The executive showed imagination and vigor in employing these clauses. At the very outset, it recognized that part of every price is the tax levied on the product. When goods traveled freely from country to country, as they did on the common market, divergencies between the tax structure of the country of origin and the country of destination became potential causes of discrimination. Accordingly, an inquiry was immediately launched into the extent and significance of such variations. A commission of experts recommended that all member countries adopt "exemptions for exports and compensating duties on imports" which "would result in the products being liable to turnover tax only in the country of destination."[55] The recommendation was adopted, despite strenuous German objections. Representatives of the Federal Republic objected that such a policy would interfere with the sale of German steel in France, where turnover taxes at the destination were high, while facilitating the movement of steel from France to Germany, where similar imposts were considerably lower. The Bundestag gave the government authority to enact a stiff increase in its import equalization tax. Both Adenauer and Erhard, however, interested at this point in making the Community work, never used the law, and the tax crisis passed without detracting from the initial momentum of the newborn Coal and Steel Community.[56]

This turned out to be neither the first nor the last clash with the national interest. In the coal sector, the ECSC faced nationalized mines in France as well as a government-sponsored import cartel, the latter selling foreign coal at the same price as domestic. Germany controlled prices at home while allowing export schedules a free rein. In Belgium, German coal, though cheaper than the local product, was sold at domestic prices, and the resulting revenue ploughed into a subsidy fund for mine modernization.[57] Steel prices were controlled in France and Germany by employing one arbitrary basing point for each country's output. In addition, the

[55]ECSC, HA, *Report on the Problems Raised by the Different Turnover Tax Systems Applied Within the Common Market* (Luxembourg, 1953), 32, 37-38: Derek C. Bok, *The First Three Years of the Schuman Plan* (Studies in International Finance, No. 5) (Princeton, 1955), 31.

[56]Diebold, *The Schuman Plan*, 223-36, provides a clear summary of this episode.

[57]For government regulations in effect in 1952, see Lister, 284-86.

French government controlled prices, licensed exports and as a rule blocked imports. In Belgium and Luxembourg, price agreements between producers and major consumers were subject to government approval.[58]

The power to establish such rules and restrictions now passed from the governments to the European Coal and Steel Community. The latter's "new deal" began with the promulgation of two decisions that outlined the procedure governing publication of prices. Each enterprise must report the charge per ton, manner of computation, loading and transport costs, trading discounts and conditions of payment. This information had to reach Luxembourg five days before going into effect and be available to all interested parties.[59] Once in effect, such schedules were to apply to all customers, and a later amplificatory decree took particular pains to outlaw all discriminations against purchasers on the basis of nationality.[60]

The High Authority made very limited use of its right to fix prices. Steel was decontrolled at once. Certain producers of special steels were even relieved of the necessity of publicizing their schedules, provided the items on them were manufactured for one specific client only. One sale to one customer ruled out the possibility of discrimination against others.[61] By the end of 1958, this had freed 8 per cent of the total volume and 17 per cent of total sales in special steels from surveillance of any kind.

Coal prices were fixed, but only for a year. In 1954 controls were confined to the two major producing areas, France's Nord and Pas-de-Calais and the German Ruhr.[62] The following year they were discontinued in the former region. This decision raised an interesting problem and provided some suggestive answers. Members of the German Bundestag complained that the Community itself was discriminating instead of spreading the light of equal opportunity. Erstwhile foes of the Schuman Plan uttered grimly: "We told you so." But the German government was once more unwilling to join the plaintive chorus. It opposed price increases and was pleased to have the High Authority assume the onus for continued

[58]ECSC, HA, *Besonderer Bericht über die Errichtung des Gemeinsamen Marktes für Stahl* (Luxembourg, 1953), pp. 29-30.
[59]*JO*, March 7, 1953. [60]*Ibid.*, May 4, 1953. [61]*Besonderer Bericht*, p. 32.
[62]*Dritter Gesamtbericht*, 91-92.

controls. Thus the executive was not involved in a head-long clash with the national interest, but rather caught between two German factions: on the one side were certain labor and producer interests in parliament which demanded higher prices, higher wages, and higher profits; on the other stood the government, beholden to the inchoate mass of consumers, trying to keep the index stationary. This triangle opened a new avenue to the supranational institution. It revealed that some forces on the national level might be induced to cast their lot with integration, undermining the solidarity of "state's rights" elements in the member nations and opting for strengthened federal organs. Supranational jurisdiction might emerge as an ally of the governments in their struggle against predatory private interests or provide an escape from government control on the national level.

The latter possibility was highlighted by a division on the national plain that reappeared after the last vestiges of price control had been discarded by the High Authority in 1956. A year later the Ruhr mines submitted new price lists, despite objections from the German ministry of economic affairs. The Community accepted the new schedules, this time siding with the industry against the government. The mines needed the revenue. The Community, interested in raising investment incentives but unable to do anything decisive on its own, viewed higher prices as one step in the right direction. For the Bonn authorities, the defeat was painful. As long as they remained responsible for the German economy as a whole, it was annoying to be crossed on such an issue.[63]

Continued government pressure on steel prices was another challenge which the ECSC was disposed to meet. In 1955 both the French and Italian governments were caught in treaty violations on this score and forced to conform.[64] The French, nevertheless, continued to find new ways of circumventing the Paris agreement. In 1957 the High Authority learned that French steel producers were being promised government loans, provided they agreed not to raise prices.[65] Another inquiry elicited the promise to desist, but it was clear that Luxembourg had most likely reached the actual

[63]Diebold, *The Schuman Plan*, 247-51.
[64]*Vierter Gesamtbericht*, 135-36; *Sechster Gesamtbericht*, 67-70.
[65]*Fünfter Gesamtbericht*, 106-07.

limits of what it could obtain. *Sub rosa* pressure continued, and re-peated Community intervention merely led to more refined meth-ods of evasion.

Through the machinery of price surveillance, the Community had assumed a role hitherto played by the governments. As a result, it could drive a wedge between business and government, cham-pioning either against the other. Still, its freedom of action must not be overestimated. Its own policies and decisions based on the treaty turned out to be a fairly rigid guide that left little play for expediency. Responsible judgment, furthermore, must recognize that the governments no less than the Community exercised partial jurisdictions, each of which must to some extent remain aligned with the other. If supranational and national policies continued to clash, a show-down, precluding coexistence, loomed inevitably: undivided control of the national economy would have to be re-turned to national spokesmen or else one must accept a progressive integration of all economic sectors. The ECSC was either the pre-lude to a more perfect union or an isolated experiment succeeded by capitulation. Current conditions tilted the balance of power to-ward the governments. Who could force the French government to eschew discrimination if it was really determined to violate the treaty? Here, by the way, the Community's limited capital re-sources once more came home to roost. Until they were sufficient to make enterprises independent of government loans, a prospect not likely to materialize in the foreseeable future, they would have to yield to determined pressure regardless of Community wishes and policies.[66]

Enforcing the rules of the game against individual firms was, of course, easier. Between 1953 and 1956, for instance, twenty-five proceedings were instituted against concerns violating price regu-lations, generally involving illegal rebates on published prices. In the most flagrant case a fine of $16,000 was successfully imposed.[67]

The price battle illustrated the inseparable nature of politics and economics. The fight against illegal government pressure on coal and steel prices disclosed the extent and limits of concrete Com-munity power. For this reason, it was equally important to deter-mine where prices stood after seven years of ECSC policy. In coal,

[66]Diebold, *The Schuman Plan*, 285.   [67]*Dritter Gesamtbericht*, 141.

the period following controls happened to be recessive. The pressures that had prompted regulation waned, and after two years of relative stability, the market buckled. Concurrently, the alignment of coal prices throughout the common market became for the first time a recognizable, if overdue, result of economic fusion.[68] Surveying trends for the period covering 1953 to 1959, the High Authority also noted with satisfaction that the steel index had risen only moderately. At the terminal point it stood between 105 and 110 while English and American prices during the same span had soared to 131 and 140 respectively.[69] The steel market in the Community had been more stable than in the rest of the world, and it was suggested that this had resulted from the application of two weapons: surveillance of business practices in general and publication of prices in particular.[70] The weight of the latter could not be denied. Considering that the public generally overestimated the impact of steel prices on the general index, any price boost in that industry could expect a hostile reception. Its damaging impact was enhanced if it must appear in print before going into effect. The Higher Authority's contention, therefore, that it had helped slow upward trends seemed to be well founded. Community price policies, while hampered by the limitation of executive power, were nonetheless a discernible factor in the general economic picture.

These limitations of power were far more serious, and the Community's effectiveness declined correspondingly as it tackled the harmonization and standardization of transport rates. On this subject the treaty was cautious as well as inconsistent. In accordance with Article Two, discrimination "in transport rates and conditions of any kind" was outlawed.[71] "Rates, prices, tariff provisions of all sorts applied to coal and steel" must be "published or brought to the knowledge of the High Authority." Special domestic tariff regimens had to be "subject to the prior agreement" of the executive.[72] On the other hand transport policy and all that the term implied remained "subject to the legislative and administrative provisions of each of the member States."[73] Was it possible, under these cir-

[68]*Achter Gesamtbericht*, 118-26.
[69]*Siebenter Gesamtbericht*, 129-35.   [70]But cf., above, 165.
[71]*Treaty*, Art. 70, Sec. 2.   [72]*Ibid.*, Art. 70, Sec. 3 and 4.
[73]*Ibid.*, Art. 70, Sec. 5. For an early analysis of this article and its compli-

cumstances, to eliminate differences between national codes and to combat discriminatory practices by national transport systems directed against foreign clients and carriers? From the point of view of the ECSC the need to do so was urgent. Rarely, if ever, could coal and ore on the one hand, and the facility to produce pig iron and steel on the other, be combined at one site. Luxembourg had the ore but not the coal. Conversely, the Ruhr had the coal but not the ore. Italian steel producers frequently had to ship in both from afar.[74] Hence the traffic carried on the common market "accounted for 50 per cent of the volume and 40 per cent of the receipts" realized by rail, waterways, and roads of the Community.[75] Community producers accounted for a decisive volume of goods shipped by a variety of media.

The six nationalized railroad systems were most susceptible to supervision. Here the High Authority claimed as early as 1954 that all discriminatory practices had ended.[76] This premature assertion was contradicted by later pronouncements on the same problem from the same source. While through rates for international traffic on the common market had in several cases been established, no uniform schedules had been adopted by the Community governments. Special preference rates were still being granted internally without consulting the High Authority. Early in 1958, for instance, the German government protested a High Authority ruling which outlawed special rates on coal shipments from the Ruhr to southern and southwestern Germany. Bonn took the position that the ECSC erroneously presumed every special tariff to be discriminatory. It pointed out that one beneficiary of the schedule under discussion was an agglomeration of small rolling mills in the Siegerland, which produced a type of pig iron unique in the Community. Transport rebates in this instance, therefore, harmed no one, but reduced producer's overhead and consumer's price. The Germans concluded that the executive should withdraw its objections.[77]

---

cating implications, see Paul Schulz-Kiesow, "Montan-Union und Verkehr," *Zeitschrift für Verkehrswissenschaft*, XXIV (1953), 69-88.

[74]Cf., A. Delmer, *La géographie de la Communauté Europeénne du Charbon et de l'Acier* (Brussels, 1953), 2.

[75]ECSC, HA, "Transport in the Community." *Doc. 1199/2/55a*, 7.

[76]Diebold, *The Schuman Plan*, 160.

[77]*Frankfurter Allgemeine Zeitung*, February 21, 1958.

While the Court ruled against the Federal Republic,[78] the clash nevertheless illustrates that governments can easily obstruct High Authority action wherever jurisdictions overlap. For, procedurally speaking, the Federal Republic was clearly in the wrong. Article 70, Section 3, of the treaty charged the High Authority to ascertain whether or not a special tariff was discriminatory *before* it went into effect. The need for a prior permit was indicated in each case. The German government had chosen to disregard this provision, by usurping a right of decision which clearly belonged to the Community. The imbalance of power suggested by this example explains why all attempts to draft one common market schedule and a Community code of exemptions have so far ended in total failure.[79]

Water transport still functions as if the Community had never existed. Although the Six signed an agreement in 1957 in which each promised to provide the High Authority with a precise and complete description of river tolls on the Rhine,[80] the executive's most recent annual reports indicate that the governments have failed to carry this out. Replies to repeated proddings "do not permit the expectation that this problem will be solved soon."[81] Road transport offers the same frustrations. Negotiations begun in 1956 resulted in an official Council communiqué, dated July 22, 1958, which admitted that an agreement on the application of the treaty to community trucking could not be obtained. The High Authority retaliated with a decision which demanded that all relevant rates and regulations henceforth would have to be forwarded to Luxembourg before going into effect.[82] This, too, was challenged by both Italy and the Netherlands. In its decision the Court responded by voiding the High Authority ordinance. While Article 70, Section 3, required that "rates, prices and tariff provisions . . . applied to the transport of coal and steel" must be published "or brought to the knowledge of the High Authority," the judges held that this did not invest the Community with the right of decision in the transport

---

[78]*Neunter Gesamtbericht*, 45.   [79]*Achter Gesamtbericht*, 198-99.

[80]ECSC, Council of Ministers, "Accord rélatif au frets et conditions de transport pour le charbon et l'acier sur le Rhin." *Doc. 416f/57.*

[81]*Achter Gesamtbericht*, 202; *Neunter Gesamtbericht*, 211-13; ECSC, CA, *Zwischenbericht im Namen des Ausschusses für Verkehrsfragen* (Luxembourg, 1957), 7-12.

[82]*JO*, March 7, 1959.

sector. Under existing provisions the executive could not demand prior publication of rates.[82a]

William Diebold, Jr., in his thorough economic analysis of the ECSC, has concluded that its achievements in the transport sector have been substantial. Through rates for transit traffic were not only applied among the Six, but successfully negotiated with Austria and Switzerland. A general liberalization of Western European transport is claimed to have been the result.[83] Up to a point this was true, but progress had only gone as far as the governments were willing to support it and had often stopped short of the modest minimum set by the treaty. Transport has been one test of the European spirit in which the member governments of the ECSC have failed.

The problem of distribution involved more than conveyances. Restrictive business practices were another obstacle in the path leading from producer to consumer. Here the treaty was voluble. Article 4d prohibited "restrictive practices tending towards the division or exploitation of the market." Article 60, Section 1, not only outlawed unfair pricing *sui generis* but singled out "purely temporary or purely local price reductions the purpose of which is to acquire a monopoly within the common market." Article 63, Section 2a, barred cartel agreements by insisting that "enterprises shall establish their conditions of sale in such a way that their customers or their agents shall be obliged to conform to the rules established by the High Authority . . ." Yet the heart of the matter was reserved to Articles 65 and 66, the latter of which alone covered three closely printed pages. The sum of their terms forbade producers' agreements designed to restrict competition and only sanctioned a merger after the High Authority had satisfied itself that it would not control the market.

Contrary to many prevalent notions, these terms do not constitute an antitrust law in the American sense. They provide for no prosecuting authority apart from the executive. High Authority decisions on the subject take the form of permits or injunctions after a request for authorization has been submitted. Violations at worst result in the levying of a fine, not in criminal prosecution.[84]

[82a] *Neunter Gesamtbericht,* 50.
[83] Diebold, *The Schuman Plan,* 191.
[84] ECSC, HA "Report on the factfinding (sic) Mission to the United States

The manner in which the High Authority collects its evidence is hampered by its inability to administer oaths. It can gather data to satisfy itself that an infraction of the Treaty has occured. Whether they will stand up in court then remains to be seen. On the other hand, enterprises risk punitive levies of considerable magnitude if they act illicitly. Moreover, agreements violating rules of competition are automatically void, so that no party can be held to them, once they have been exposed by the High Authority.

While the treaty outlaws cartels and subjects concentrations to prior authorization, it does not prohibit monopolies. As long as it plays the game, an enterprise may acquire a monopoly on the common market. As long as it does not use its position to violate or circumvent the law, it will enjoy the fruits of its achievement undisturbed.[85] Mergers require permission, monopolies merely have to watch their manner.

As it turned out, neither developments have assumed threatening proportions. Local monopolies, like the nationalized coal mines in France, have not become Community-wide. Concentrations did not become the problem which some observers had anticipated. At the outset, the largest private coal producer in the Community had a capacity of fifteen million tons per year, or 6 per cent of maximum ECSC output. The largest steel producers, Luxembourg's ARBED (Acieries Réunies de Burbach-Eich-Dudelange) and Germany's Dortmund-Hoerder Hüttenunion, each accounted for some three million tons or about 5 per cent of total production.[86] The threat of market domination was obviously remote. Hence not a single request involving concentrations has had to be refused.[87] This apparent leniency nurtured intermittent fears, among Germany's neighbors in particular, that the Community was not guarding against the revival of big steel for big armament in the Ruhr. Michel Debré, who had justly warned his colleagues in the Nation-

---

... for the Purpose of Studying Anti-Trust Practices There, 8.3-6.4, 1958." *Doc. 5879/58e,* 22-23.

[85]*Treaty,* Art. 66, Sec. 7.

[86]*Die Neuordnung der Eisen—und Stahlindustrie im Gebiete der Bundes— republik Deutschland* (Munich, 1954), 276-81.

[87]*Achter Gesamtbericht,* 194. A contemplated merger of August Thyssen— Hütte AG and Phönix—Rheinrohr AG might have resulted in the first exception, but the request was withdrawn on April 27, 1960 before a decision had been rendered. *Neunter Gesamtbericht,* 198-99.

al Assembly that the Schuman Plan did not commit its agencies to uphold the deconcentration laws of the occupying powers,[88] pursued this point doggedly down to the last meeting of the Common Assembly in 1958. "Recartellization," as he put it, "if continued, will render useless both High Authority and Common Assembly, because [at the present rate] they will no longer be able to exercise their powers."[89] His point was difficult to support. Although a number of smaller units had been allowed to merge, the production leaders remained the same. Not a single steel firm in the Community, for instance, produced more than 5 per cent of the total. For this reason, the High Authority persisted in a policy of sensible moderation which could be summarized in the following terms:

It justified mergers below the existing 5 per cent maximum as conducive to effiency and increased production. It rejected any responsibility for allied legislation in Germany or French misrepresentations of the treaty. On the positive side it affirmed, however, that it would not agree to "restore an enterprise of the importance of the Vereinigte Stahlwerke" of prewar memory,[89a] warning at the same time that this did not mean that concentrations falling short of the dimensions of this defunct colossus would be automatically sanctioned.

The relative smallness of producing units has not necessarily assured "normal conditions of competition." In the steel industry different districts of the common market vied for customers, but in the coal sector monopolies prevailed. Sometimes they dated back to the 1890's. They were known and their *modus operandi* had become traditional. The Community kept them under continuous observation, and especially in times of penury, care was taken to assure that all consumers obtained a fair share of the supplies. But of competition there was none. When coal was scarce, producers could only join forces in order to meet demand to the fullest extent possible. When recession struck in 1957, the mines on a Community

[88]See above, 73.
[89]*Debats*, XXXVI, 286. (a) *Ibid.*, 294-95. In all fairness it must be added that the 5 per cent limit has been passed in special production sectors. The recent merger of Dortmund-Hörder Hüttenunion AG with Hüttenwerk Siegerland AG, Siegen brings together facilities that account for more than 7 per cent of the cold rolled steel production on the common market. *Neunter Gesamtbericht*, 199-200.

basis joined to devise ways and means that would reduce rivalry from other energy sources. Now they were even less interested in cutting one another's throat.[90] The High Authority sympathized with their predicament, and although it recognized that some sales organizations in particular were violating Article 65 of the Treaty, it authorized their continued operation on a year by year basis.[90a]

Unlike Article 70, the provisions dealing with cartels and concentrations provided for independent High Authority action. "Its decisions" were "reached without either consultation with the Consultative Committee or advice from the Council of Ministers." It was accountable "only to the Parliamentary Assembly and of course for jurisdictional matters to the Court of Justices."[91] Yet its impact was difficult to assess. Its most common function, the licensing of mergers, had under prevailing circumstances become almost routine acquiescence. A final judgment must, however, take into account what has been forestalled as well as what has been accomplished. "The threat to the successful functioning of the common market was above all the establishment of supranational cartels and monopolies," which would stifle competition and, worse, neutralize the power of the entire Community. After seven years, it seemed a *coup de force* by any high-powered concentrations of economic power had been prevented. The treaty and its guardians had preserved the *status quo* and cut violations to the vanishing point.[92]

So far this survey has dealt with sectors of activity in which the ECSC addressed governments and industries. It must not be for-

[90]See, for instance, Studienausschuss des Westeuropäischen Kohlenbergbaus, *Die Anwendung der Kernenergie zur Kraft—und Stromerzeugung und ihr Einfluss auf den Kohlenbergbau* (Essen, 1956), *passim*. (a) For a good general survey of High Authority policies, particularly in respect to Article 65, see the excellent Karlheinz Kleps, *Kartellpolitik und Energiewirtschaft in der Montanunion* (Ökonomische Studien, Heft 7) (Stuttgart, 1961), 49-140. On current efforts to revise Article 65, cf., *Neunter Gesamtbericht*, 191-92; ECSC, HA, *Bulletin . . .* , VI, No. 3 (1961), 15.

[91]Fernand Spaak, "Competition in E.C.S.C.," *1960 Institute on Legal Aspects of the European Community* (Washington, D.C., 1960), 129.

[92]Richard A. Hamburger, "Coal and Steel Community. Rules for a Competitive Market and Their Application." Luxembourg, unpub. manuscript, 1960, 35.

gotten, however, that the treaty also promised sweeping but vague accomplishments in the realm of wages and living and working conditions.[93] Thus it also loomed as a potential medium for the kind of supranational action which could directly affect millions of humble folk to whom "integration" had remained a lustreless technical term.

The negotiators at Paris had taken great care to confine the social jurisdiction of the ECSC within modest limits. Nowhere did they handle national prerogatives with greater delicacy. Differences in social legislation from country to country, varying methods applied to regulation of wages and labor contracts, divergent laws governing hours and safety, all made it technically impossible to remove these areas of responsibility from national control.[93a] Economic and political considerations prevented the governments from relinquishing supervision over the welfare of any part of the national labor force. Unions refused to exchange well-established channels of communication with local political leaders on whom they could exert a variety of constitutional pressures for an uncertain entente with supranational officials from whose seat of power they remained one step removed.[93b] In some very specific instances (*e.g.*, abnormally low prices as a result of abnormally low wages), the Community might step in after consultation with the Council and the Consultative Committee, but its role remained purely advisory even then.[94] Although Article 69 provided that skilled labor was to have access to jobs throughout the Community, it reduced the High Authority to the role of a handmaiden who must promote but not actually enforce "the application by the member states of the measures provided for in this Article." As in the case of transport, the Six were charged individually to carry out certain policies while the supranational authority remained without means to pro-

[93]*Treaty*, Arts. 2 and 3e. For a basic introduction to social action by other European organizations, see Albert Delperée, *Politique sociale et intégration europeénne*, (Liège, 1956), 58-71. [a] Jack Schiefer, "Sozialpolitik der Hohen Behörde—Möglichkeiten und Grenzen," *Bergbau und Wirtschaft*, X (1957), 26. [b] ECSC, HA, "Déclaration par M. Finet au nom de la Haute Autorité au sujet du rapport de M. Mutter sur les aspects sociaux du Memorandum de la Haute Autorité sur la définition des objectifs généraux (Document no. 11, février, 1957)." *Doc. 1261/57f*, 4. Finet went on to claim that some leaders have since recognized that this was a fundamental error on their part.

[94]Wilhelm Langwieler, *Die sozialpolitische Problematik der Montanunion* (Bonn, 1953), 7-9.

mote effective unification and coördination of policy. Finally, the High Authority, in line with its task to promote new methods of production and research, might provide grants for scientific investigation and contribute financially to the easing of unemployment resulting from technological change. States were required to match this aid unless the Council by a two-thirds majority gave the High Authority license to proceed on its own.[95]

The results of these provisions were mixed. Some ventures were suprisingly successful, others were disappointing, still others brought results that were just about on a par with expectations.

The High Authority has not been involved in the shaping of wage policy. If the assertion has nevertheless been made that "differences in miners' and steelworkers' wages as between one country and another have in general decreased,"[96] one can only assume that this trend forms part of a general alignment in prices, costs, and profits, resulting from the common market. For the executive's direct action has been confined to investigation, research, and the periodic publication of their results.[97] These reveal that wage earners of the Community have benefited from the continuous boom of the 1950's. In their own minds, they may credit their well-being and abiding full employment to the ECSC, but the requisite studies of evolving labor attitudes toward the supranational remain to be undertaken.

Though the common market for coal and steel opened almost immediately after Community institutions had begun their work, it remained confined to the products and excluded their producers. The nature and extent of labor mobility had to be negotiated before it could become a reality. A list of skills and job specifications had to be drafted to determine which workers were *bona fide* members of the Community's work force. Channels of information had to be developed to enable employers to find suitable men in

[95]ECSC, CA, Ausschuss für Fragen der Sozialpolitik, *Übersicht über die sozialpolitischen Bestimmungen des Vertrages* (Luxembourg, 1953), *passim*.

[96]ECSC, HA, "The social mission of the European Coal and Steel Community." *Doc. 1697/57e*, 16.

[97]Most recently: ECSC, HA, *Entwicklung der Löhne und Lohnpolitik in den Ländern der Gemeinschaft im Jahre 1958* (Luxembourg, 1959). For a significant contribution to comparative wage statistics, see "Methoden des Reallohnvergleiches zwischen den Ländern der Gemeinschaft," *Statistische Informationen*, I, No. 7 (1954), 10-13.

other countries. Immigration laws had to be adapted to a free flow of labor across boundaries, and wage and social security policies had to be harmonized to prevent discrimination against foreign workers. The High Authority was called upon to "guide and facilitate" these reforms. Since men like Monnet had a healthy respect for public opinion, they saw the social sector as an ideal sphere in which the Community and its peoples could meet and understand each other. The High Authority began to guide social policy at once. In March 1953 it convened an *ad hoc* committee, including experts from the International Labor Office in Geneva and the OEEC, to prepare the ground work for an agreement on the execution of Article 69.[97a] On the basis of their report the executive recommended to the governments

1) the creation of a Community labor passport.
2) measures to coordinate national employment offices, to join supply with demand on a common labor market.
3) the establishment of a descriptive list of occupations in Community industries.
4) several bilateral or one multilateral social security agreement, applying to all migrant workers if possible.

An intergovernmental conference took this program under advisement, and by May 26, 1954, it had worked out a draft agreement which encompassed three of these suggestions, but remanded social security to a later, separate negotiation. The draft was accepted by the Council and sent to the governments on December 8, 1954.[98]

The agreement reduced obstacles to labor mobility, but it did not altogether remove them. It applied only to skilled workmen who had undergone specific vocational training and/or a minimum of job experience. The *carte de travail* was not a passport in the strict sense of the word. It provided merely the right to cross borders in

[97a]The inclusion of an OEEC official made sense in view of the Manpower Liberalization Code adapted by that organization in 1953. Cf., David E. Christian, "Resistance to International Worker Mobility; a barrier to European Unity," *Industrial and Labor Relations Review*, VIII (1954), 387.

[98]Rudolf Petz and Helmut Zöllner, *Die Beschäftigungsfreiheit der Montanfacharbeiter* (Frankfurt/Main, 1956), 12-15; provide the history of the negotiations. See also *Gesamtbericht 52/53*, 104-06; *Zweiter Gesamtbericht*, 176-79. For the text: ECSC, *Décision relative à l'application de l'article 69 du Traité du 18 avril 1951 instituant la Communauté* . . . (Luxembourg, 1955).

response to a definite job offer. The search for men and jobs was delegated to the national employment agencies rather than to a supranational clearing office.[99] Holders of the card were warned on an accompanying set of instructions that each government reserved the right to deport Community aliens for reasons of health or in the interest of public order. Nor could the decision remove a variety of political and sociological obstacles to the free circulation of labor. Skilled workers covered by the arrangement frequently had no reason to seek positions abroad while the less secure of their comrades, the less experienced and less instructed, were not included. It was estimated that only 350,000 of a total of 1,600,000 in the community could legitimately apply for the labor card. Then there were ties of home, reluctance to leave families even temporarily, language barriers, and a host of other adjustment problems which perpetuated an imbalance of supply and demand on the labor market that no amount of goodwill on the part of High Authority or governments could dent in a free society.[100]

Finally the decision itself, though promulgated in the waning weeks of 1954, did not go into effect until September 1957, due to some national hesitations to ratify. During the first year after that date only 283 cards were issued, hardly enough to justify so much labor, debate, and maneuvering. The industry with the largest labor deficit, coal mining, was in a crisis, but new hiring had slowed down in general. The new unemployed who would have desired to benefit were not eligible. After much travail, the total result appeared disproportionately modest, the prospect dismayingly uncertain.[101]

The personal imponderables which were the source of much inflexibility in the labor supply on the common market also dogged High Authority attempts to rehabilitate and relocate workers en masse. As a result of the growing competitive tempo, some enter-

[99]ECSC, HA, "Note de la Haute Autorité de la Communauté Europeénne du Charbon et de l'Acier concernant l'application de l'article 69 du Traité . . ." *Doc. 5749/55*, 2-4.

[100]For a good discussion of these elusive human factors, see ECSC, HA, *Hindernisse für die Beweglichkeit der Arbeitskräfte und soziale Probleme der Anpassung* (Luxembourg, 1956), 39-52.

[101]*Siebenter Gesamtbericht*, 258-60. For different and more impressive accomplishments in EEC, cf., EEC, Commission, *Vierter Gesamtbericht*, 170.

prises had to reorganize and retool in order to survive. This often involved major interruptions of production and led at the very least to temporary loss of work, if not to permanent technological unemployment. The High Authority's task under these circumstances was either to provide assistance for training men to assume new jobs or to help them find positions elsewhere.[102] As a rule, requests for such aid went from the enterprise to the government, which in turn would commit itself to help but ask the ECSC to assume half the burden. If the Community was satisfied that the problem under review resulted from disturbances created by the common market, it would then come to terms with the national authorities on the modalities of collaboration.

The results produced some surprises. The simpler the procedure and the task, it seemed, the more substantial the returns. In Italy the High Authority agreed to pay tide-over relief to dismissed workers training for new positions. It contracted to assume the entire load with the understanding that the government would in turn finance new ventures and provide additional opportunities for employment. This agreement was expected to involve some eight thousand persons, and it has since provided assistance for a considerable percentage of that total.[103] Another, more limited instance of temporary aid was provided by the much publicized case of the *Compagnie des Ateliers et Forges de la Loire* at St. Étienne. Four medium-sized steel plants, traditional producers of a certain acid, high quality steel for armaments, were trying first to extricate themselves from the ruin of 1940, next to survive changes in the market to which four small competitors within a radius of fifteen miles simply could not adjust. As orders declined, they kept taking each other's bread. None of them had enough to survive, let alone to buy out his rivals. As early as 1946, the Monnet plan had urged a merger, but the idea did not gain unanimous acceptance until 1953. To keep the affected workers employed during a reorganization that involved increased specialization of each component, the ECSC and France contributed $450,000 each. Specialists at one plant were gradually transferred to commensurate jobs at others. Others received subsistence while undergoing additional training.

[102]*Convention Containing the Transitional Provisions*, Sec. 23.
[103]*Vierter Gesamtbericht*, 226-27; *Siebenter Gesamtbericht*, 256-57.

After initial complaints, union representatives were added to a mixed committee of government and High Authority representatives which consulted periodically as the work progressed. The case of CAFL brought the Community to the grass roots. It preserved production installations of some importance and saved a town from serious industrial blight.[104]

The happy issue of this readaptation enterprise glosses over a number of setbacks along the way. Some highly skilled personnel were not disposed to wait until the reorganization and merger of the four enterprises had been completed. Within six months, one hundred of these industrial artisans had given notice and found employment elsewhere. On the other hand, there was a marked hostility to change. Some men refused a new job five or six miles away, even if better housing was available at the new location, and preferred low-category employment with reduced wages at the old shop. Such reluctance to move was especially frustrating when the rehabilitation process involved large-scale removals to other regions. In 1953 mine owners in the Centre-Midi of France agreed to some closings and prepared to transfer five thousand miners to Lorraine. The High Authority offered some $2 million in aid, providing a payment of $400 to heads of families and $150 to single employees, plus moving and transport costs. It also promised loans to promote the construction of necessary housing at the new work site.[105] Two years later 258 miners had volunteered to depart, and 145 had actually gone. By 1956, a total of 560 had moved. About 4,500 out of 5,000 showed absolutely no predisposition to participate.[106]

Several reasons accounted for this failure. Even before the opening of the common market, some miners from Centre-Midi had gone to Lorraine and returned dissatisfied. The raw climate and the language difficulties persuaded them to brave the risks of unemployment at home. The first group of 125 transfers in December 1953 consisted mostly of North-Africans who were peremptorily told to pack for departure on a certain date. Nine refused and were fired. Rehabilitation on these terms smacked of deportation. Christian and Socialist unions intervened and so did the ECSC. Pains

[104]ECSC, HA, "New Deal for French Steel." *Doc. 2684/55e*, 3-7.
[105]*Zweiter Gesamtbericht*, 173-74. [106]*Vierter Gesamtbericht*, 223-26.

were now taken to explain to the miners what benefits they could expect under resettlement, which included new jobs and pay equal to the old. But the response did not quicken. Of the small number that chose to go, 70 per cent were foreigners, frequently Spaniards driven across the Pyrenees by the Spanish Civil War, who feared unemployment and deportation if they did not cooperate. The natives of the region simply preferred to remain in the homes that some of their families had occupied for more than a century and to look to their truck gardens for survival in case of a shut-down. Foremen discouraged good men from leaving. Local union organizers worked at cross purposes with their national headquarters, afraid that mass resettlement would eventually wipe out their cells. The Bishop of Rodez, Msgr. Dubois, wrote to the members of a Christian union local: "You are right . . . to refuse exile from your *petite patrie.* . . . You are right to proclaim your attachment to the soil and to your region, to your living parents and the graves of your ancestors." Local business men and shop keepers swelled the opposition. The region was not urbanized. Alès with 37,000 inhabitants was its largest town. If it could retain its population, there was always the hope of reopening the mines or attracting new industry. The loss of five thousand families would doom it forever. When the chips were down, the theories of readaptation succumbed to the actual desire to stay and try to survive in accustomed surroundings.[107]

Another smaller French resettlement venture in the Auvergne had the same results. Of 495 idled miners, 270 found new jobs, 150 underwent prolonged unemployment, 21 chose retirement, and only 44 moved to Lorraine. As a result, the Community abandoned resettlement. The experience showed that a distressed area could be aided by mergers to eliminate superfluous competition. Failing this, attempts would have to be made to attract new industries.[108] One could only add that the fortunate economic situation left ample time to experiment with all feasible alternatives.

Lastly, the High Authority made imaginative use of Article 55, Section 2c, of the treaty. This provision allowed for the use of tax

[107]ECSC, HA, "Les transferts de main d'oeuvre du Centre-Midi vers la Lorraine." *Doc. 2129/56f,* 1-12.

[108]Writer's interview with Mr. Paul de Boer of the High Authority, March 2, 1957.

revenue in subsidizing research. At the instigation of the Common Assembly, the executive decided to devote some of these funds to develop inexpensive housing, first on an experimental basis, then on a large scale. The purpose was to attain the objective of higher levels of living, to provide greater stability in the labor force—inadequate housing in Belgium, for instance, led a large annual turnover among Italian migrants—and to attract workers to areas and industries suffering from a labor shortage.[109] By the end of 1960, it had provided over $44 million in credits, succeeded in inducing others to contribute another $17 million, and thus provided three-fifths of a construction program that resulted in the building of 36,208 houses and apartments.[110] Although this did not resolve an estimated shortage of 250,000 dwelling units, it was a substantial and deservedly publicized contribution. Added to the Community's vital concern in and financial contribution to safety research, industrial medicine, and statistical studies of price indexes, it launched the ECSC into another activity that reached the individual worker. Every opening of a housing project under Community auspices provided a lasting monument to its work and its progress.

The European Coal and Steel Community has grown into a diversified microcosm. It has been active: endowed with independent powers, it has combined energy and realism in their application. But in the ECSC's first seven years, it had been amply demonstrated that partial integration could only bring limited success. The number of areas in which High Authority and national governments trod on one another's toes was uncomfortably large. True, there was not a single government which obstructed the Community in principle. But the spirit of cooperation rose in proportion with the powers delegated to the ECSC by the treaty. In any case, accomplishment was spotty.

Production had risen, but the Community could not claim more than a contributory share. Prices failed to rise disastrously, but Community controls over their movements proved in some instan-

[109]*Zweiter Gesamtbericht*, 179-82; Helmut Zöllner, "Die Montanunion fördert den Arbeiterwohnungsbau," *Bergbau und Wirtschaft*, IV (1957), 38.
[110]*Achter Gesamtbericht*, 320.

ces illusory. The movement of goods on the common market was no longer impeded by tariffs, and restrictive cartels had been contained, but transport discriminations survived. The ECSC lacked the resources and powers to effect a common capital market. Governments could continue to bribe or intimidate enterprises to favor the national over the supranational interest. On the basis of the treaty alone, the worker continued to look to his union and his government for redress. Yet the fact that the Community had injected itself successfully into the welfare picture was one of the strongest indications that an independent supranational institution could survive even under less than ideal conditions.

The greatest danger under the circumstances was stagnation. Jean Monnet, the creator of the European Coal and Steel Community, had conceived of it as a pilot project. As the reader closed the eighth annual report of the High Authority for 1960, he was bound to ask himself: "What more is there to integration? To what other experiments has the ECSC contributed its impetus and experience? What new dimensions have been added to Robert Schuman's original 1950 model?" It is time, then, to look beyond the ECSC and to contemplate the European spirit in travail during the opulent Fifties.

CHAPTER ELEVEN

Europe in Suspense

IT IS TIME TO RESUME THE CHRONOLOGICAL THREAD OF THIS NARRA-
tive. Integration of coal and steel in Western Europe, and the partial harmonization of the economic and social functions associated
with these industries, had been the hallmark in the sixth decade
of our century. The taboos of national sovereignty had under certain circumstances retreated before the desire to revive the Continent under new auspices. Still, in other respects, political life proceeded as usual. The extent to which the Schuman Plan would sell
itself remained unpredictable. The political scientist's hope that
there would emanate from this first experiment an overflow of in-
tegrative energy into their other economic sectors[1] was both too
narrow and unwarranted. It was too narrow because the potential
effect need not be confined to economic life. In the halls of the
Common Assembly new forms of political organization burgeoned,
and the new rows of homes in many centers of the Community
symbolized a fight against gloom and grime which was only partially economic. It was unwarranted because the tempo and extent
of the "spillover" remained conjectural. Might there not be an
equally significant "damming in" of supranational forces? In transport, in its attempt to solve structural problems of the coal industry,
and in the effort to mobilize investment capital, the ECSC had
been contained by adverse powers. Progress was not inevitable,
and the survival of the institutions called into life by the Schuman
Plan could not be taken for granted. The prediction of new advances beyond sector integration was at the outset little more than
a declaration of faith.

Of this faith there seemed to be an abundance. Even as the effort

[1]Haas, *The Uniting of Europe*, 105-06.

of Robert Schuman laid the ghost of Franco-German economic conflict, the Consultative Assembly, holding its first meeting after the North Korean Red Army crossed the 38th Parallel, called for military integration.[2] Both French and British spokesmen, for different reasons, led this trespass which the Assembly's statute had specifically forbidden. The French feared unilateral German rearmament, the British an American withdrawal from Europe in order to counter more vigorously Communist thrusts in Asia. Both fears were vindicated when the decision to rearm Germany ripened with autumn, largely at America's behest.

Fear of the revival of an old foe, even as a more recent adversary made the quick settling of traditional conflicts imperative, forced the European army project out of the powerless hands of the Council of Europe onto a more responsible level. On October 28, 1950, French Premier René Pleven put the plan that bears his name before the NATO Defense Committee. He called upon the same six nations that were in the midst of negotiating a coal and steel pool to merge their armed forces.

In defense as in industry a German contribution to a war, now both hot and cold, was recognized as indispensable, and integration was proposed as the tool that would take the sting out of the Teutonic revival. Accordingly, Pleven applied the Schuman formula to the military sector in order to avoid unilateral rearmament pure and simple as well as unlimited German control of a new national army under expanded provisions of the NATO pact.

The first reactions to the French proposal were frigid. NATO experts doubted that it would work. Predictably some of Pleven's countrymen—not all extremists—opposed German rearmament under any condition, although in October 1950 a majority supported it. Britain once more declined to abet supranationalism in defense just as she had rejected it in economics. The Germans, finally, refused to participate in a scheme which consigned them to a status of inferiority.

Two events "unfroze" the Pleven Plan. On November 7, 1950, Konrad Adenauer received the French High-Commissioner, André François-Poncet. The French diplomat was apparently able to dispell some of the Chancellor's doubts, for the following day he

[2]See above 36.

went before the Bundestag favoring German participation.[3] In December, Chinese intervention in Korea bode fair to prolong the Far Eastern War beyond the optimistic "home by Christmas" deadline. It forced the United States to reappraise its stand on the European army. The upshot was a proposal from the American NATO representative, Charles M. Spofford, to add German combat teams to NATO forces, pending the effectuation of the Pleven Plan. In return for French acquiescence to this interim, Washington agreed to support a European Defense Community.[4]

While the content of the François-Poncet-Adenauer conversation is unknown, the vital German shift is not hard to explain. From Bonn's point of view, the Pleven Plan no less than its predecessor offered egress from a frustrating impasse. The brainchild of Jean Monnet had ended the wardship of German industries under the International Ruhr Authority. The European army would provide ways of ending Allied occupation west of the Soviet zone, speed the recovery of complete sovereignty, and offer simultaneous reinsurance for Germany's second democratic experiment against the resurgence of traditional militarism. At the same time, the Federal Republic accepted certain special limitations. She agreed to forego manufacture of atomic and bacteriological weapons. Her forces would be entirely committed to the supranational army, and she had to accept being the only member of the European Defense Community who did not belong to NATO.

Not all concessions were German, however. The most remarkable aspect of the Pleven Plan was, after all, that it bound six nations not merely to keep the peace among each other, but to surrender the means of making war or of defending themselves unilaterally against any enemy in Europe. They were to retain jurisdiction only over troops recruited to police non-European territories, contingents on international missions, and their respective police forces.[5] The bulk of military manpower was to be controlled by a supranational commission, modeled on the High Authority, which

---

[3] *Die Vertragswerke von Bonn und Paris vom Mai 1952* (Dokumente und Berichte des Europa-Archivs, Band 10), (Frankfurt/Main, 1952), xxiii-iv.

[4] Zurcher, *The Struggle to Unite Europe*, 89-90; for the English text of the EDC treaty see RIIA, *Documents on International Affairs, 1952* (London, 1955), 116-70.

[5] RIIA, 119.

functioned within an institutional framework faithfully copied from the ECSC treaty.[6]

Once forced past initial hurdles, the project gained ground. The Spofford Plan had succeeded, temporarily at least, to steer it through two tricky eddies. German rearmament began on a scale sufficient to add to Western strength, but not with enough precipitation to elicit Russian intervention in Europe at a time when the United States was engaged elsewhere, nor so uncompromisingly as to create a crisis of morale among the original NATO partners.

Persistently divided reactions served as a continuing reminder of a most delicate task, but the returns to Germany for the concessions she was willing to accept were quick in coming and were, in her instance at any rate, more persuasive than words. In May 1951, the Federal Republic regained control of her foreign affairs and foreign trade. After the Spring of 1951 had passed in further barren debate with Russia over an agenda for another foreign minister's conference on Germany, September found the Big Three in accord to integrate the Bonn Confederation into the Western community; and in October German uniforms made their postwar debut at a crucial six-power conference on the EDC treaty.[7] Despite Adenauer's subsequent failure to obtain for his country full membership in NATO, Bonn's overwhelming support for the European army could from this point onward be taken for granted.

Meanwhile, the project had won preliminary approval in the French National Assembly by the same substantial margin which that body accorded the ECSC pact in December of 1951. After the United States and Great Britain gave it emphatic support the negotiations, begun in February 1951, led to completion and signature of the treaty on May 27, 1952.[8]

The excitement among stalwart Europeans mounted. The European Coal and Steel Community had been ratified in April. Now the second experiment in sector integration had been drafted and

[6]*Ibid.*, 122-29.

[7]Ellinor von Puttkamer, "Der Entwurf eines Vertrages über die Satzung der Europäischen Gemeinschaft," *Zeitschrift für ausländisches öffentliches Recht und Völkerrecht*, XV (1953), 104n, rightly points out that for the rest the effect of the September communiqué on the October deliberations was slight.

[8]See *Die Vertragswerke von Bonn und Paris*, xxvii-xxxviii for an excellent resumé of these negotiations.

launched. The next problem was how to tie them together. Could it be "imagined that the six participating countries would willingly send their sons to serve in this European army unless a fundamental unity existed in their foreign policies? The establishment of a six-nation defense community must lead to a unification . . . in the field of foreign policy."[9] A broad roof was needed to shelter the narrow efforts of partial integration from the centrifugal forces of national resistance. Carried along by the tide of enthusiasm, the foreign ministers of the Six on September 10, 1952 advanced to this third line of attack. The next day Chancellor Adenauer, in his capacity as president of the Coal and Steel Community's Council of Ministers, brought their proposal to the floor of the Common Assembly, coupled with the mandate that the Community parliament, suitably enlarged, would draft yet another treaty establishing a European Political Community.[10]

The mandate was willingly received, but not without reservations. Ensuing discussion revealed some legal difficulties. The designated instrumentality was to be an *ad hoc* assembly, not the

Chart VII.

THE EUROPEAN DEFENSE COMMUNITY

Council of Ministers		Court		Assembly
National Governments	Consulting Committees	Commission	SHAPE	National Parliaments
	European Military Territorial Organization	European Procurement Office	European Defense Forces	

Source: *Die Vertragswerke von Bonn und Paris vom Mai 1952* (Dokumente und Berichte des Europa-Archivs, Band 10) (Frankfurt, 1952), p. ix.

[9] These were Chancellor Adenauer's words when he spoke to an American audience at the Waldorf-Astoria on April 6, 1953; Zurcher, *The Struggle to Unite Europe*, 96. The initiative for the EPC came, however, from DeGasperi, see above, note 7.

[10] *Débats*, I, 22-23.

ECSC parliament, whose limited functions did not lend themselves to this task. Thus the ministers were addressing themselves
to the members of the Assembly rather than to the Assembly itself.
The basis for their request was Article 38 of the EDC treaty, which
called for a democratically elected assembly to explore the matter
of coordinating sector integration in a political federation. Could
the *ad hoc* group legitimately proceed if its only authority was an
agreement which had not yet been ratified?[11] Could Europe be
constructed in this headlong rush? On the other hand, this legalistic
timidity was assailed by those who in the Consultative Assembly
"session after session, had supplicated the governments with ve-
hemence, anxiety and anguish to agree to the establishment of a
common political authority."[12] Who could call it a headlong rush if
four years after the event six powers had at last decided to make
good the promises of the Hague Congress of 1948?[13] Between these
two views stood an objection which refused to accept ministerial
mandates as sufficient cause for action and feared a precedent that
would make the Assembly the messenger boy and workhorse of
the governments.[14]

The most determined opponents of early political coordination
brought in a resolution which merely called for a study commission of twenty-five to consider the ministerial proposal and report
on it by the required deadline. The overwhelming majority, however, rallied behind two motions sponsored by Guy Mollet and
Paul-Henri Spaak, signifying acceptance of the task and asking
the German, French, and Italian delegations to select from among
their compatriots in the Consultative Assembly the additional three
members to which each was entitled in the constituent body. Finally, they provided that the *ad hoc* group would hold its first
meeting on September 15, 1952. These affirmative proposals were
adopted 58-4, with an unrecorded number of absences and absten-
tions.[15]

The hard work of the *ad hoc* assembly was entrusted to a constitutional committee of twenty-six members, with Heinrich von
Brentano in the chair.[16] Their proposal, embodied in a draft treaty

[11]*Ibid.*, 76-78.   [12]*Ibid.*, 79.   [13]*Ibid.*, 81.   [14]*Ibid.*, 84.
[15]*Ibid.*, 101-04.
[16]Basil Karp, "The Draft Constitution for a European Political Community,"

tabled at Strasbourg on March 6, 1953, promised only limited political integration. The key passage in the formulation of its objectives demanded that the European Political Community "ensure the coordination of the foreign policy of member states" but only in "questions likely to involve the existence . . . security" and "prosperity of the Community."[17] This entailed no blanket surrender of national jurisdiction in the realm of international affairs but merely established, so it would seem, supranational coordination on diplomatic questions emanating from the operations of the ECSC and the EDC. In this limited field the EPC could make proposals, conclude treaties with third countries, and harmonize the foreign policy of its members.[18] These were bound to inform the EPC of any foreign policy agreements "they are in progress of negotiating" which would affect the Community. Disagreements arising from this procedure must be submitted to arbitration. Finally, the new community could "to the extent required for the achievement of its aims and within the limit of its powers and competence, have the right to accredit and receive diplomatic representatives."[19]

The projected institutions of the European Political Community consisted of a bicameral legislature, including a lower house directly elected by the peoples, and a Senate chosen by the national parliaments. Upon ratification of the treaty, they would also assume the parliamentary functions under the ECSC and EDC treaties. This feature bore the undeniable imprint of a treaty drafted by legislators. Not only did it repose on a direct international mandate, but the European parliament could also legislate and exercise budgetary controls.[20] Bills must pass both houses by a simple majority, but one fourth of the Senate could return a legislative proposal to the chamber for reconsideration. Nor did this parliamentarian's utopia provide for executive independence. On the contrary, the president of the executive council was elected by the Senate, and his colleagues had to be confirmed by a vote of confi-

---

International Organization, VIII (1954), 183; Elinor von Puttkamer, "Der Entwurf eines Vertrages über die Satzung der Europäischen Gemeinschaft," *loc. cit.,* 106-119.
    [17]*Ad Hoc* Assembly instructed to work out a draft treaty setting up a European Political Community, *Draft Treaty Embodying the Statute of the European Community* (Luxembourg, 1953), Art 2. hereafter cited as EPC treaty,
    [18]*EPC Treaty,* Arts. 55, 67-69.   [19]*Ibid.,* Arts. 73-74.   [20]*Ibid.,* Arts. 10, 13-17.

dence in both houses. An adverse poll in either chamber would suffice to force the Council's resignation.[21] Finally, the draft provided for liaison through the Council of Ministers, except that the EPC group was to "communicate with each member state through the minister of the latter" rather than its president.[22] The judiciary was identical with that of the two pre-existent communities.

The debate over this interesting document consumed several days. In view of the large margin by which the ministerial proposal had been adopted originally, and in the absence of any visible major shift in public opinion since then, there was no likehood of its rejection. Yet some critical questions were raised which deserved a hearing. Certain French spokesmen wondered about the EPC's effect on overseas territories. How could one expect continued fidelity from the natives to a colonial power which on the European continent had surrendered its sovereignty? This might appear to be an academic question in 1962, but the *status quo* of 1953 still invested it with an aspect of seriousness.[23] Other questions, posed in a less negative spirit, sought to untangle the nebulous hierarchical relationships between the various European executives. Even so experienced a constitutional authority as Fernand Dehousse of Belgium was unable to clarify the scene. According to him, the High Authority of the ECSC and the EDC Commissariat would be controlled by the European Executive Council. He went on to explain that as soon as the EPC treaty went into effect, these executives would all be responsible to the new European parliament.[24] This would indicate that they were all three equal in their relationship to the legislative branch but not equal among each other. Moreover, it was not explained how that parliament could legislate bicamerally under the political community, while resting content with its review functions unicamerally under the aegis of ECSC.

There was much debate and division this time on the question of national representation. In the chamber France and Germany had one seat for approximately 750,000 inhabitants, while Luxembourg's population of 300,000 was to be represented by twelve dep-

[21]*Ibid.*, Arts. 28, 31. [22]*Ibid.*, Art. 37.
[23]*Ad Hoc* Assembly, *Summary Report of Debates, March 6, 1953*, II, 1.
[24]EPC treaty, Art. 60; *Ad Hoc* Assembly, *Summary Report of Debates, March 9, 1953*, I, 8.

uties. The distribution of Senate seats was likewise subject to much controversy. Both sections dealing with legislative apportionment passed by surprisingly slim margins. The love feast which four years earlier had attended this ritual prior to the establishment of the Consultative Assembly was not repeated when the exercise of concrete powers was at stake.[25] One project article defining representation of the Saar was dropped into the bottomless well of silence to avoid a painful discussion on an increasingly painful subject.[26]

In the end there was a deceptive show of unanimity. Fifty votes were cast for the project, none against. But thirty-seven members had either boycotted the assembly's work altogether or remained silent when its labor was completed. Three French Socialists, including Guy Mollet, formally abstained because they saw no way by which Great Britain could be drawn into the European circle. The German Socialists never attended because they opposed any strengthening of the EDC, which they regarded as a French conspiracy to keep Germany disarmed. Several conservative deputies from France, on the other hand, chose silence because to them the community symbolized the road back to German hegemony over Europe. One lonely Luxembourg liberal felt, surprisingly, that the small members had not been accorded adequate representation.[27]

What it finally boiled down to was several rounds of lively but unsubstantial shadow boxing. On March 10, 1953, the draft treaty was duly presented to a somewhat less than expectant Council of Ministers. It formed the subject of a number of high-level deliberations in the months that followed, the last of which in December at The Hague adjourned in "a blaze of ambiguity." Another session, scheduled for March 1954 to consider a final report presented by a lower administrative echelon, never convened.[28]

The European tide seemed to have passed its crest. This was hardly the fault of the ministers. The EPC had been conceived as

[25]*Dto., March 7, 1953*, II, 6-10. [26]*Dto., March 10, 1953*, II, 11-12.

[27]Karp, "The Draft Constitution for a European Political Community," *loc. cit.*, 184.

[28]Zurcher, *The Struggle to Unite Europe*, 108-09n; RIIA, *Britain in Western Europe: WEU and the Atlantic Alliance* (London, 1956), 42-43, somewhat unfairly and misleadingly adds that the foreign minister's meetings on the EPC "decreased in productivity when M. Schuman was replaced by M. Bidault."

a link between two communities of which only one existed. The
EDC treaty had produced only intermittent labor pains; delivery
was not imminent. As of March 10, 1953, none of the signatories
had ratified the pact. Efforts to that end in the Bundestag and the
Benelux parliaments corroborated expectations that four countries
at least would put their stamp of approval on the document early
in 1954. But Italy procrastinated, waiting to be pushed over the
brink by the French. In Paris the road-blocks were the highest.

The story of the EDC treaty in the National Assembly is protracted, dreary, and at the outset not devoid of mystery. After it
was signed, Robert Schuman waited six months before sending it
to the chamber. On this occasion his timing was off. He submitted
the pact at a time when the press was spotlighting the Bordeaux
trial of several Alsatian SS men accused in the gruesome mass
slaughter of civilians of all sexes and ages at Oradour during World
War II. This tragedy not only raised a host of internal controversies; it also recalled just how much unfinished business had been
held over from the all too recent occupation by a country whose
armed forces were to be merged with those of France.[29] Was it
coincidence then that the defense committee of the National assembly began its labor on the military integration plan by appointing two *rapporteurs,* Jules Moch (Socialist) and Pierrre Koenig
(Gaullist), who were both known to oppose it?

Apart from the imponderable impact of Schuman's departure
from the Quai d'Orsay on January 7, 1953, this slowdown was not
merely of local provenance. In the USSR Stalin died on March 5,
1953. Two months later, his successors rather demonstratively
dropped territorial claims against Turkey. The signing of a Korean
armistice followed on July 27. New conference proposals by Stalin's heirs made headlines throughout the world and fortified the
belief that the Cold War was thawing.

In France meanwhile a succession of shaky cabinets (Pinay,
Mayer, Laniel) saw less and less reason to risk their existence on a
controversial measure, the need for which appeared to evaporate
in the rising sun of renewed international goodwill. In actuality,
the conditions that had aided the gestation and birth of the Schu-

[29]Alexander Werth, *France 1940-55* (London, 1956), 597.

man Plan—economic crisis, compounded by Communist aggression
—were not repeating themselves. To the extent that the Russian
threat receded, the sacrifice of national sovereignty appeared unnecessary. To overcome the handicaps of the *détente* of 1953, the
supporters of the EDC came to rest their case increasingly on the
negative proposition, grist to the mill of the German Socialists, as
we have seen, that it alone would insure France against German
military revival. This argument revealed that the European spirit
was withering. More than that, it elicited the obvious rebuttal: if
German rearmament was such a danger, how could it be met by
destroying the freedom of action of the French army?[30] One fact
alone might arrest this reversal of opinion: British participation.

Here was the theme that imposed the many minor modulations
on European harmony. Britain had refused to join the ECSC, and
the treaty of association concluded between the two in 1955 would
not bring them together to any significant respect.[31] The ally across
the Channel was not ready to pool her sovereignty with any group
of continental friends. Foreign Secretary Anthony Eden's answer
to the Pleven Plan was to recommend support without participation and to hold in readiness "a more modest scheme . . . based upon the technical military arrangements, *but without* elaborate political superstructure."[32] The French, however, wanted more than
ill-defined "close political and military links." As insurance against
Germany, they aimed at a full-fledged mutual defense alliance
between the EDC and the United Kingdom. According to the Eden
memoirs, this would have included British participation against
any member of the Community who broke the Pleven Pact, an un-
usual and consequential commitment indeed. Eden has claimed
that he would have been willing to sign a formal treaty, under
which "each party would be obliged to give military assistance to

[30]Raymond Aron and Daniel Lerner (eds.), *La querelle de la CED* (Cahiers
de la Fondation Nationale des Sciences Politiques, No. 10) (Paris, 1956),
3-13.

[31]See, Council of Association between the Government of the United Kingdom of Great Britain and Northern Ireland and the High Authority of the European Coal and Steel Community, *First Annual Report, November 17, 1955-
December 31, 1956* (Luxembourg, 1957), *passim.*

[32]Sir Anthony Eden, *Full Circle* (London, 1960), 34.

the other, if either were the object of an armed attack in Europe."
He has credited this concession, valid for the duration of NATO,
with hastening the signing of the defense treaty in May.[33]

This was as far as Britain was willing to go. To the hesitant
French, who pointed out that the NATO arrangements would lapse
in 1969, whereas EDC was to run until 1994, Eden conceded in
April 1954 that he considered "the North Atlantic Treaty as being
of indefinite duration . . . ," while assuring them that his country
had no intention of withdrawing from the continent.[34] French
suspicions that the gaps in the British commitment were more substantial than London admitted were nourished by past British opposition to integration as such. Had not Eden himself attempted
only two years previously to effect an impossible juncture between
the independent institutions of the ECSC and the consultative organs of the Council of Europe?[35] A more sympathetic observer
might admit that Whitehall could not be solely concerned with
protecting France from the necessity of a painful decision. The
British had troubles of their own.

> After 1951, . . . the Conservatives, who had come to power,
> could never quite make up their minds whether EDC corres-
> ponded to either Continental or British interests. If it failed
> through military inefficiency, then it was a bad form of Ger-
> man rearmament. If, on the other hand, it succeeded militarily,
> then it would certainly be a decisive installment of Continen-
> tal federation. British official thinking had formally aban-
> doned the two-centuries'-old policy of opposing Continental
> unity under a "greatest power."

What might seem insufferable deviousness was in reality a definite inability to arrive at a clear-cut decision. "The paralysis was
characterized by public exhortation but private coolness towards
. . . EDC."[36] As a result, the hope of substantial British participation
by French standards had had to be abandoned by the time the

[33]*Ibid.*, pp. 44-45; *Britain in Western Europe*, 43.

[34]*Britain in Western Europe*, 45.

[35]Ball, *NATO and the European Union Movement*, 177; Eden's failure to
comment on his own 1952 project in his memoirs is revealing, cf., *Full Circle*,
47-48.

[36]*Britain in Western Europe*, 53.

committees of the National Assembly were ready to pronounce on the Pleven treaty.

The United States government, on the other hand, impatiently pressed for French ratification. At the three-power conference in Bermuda (December 4-8, 1953), this insistence seems to have taken rude and insulting forms, which rankled in the mind of Foreign Minister Bidault. This brusque tone sprang from Secretary Dulles' fear that Congress would turn its back on NATO if the EDC was not constituted soon, and his mistaken view that the alignment in the National Assembly presaged certain passage of the treaty as soon as the French government gave up its international blackmail and got down to business.[37]

Buffeted by divergent counsels of friendship, France was also facing military defeat in Indo-China. On May 8, 1954, the Asian empire of the French, which had been founded by Napoleon III and buttressed by the policies of Jules Ferry, was buried under the crumbling walls of Dien Bien Phu. Not many French politicians were now willing to surrender military sovereignty. Despite the reservations in the Pleven treaty which guaranteed national jurisdiction over troops fighting overseas, the Indo-China tumult drowned out everything else. Bleeding severely from the wounds inflicted by Ho Chi Minh's legions and faced in the foreseeable future by similar onslaughts in North Africa,[38] France could not compartmentalize her troubles politically, strategically or emotionally. The late spring and early summer of 1954 turned into one protracted government crisis. In April Marshal Juin exploded a bomb when he opposed the EDC and paid for his temerity with dismissal from the NATO command. With the beginning of peace negotiations in Geneva, rioting erupted in Paris. Defense Minister René Pleven was manhandled by outraged patriots at the Arc de Triomphe. On May 13, the Laniel government survived one Indo-China debate by two votes. A month later it chose an adverse vote on a procedural question in connection with the same issue to shed the crushing burden of responsibility.

[37]Roscoe Drummond and Gaston Coblentz, *Duel at the Brink, John Foster Dulles' Command of American Power* (New York, 1960), 98; *Full Circle*, 55.
[38]Cf., Pierre Mendès-France's well-founded prophecies in Assemblée Nationale, *Séance du 9 juin, 1954*, 2854.

At this very moment—on June 9 and 18, 1954, respectively—the foreign affairs and national defense committees reported adversely on the European defense pact. The first result was more Anglo-American pressure. Both London and Washington expressed the determination to introduce Germany into the Western community as an equal partner, if necessary without consulting France. This accord between the trans-Atlantic allies was really surprising. England was not committed to European integration and had helped retard it. The United States viewed it with hope and affection and refused to accept the defeat of the EDC long after it had become virtual certainty. The only provisional conclusion one can draw at this point is that Britain, better informed on the declining prospects of the defense community, saw no danger in paying lip-service to a moribund project—and no profit in antagonizing John Foster Dulles on an issue in which she was going to have her way.

These domestic and international crosscurrents generated much thunder and lightning over the head of Joseph Laniel's spectacular if unlucky successor, Pierre Mendès-France. His investiture was more than a routine personnel change. At the Quai d'Orsay the Schuman-Bidault lease had run out, and the new prime minister, doubling in foreign affairs, was moving in. For the first time since 1945, the MRP became the hard core of opposition. At the same time, a larger segment of "ministerial" Social Republicans split from General de Gaulle's Union for Republican and Social Action. Pierre Koenig, the victor of Bir Hakim, replaced René Pleven as minister of defense. Because of his pledge to make peace in Indo-China, Mendès-France received the embarassing offer of Communist support, which he refused. It was an unorthodox, unstable coalition, resting on votes from the extreme Right and the extreme Left, headed by a Radical with an independent mind, reformist zeal, and clean hands.[39]

Mendès-France promised action on the EDC, but he promised this to his countrymen rather than to the treaty partners or the Anglo-Saxon powers. While his most immediate problems remained at Geneva suspended in mid-air—a conference of the EDC pow-

[39]He was invested with the support of 414 members, enough to forego the 100 Communist votes. See also Alexander Werth, *Lost Statesman, the Strange Story of Pierre Mendès-France* (New York, 1955), 88.

ers called by the Benelux states on June 22 could not meet until August 19 for this reason—he outlined his European policy in the investiture debate. First, he intended to bring together the opposing points of view. These were represented in his own cabinet by Pierre Koenig on the emphatic negative, and by his Radical colleague Bourgès-Maunoury in a rather more lukewarm fashion on the positive side. These two were to negotiate terms of French acceptance after which Mendès-France promised to meet with the other five neighbors. The third step would be up to the National Assembly. In that last showdown, he pledged no support to either side. He was doubtful about the outcome and made it clear from the outset that he would comply with the wishes of the majority and would not stake his government's existence on the ratification of M. Pleven's utopia.[40]

The Geneva parleys ended in July. Warnings multiplied that the French refusal to make good on the EDC would be followed by unilateral German rearmament. On the 16th, in retribution, Mendès-France stunned a still incredulous John Foster Dulles with the point-blank assertion that the defense treaty as it stood could not pass the Assembly. Three weeks later the intra-French *pourparlers* between Bourgès-Maunoury and Koenig collapsed. On August 13, the French parliament scheduled the EDC debate to begin on the 28th.

Before this last act began, a final attempt was made at Brussels to save the EDC wholly or in part. To this three-day conference the French premier came with a series of revisions whose acceptance he felt to be indispensable if the treaty were to be ratified. The EDC was to be coterminous with NATO. The moment British or American troops were withdrawn from the Continent, it would automatically lapse. Only troops in "forward areas" (*e.g.,* French and Benelux contingents in Germany) were to be integrated. For the first eight years the treaty was in force each member was to retain a veto over community decisions. Officers were to remain under national jurisdiction.[41]

[40]Assemblée Nationale, *Séance du 17 juin, 1954,* 3003; Hermann Volle, "Die Agonie der Europäischen Verteidigungsgemeinschaft," *Europa-Archiv,* IX (1954), 7117.

[41]Edgar S. Furniss, Jr., *France, Troubled Ally: De Gaulle's Heritage and Prospects* (New York, 1960), 97-99, *Dilemma in Western Europe,* 48-49.

Each amendment was a torpedo. Yet even going as far as Brussels cost Mendès-France the very price he had not wanted to pay: a government crisis. The Gaullists in the cabinet resigned so as to avoid association with any compromise treaty the Radical leader might be able to negotiate. To the defection of his moody friends on the Right came the machinations of his avowed enemies. Robert Schuman advised Adenauer not to yield, as the National Assembly would ratify, while André Philip similarly urged Spaak to stand firm.[42] The effect of these international maneuvers remains to be determined, but they revealed Mendès-France faced by a solid, hostile front at Brussels and backed against a crumbling coalition in Paris. This alone excused a last shabby move, which consisted in creating the impression that the French treaty amendments had some measure of American support. It took a trip by Ambassador David Bruce to the Belgian capital to contradict this amazing announcement. The State Department's rectification has been described as a violent diatribe. In any case, it killed whatever case Mendès-France might have appeared to possess.[43]

After the abortive six-power meeting in the Belgian capital, the French premier proceeded to England, where he met Churchill and Eden at Chartwell. According to his own recollections, his British counterpart at Downing Street was obsessed "by the idea that ... America might get so fed up with France that it might ... pull out of Europe. In that case, Churchill saw the Iron Curtain moving further West."[44] Eden has admitted that Mendès-France recognized the need for alternative forms of German rearmament. But the British Foreign Secretary relished his own position of moral superiority. New approaches to the problem, he said, would not be easy to find. He impressed upon Mendès-France "that we intended to work in close agreement with the U.S. government and that we had a debt of honor to Adenauer and those European countries who had ratified EDC."[45]

[42]Eden, *Full Circle*, 147.
[43]Drummond and Coblentz, *Duel at the Brink*, 99-101.
[44]Werth, *Mendès-France*, 100.
[45]Eden, *Full Circle*, 148-49. Dulles persisted in believing that sins of omission rather than commission on England's part had killed a scheme which he had so ardently and ineffectually supported. Cf., Drummond and Coblentz, *Duel at the Brink*, 102-03.

There was no comfort to be had anywhere as Mendès-France returned home to preside at the trial of the EDC. Since the only formula which he felt might ensure ratification had been turned down by Germany, Italy, and the Benelux powers, he reiterated his refusal to commit his government on the outcome. He demanded a settlement, but left its terms to the discretion of the French parliament.[46]

In fairness to Mendès-France one must recognize his remarkable objectivity on the rostrum. He did not urge the Assembly to ratify, but he told it in no uncertain terms what it could expect if it did not. Consideration of German rearmament would be postponed, not ruled out. Instead of accepting it as a part of a supranational arms pact, France would have to yield to Anglo-American pressure and accept a German national army.[47] Although he did not champion the EDC, there is no evidence that Mendès-France pretended to share the illusion of its national opponents. For the rest, he preserved the aloofness he had promised. To the spirited attacks of the supporters of the EDC he offered no response. Though René Mayer contemptuously flayed him for letting delusion run wild without assuming the responsibility of either fighting or leading it,[48] he remained impassive. The last word came not from the government benches but from the tired old man of the Third Republic: Edouard Herriot. This relic of a past age, himself once an advocate of the United States of Europe during the Briand-Stresemann era, now called the supranational concept "monstrous and ridiculous." "For me, for us, the European community spells the end of France," he cried.[49] In the end, the procedural device of moving the previous question brought the stormy debate to a close. The motion passed 319-264, with the majority of the cabinet abstaining. Paul Reynaud, shaking with fury, rose to protest the legislative maneuver. The chair ruled him out of order. Someone shouted: "Let the gravedigger speak." On the right, deputies intoned *La Marseillaise.* "Let the supporters of EDC sing *Deutschland über alles,*" cried others. The impotent banging of the gavel merged with

[46] Assemblée Nationale, *Séance du 29 août, 1954,* 4436.
[47] Assemblée Nationale, *loc. cit.,* 4435.
[48] For Mayer's remarkable effort, see Assemblée Nationale, *loc. cit.,* 4446-49.
[49] Assemblée Nationale, *Séance du 30 août, 1954,* 4465-67.

general chaos as the session disintegrated.[50] A year before the Netherlands Foreign Minister had asked whether "Europe" would come about "voluntarily and freely" or as the result of threatened intervention from outside.[51] France's decision on August 30, 1954 constituted one answer.

France had deserted Europe, and Mendès-France had let it happen. No one hated him more bitterly for it than Europeans outside and inside of France. It was understandable and inevitable enough. The disciples of Jean Monnet wanted to build a new order, Pierre Mendès-France wanted to save the country whose name was part of his own. Under the cold exterior of a man who took to politics as a fortyish spinster to unexpected matrimony, and who was as much an economic expert as Monnet, lay concealed an anguished, sentimental nineteenth century patriot. Like General de Gaulle, like Michel Debré, he advocated a *redressement nationale* before embarking on what he described as an international policy of pretentious promises and broken pledges.[52] Unlike the revered general, he realized as early as 1954 that such an internal reformation would also mean the end of empire. Mendès-France saw his mandate as the prelude to peaceful revolution. He hoped to do for France under the constitution what the General in 1958 began with an act of usurpation. But he and his cabinet did not survive 1954. Like Léon Blum, whose career was not dissimilar, he received a few piecemeal concessions in the economic realm. He was not given the time to succeed or fail in any sweeping sense, merely the opportunity to desert Europe. What has happened since his resignation has vindicated his European enemies and inculpated the nationalist "bitter-enders" of 1954, who now must let De Gaulle perform belatedly what could have been accomplished more advantageously before.

For Pierre Mendès-France there is neither reward nor vindica-

[50]Assemblée Nationale, *loc. cit.*, 4471. Furniss' statement that "the National Assembly interred the treaty with relative calm and dignity" [p. 99] is not borne out by the record.

[51]J. F. Koevér, "The Integration of Western Europe," *Political Science Quarterly*, LXIX (1954), 355.

[52]Compare his words in *Assemblée Nationale, Séance du 9 juin, 1954*, 2854, with Debré, 42, 109.

tion. In respect to France's surrender overseas and on the issue of republican reorganization, he was wrong because he was right too soon. In regard to France's European mission, a verdict is more difficult to arrive at. The EDC treaty, like its EPC pendant, was not a work of unadulterated wisdom. Some of its provisions were, in fact, shockingly anachronistic. Under Article 68-2, certain strategic reorganization measures required recommendations by the Commanding General, agreement by the Commissariat, and unanimous consent of the Council of Ministers. What could eventuate from such a complex procedure in a war in which minutes could spell the difference between victory and disaster? Article 75 left the decision to mobilize in the hands of the member states. Could the integrated command really accept this reservation when the chips were down? What does mobilization mean in a nuclear contest? Either it is permanent or it is nonexistent. Finally, what was a European army without a European state? In other words, what did Mendès-France help inter? A living organism or a phantom? As long as we can ask that question, he can justify himself. Surrounded as he was by illusions on both sides, he was wise when he refused to make a choice.

The depressing effect of the French vote on August 30, 1954 cannot be gainsaid. Whether anything was lost in military terms or not, the political damage called for immediate repairs. Ever since July 4, an Anglo-American study group had been working on ways and means of restoring German sovereignty without EDC ratification. There is no evidence that their work contributed substantially to the events of autumn and winter. What followed the defeat of the Pleven Plan was largely set in motion by Anthony Eden.

Great Britain had refused to join the EDC, but the British had agreed to remain on the Continent, accepting NATO as an alliance of unlimited duration. At the same time, the refusal of the French National Assembly to continue on the European avenue left German rearmament and independence in a state of suspense which could not be allowed to persist indefinitely. The eventual way out of this maze of loose ends was a military pact sufficiently orthodox in structure to permit British participation and sufficiently restrictive in nature to include Germany on terms acceptable to France.[53]

Britain was ready to initiate this salvage operation. It would require unprecedented concessions at the expense of her diplomatic traditions, but it would also tie the European partners so closely to her apron strings "that it would be difficult and damaging" for any of them "to break these ties quickly."[54] Eden saw both sides of the coin and grasped his opportunity. On September 2, his commissioner in Germany successfully sounded out Adenauer on German membership in NATO with limited rearmament. The Chancellor agreed to both. Next the British Foreign Secretary approached the other governments concerned, proposing an early conference to create a new instrument of military cooperation. On Sunday, September 6, as Eden was relaxing in his bath tub, so he tells us, it occurred to him that the Brussels Treaty would be the ideal basis for these imminent negotiations.[55] On September 11, he left London for a tour of Western European capitals, making Paris his last stop. He did not want to open preliminaries in the French capital without being able to confront Mendès-France with a solid phalanx of support.

Eden's project received the warm support of the Benelux foreign ministers with whom he conferred at Brussels on the 11th. Over the weekend Konrad Adenauer agreed to a four-point program: a German national army with quantitative limitations, entry into NATO, expansion of the Brussels Treaty into a seven-power pact, and a conference to be held in London at the earliest possible date. The scheme was sanctioned by the Scelba government in Rome, where the British leader called on the 14th, but the following morning as he was getting ready to fly to Paris he received a jolt: John Foster Dulles was on his way to Bonn. He was going to stop in London. He would make it a point not to alight in Paris. Not satisfied merely with antagonizing France at this juncture—the French had been fairly uncompromising themselves of late—he also criticized Eden's plan as makeshift and unsatisfactory. The master of Whitehall felt crossed, but he need not have worried. For Dulles' jaunt, despite

[53]Per Fischer, "Dreijährige Bilanz der Westeuropäischen Union," *Europa Archiv*, XIV (1959), 47.
[54]*Britain in Western Europe*, ix.   [55]Eden, *Full Circle*, 150-51.

America's stubborn attachment to the supranational army, proved unexpectedly helpful. Mendès-France was not so much offended by the American gesture as frightened. He thought that "Dulles was fully perepared to agree unilaterally to the rearmament of Germany: a straight German-American deal, . . . which, he thought, England would accept, more or less willingly, as a *fait accompli.*" He was relieved that Eden at least still spoke to him and was eager to help him close the circle. After initial hesitations about *immediate* German membership in NATO, he followed the British lead without reservation.[56] On September 18, after a busy and eventful week, Eden persuaded the reluctant American Secretary of State to join the other powers in a conference scheduled for the 28th, despite continuing disagreement over the merits of the stillborn EDC.

As things stood, Eden saw the impending conference in these terms: he had to get Germany rearmed and into NATO. He must devise safeguards that would make this eventuality palatable to the French and overcome American reluctance to support a defense pact of national armies. His inducement was a promise to keep British troops on the Continent and "not to withdraw them against the wishes of the majority of the enlarged Brussels Treaty powers."[57] The United Kingdom would thus concede to her partners a certain right to dispose of a small part of her own armed forces.

Churchill's deputy proved himself in the post-EDC crisis, and he got rapid results. The London Conference worked at a brisk pace. Although the French had come ready to hedge, the fear of a German-American entente made them more pliable than usual. By the time the conferees reconvened in Paris on October 21 to sign the agreement which established the "Western European Union," John Foster Dulles had not only gone along but made some handsome verbal amends to Mendès-France. He "said he had received many false reports from Paris at the height of the Indo-China conference. . . . He noted that these reports had poisoned his mind. He said he had come to realize their falsity and that he wanted Mendès-France to know this."[58]

[56]Werth, *Mendès-France,* 100; Eden, *Full Circle,* 151-61; Drummond and Coblentz, *Duel at the Brink,* 103-04.
[57]Eden, *Full Circle,* 165.
[58]Drummond and Coblentz, *Duel at the Brink,* 108-09.

The disappointment over the EDC disaster did not allow Europeans to wax enthusiastic over the WEU while the opponents of the former viewed it with equal suspicion. Admittedly, the former had less reason to cheer than the latter. Gone were the common defense budget, integrated licensing and letting of arms contracts, and joint responsibility. Integration of units would only take place at the army group level, and defense policy was formally returned to national jurisdiction.[59] Yet the compromise deserved a respectful hearing, for an extensive and elaborate system had developed out of a few high-level scurryings.

This system did not consist of one detailed treaty, but a series of amendments to existing agreements on the status of Germany, the Brussels Pact, and NATO.[60] To begin with, Germany was admitted to NATO. At the same time, France, Great Britain, and the United States terminated the occupation. They agreed with Germany on the size, nature, and role of Allied defense forces henceforth stationed on the territory of the Federal Republic.[61] The WEU, as such, was established by a protocol "modifying and completing the Brussels Treaty," which dropped Germany as the potential enemy, took her into the family, and formulated a new objective "to promote the unity and to encourage the progressive integration of Europe." It endowed the old Council with powers to "set up subsidiary bodies," including an Agency for the Control of Armaments, and enabled it to make certain decisions by majority or two-thirds vote. Every year it was to report to an assembly composed of representatives of the signatories to the Consultative Assembly of the Council of Europe.[62] The WEU's armed forces were to be of the

[59]Gerhard Bebr, "The European Defense Community and the Western European Union; an Agonizing Dilemma," *Stanford Law Review*, VII (1955), 184-96.

[60]It also included an agreement on the status of the Saar which would have made it a European territory. This solution was rejected by the Saarlanders in 1955 when they opted convincingly for a return to Germany. Their wish was granted effective January 1, 1957. For a quick résumé, see Marinus van der Goes van Naters, "L'histoire de la Sarre en documents . . . ," *European Yearbook*, II (1956), 139-50; Jacques Freymond, *The Saar Conflict* (London, 1960). Ludwig Dischler, *Das Saarland, 1945-56, eine Darstellung der historischen Entwicklung mit den wichtigsten Dokumenten*, 2 v. (Hamburg, 1956).

[61]For the English texts, see RIIA, *Documents on International Affairs, 1954* (London, 1957), 102-08.

[62]*Ibid.*, 29-30.

strength laid down in the late EDC pact, including likewise limitations of German armaments in the atomic, bacteriological, and naval field. Britain stuck to her original promise not to withdraw her forces "against the wishes of the majority of the High Contracting Parties." Finally, the WEU's force-in-being was avowedly constituted as part of NATO.[63]

These agreements, sketched at London and signed at Paris on October 23, 1954, quickly ran into the same foul weather as the EDC. Although they had relatively smooth sailing everywhere else, they encountered expected opposition in Paris. On December 24, the National Assembly defeated the ratification bill 280 to 258. Clearly, Pierre Mondès-France was now forced to abandon the role of disenchanted passivity he had held to in August. This time he staked his government on the issue, aided by Anthony Eden's public assurance that Germany would be rearmed regardless of France, but that Britain would maintain her forces in Europe only if all signatories ratified the Paris agreements. If Germany wanted her own army, she could get it without the consent of Paris. If the French wanted to prevent her rearmament, on the other hand, they would face an Anglo-American retreat to a peripheral strategy. The two threats in conjunction forced a revised verdict within a week. On December 29, France stopped sulking and joined the Western European Union.[64]

No one discharged fireworks after the event. The WEU had no supranational allure to quicken the heartbeat of the Pan-European, and it went too far beyond an orthodox alliance to gain the confidence of Continental isolationists. The British contribution to the defense of the mainland was by no means its only innovation. All members were forbidden to have armed forces in Europe unauthorized by NATO.[65] In regard to national control of armies, the Supreme Allied Commander Europe had assumed the role which the Commissariat was to play under the EDC. If national contingents were to be increased, this could only be done by unanimous consent. The EDC had provided for prior authorization of defense programs; WEU required post facto inspection, which after 1957

[63]*Ibid.*, 31-36.
[64]Nathan C. Leites and Christian de la Malène, *Paris from EDC to WEU* (Santa Monica, 1956), 160-74; Eden, *Full Circle*, 171.
[65]*Britain in Western Europe*, 67.

also covered private manufacture of weapons.[66] Despite the absence of supranational institutions, the Council of Ministers and its deputies could revise the list of controlled armaments by a two-thirds vote and questions submitted to the Armaments Control Agency by a simple majority. The WEU was the first arms pact operating with a parliament. Unlike the Consultative Assembly from which it drew its membership, the WEU Assembly alone and expressly provided a link between the Six and Great Britain.[67] While the pioneering predecessor had been established by a treaty setting forth its *modus operandi* with paralyzing thoroughness, it was called into being by one sentence and left to work out its own rules.[68] Above all, it was the first international assembly to discuss defense problems. This was a novelty fully as unprecedented as any supranational feature in the ECSC.[69]

So all had not been lost. The acceptance of the WEU after the rejection of the EDC clearly indicated that under minimum conditions progress was still possible. Whatever the new pact might not be, it "was [constitutionally] more ambitious than NATO, OEEC, or the Council of Europe." Unlike the latter, "WEU was given a relatively narrow field of activity . . . with a quasi supranational organ, the Armaments Control Agency, and quite specific jurisdiction in the military sphere."[70] The battles of 1948 and 1949 did not have to be refought, nor did all the battles of 1954. At the same time, one could not help feeling that the EDC and the EPC had been hastily slapped together and driven through the parliaments at a speed dictated by panic. To wait until the effect of the ECSC had prepared the way for an evolutionary European order would have been preferable. The point has been made before, and may stand repeating at the end of this chapter: the splendid timing that

[66]*Ibid.*, 72-73.   [67]WEU, Assembly, *First Session, October 24, 1955*, 73.

[68]*Dto., Second session, April 23, 1956*, 24.

[69]*Dto., First session, October 28, 1955*, 165; Marinus van der Goes van Naters, "De huidige staat van het Europese parlamentarisme," *Internationale Spectator*, XII (1958), 124; Henry L. Mason, "The Assembly of Western European Union and European Defense," *Ibid.*, XIV (1960), 450-54; for a more detailed and general descriptive analysis of the WEU Assembly, see G. van Benthem van den Bergh, "De parlementaire vergadering van de Westeuropese Union," *Ibid.*, XV, No. 2 (1961), 5-56.

[70]Mason, "The Assembly of Western European Union," *loc. cit.*, 452; Ernst B. Haas and Peter H. Merkl, "Parliamentarians against Ministers: the Case of Western European Union," *International Organization*, XIV (1960), 40.

had aided elaboration and passage of the Schuman Plan was sadly lacking when its companion pieces were being fashioned. Haste was also apparent in their craftsmanship. The EPC was no political community, merely a crude linking of political questions arising from the integration of several scattered sectors. The EDC bore the imprint of nineteenth-century strategy. In terms of conventional military science, it still left the last word to the states; in terms of nuclear war, it was an anachronism. Neither community was the best that could have been devised. Both were a long way from foreshadowing a United States of Europe. To have put European union on so crude a frame might in the long run have redounded to its everlasting discredit and nurtured once more the superstition that an international order on a regional basis was unworkable.

The defeat of the EDC may well have been a blessing in disguise. The adoption of the WEU on the other hand was a modest but substantial consolidation of the gains made since 1945 in international thinking, institutional experimentation, and continental planning. It indicated that the tragedy following the failure of the Briand proposals of a quarter-century ago would not repeat itself. Britain remained an uncertain factor even in this compromise scheme,[71] but continental Europe was on its way, travelling more slowly than its ardent supporters had hoped, yet moving forward nonetheless.

[71] Cf., Alfred Grosser, "Suez, Hungary, and European integration," *Ibid.*, XI (1957), 477.

CHAPTER TWELVE

The Second Launching
of European Union

It is easier to see the WEU as an achievement today than it was in 1954. Then it was not so much a tribute to successful salvaging as a symbol of supranational failure. In the German Bundestag a prominent Rightist enemy of the ECSC jubilantly predicted the end of institutional integration. The *Deutsche Zeitung* echoed his remarks. British voices viewed those attitudes as a sign that the Federal Republic, too, was deserting the European cause.[1] Paul-Henri Spaak recalls that "the failure of EDC was a terrible blow to the idea of European integration. . . . It was a blow to the whole European idea, and at that moment it was a question as to whether the efforts in this direction, which had been constant since 1948, would not be halted once and for all."[2] Only the USSR seems to have viewed the WEU as a serious accomplishment. Following its adoption she annulled both her wartime pacts with Great Britain and France.

The prevalent view seemed to be that the WEU had possibly saved an alliance, but that the principle of European union continued to be in jeopardy. To rescue it became the task of all true Europeans: they now abandoned the obviously fruitless debate over the merits of the EDC in favor of a new approach. The first to exchange past quarrels for new solutions were the Benelux governments. Notably the Netherlands had for some time demanded progressive expansion of economic integration, a European tariff union, and a single European market for all goods and services.[3]

[1] *Financial Times* (London), September 8, 1954.
[2] Paul-Henri Spaak, "The New Europe," *The Atlantic Monthly*, CCII (September 1958), 39.
[3] Netherlands Information Service, *News Digest from Holland*, March 25, 1953, and January 27, 1954.

When the foreign ministers of the Six met in Messina, Sicily, at the end of May 1955, only weeks after the WEU agreements had gone into effect, Dutch, Belgian, and Luxembourg diplomats pressed for a new effort to revive European ideals and to perfect European institutions. They initiated what has come to be known as the *relance Européenne*. Both France and Germany (or perhaps more accurately, Ludwig Erhard) were lukewarm to the idea. They countered with a proposal that looked to a broadening of the OEEC, or at most the designing of new agencies operating on an intergovernmental basis. What tipped the balance in favor of the smaller powers was the support which they seem to have received from the French and German members of the High Authority. Its nature and importance has been viewed differently by different participants. An attempt to reconstruct the key developments at Messina must reckon with a Benelux version which credits the major initiative to Spaak. Monnet's admirers have added that the Belgian statesman was active enough, but that the resolution which he submitted, and which was accepted by the six ministers, had been drafted by their idol. They have credited the first president of the ECSC executive with the actual authorship of the second launching of Europe. Certain German observers, finally, have insisted that Vice-President Etzel, himself highly esteemed by Adenauer as well as by Monnet, had a "Trojan horse" on the staff of Erhard, a high ranking civil servant who prevailed on the minister of economics to affix his signature to the Spaak document. There is no reason to believe that any of these versions constitute the entire story or that any of them is a fabrication.

In any case, the meeting went on record as championing further integration. The most positive recommendations included the founding of a common organization to develop nuclear energy for peaceful purposes and the initiation of a "common European market, free from all customs duties and all quantitative restrictions." In this connection, the institutional integrationists scored a major victory by gaining the insertion of a clause which demanded "appropriate institutional means for the realization and operation" of the enlarged economic organism. As a first step, the ministers created an intergovernmental commission under Spaak's chairmanship and delegated to it the task of "drafting the relevant treaties or arrangements."[4]

Messina aroused no extravagant hopes. Two years earlier the same ministers had ordered a custom-made political community and then filed it away. By Spaak's own admission, "politicians often use big words to veil the hollowness of their policies." Yet he felt that one must grant the Messina meeting one accomplishment: it did not *ask* whether a common market was possible. It decided to establish one and instructed the intergovernmental committee: "You must now tell us how to go about it."[5] Whether they would take its advice after it was proffered remained, of course, to be seen.

The Messina conference was the last gathering of its kind attended by Jean Monnet as president of the High Authority. Following the defeat of the EDC, the author of the Schuman Plan had announced that he would resign at the expiration of his term in order to devote himself to the European cause under conditions providing greater independence of action. Following his departure from Luxembourg, he addressed a letter to a carefully selected small circle of West European leaders, who represented socialist, Christian, and liberal parties as well as all non-Communist trade unions. He invited them to join an "Action Committee for the United States of Europe." Their adherence would commit them and their organizations and would constitute a pledge to exert pressure on parliaments and public opinion "to make of the Messina resolution of June 2 a real way-station on the road to a united Europe."[6] Support of the committee was taken to mean acceptance of the principles of supranational integration.[7] Monnet made it clear

[4]Meeting of the Ministers of Foreign Affairs of the Member States of ECSC, *Resolution Adopted by the Ministers of Foreign Affairs of the Member States of the ECSC at their Meeting at Messina on June 1 and 2, 1955. Provisional Translation* (Luxembourg, n. d.).

[5]Spaak, "The New Europe," *loc. cit.*, 40.

[6]See Monnet interview in *Bonner Rundschau*, October 14, 1955.

[7]For a list of the committee's charter members, see page 234.

Chart VIII

Charter Members of the Action Committee for a United States of Europe

Socialist Parties

Barger, J. A. W.	President, Dutch Labor Parliamentary Group
Buset, Max	President, Belgian Socialist Party
Fohrmann, Jean	Executive Committee, Lux. Socialist Party
Matteotti, Matteo	Secretary-General, Social Democratic Party of Italy
Mollet, Guy	Secretary-General, French Socialist Party
Ollenhauer, Erich	President, Social Democratic Party of Germany

Christian Democratic Parties

Fanfani, Amintore	Political secretary, Italian Christian Democratic Party
Kiesinger, Kurt	Executive Committee, Christian Democratic Union
Lecourt, Robert	President, MRP group in France's Nat. Assembly
Bruins-Slot, J. A. H. S.	Dutch Protestant (Anti-Revolutionary) Party
Margue, Nicolas	Executive Committee, Luxembourg, Christian Social Party
Romme, C. P. M.	President, Parliamentary group of the Dutch Catholic Party
Lefèbvre, Théo	President, Belgian Christian Social Party

Liberal and Other Parties

Blank, Martin	Free Democratic Party, Germany
Desternay, Maurice	President, Belgian Liberal Party
Elbraechter, Alexander	German Party
Faure, Maurice	French Radical Socialist Party
Garet, Pierre	President, French parliamentary group of Independents
Malagodi, Giovanni	Secretary-General, Italian Liberal Party
LaMalfa, Ugo	Italian Republican Party
Pleven, René	Union Démocratique et Sociale de la Résistance

Trade Unions

Alders, J.	Dutch workers movement
Bothereau, R.	Secretary-General, Force Ouvrière
Bouladoux, Maurice	President, French Christian Federation of Labor
Cool, Auguste	President, Belgian Confederation of Christian Trade Unions
Freitag, Walter	President, German Federation of Labor
Hazenbosch, C. P.	President, Dutch Christian Trade Unions
Imig, Heinrich	President, German Miner's Federation
Oosterhuis, H.	President, Federation of Dutch Trade Unions
Krier, Antoine	Secretary-General, Luxembourg Worker's Federation

Source: Action Committee for the United States of Europe, *First Session, June 17-18, 1956*, pp. 10-11.

that he expected more than lip service and that his "lobby" would have to be financed by the participating organizations.[8]

Thus the Action Committee was conceived as a coalition of divergent forces, all of whom agreed, however, on one issue: the need for European unification. In Monnet's opinion, the governments had *not* made a firm decision at Messina. His first objective, therefore, was to create conditions that would rule out another retreat.[9] His committee was to be the foundation of six pro-European parliamentary majorities. He did not see himself as a propagandist, but as the head of a force of unmatched political strength. The ACFUSE included the party leaders themselves, not their substitutes or secretaries. From the very outset, its momentum derived from the remarkable achievement of persuading hitherto hostile groups, like the German socialists, to join. A year after the defeat of the EDC, Monnet was ready to forge new weapons with the aid of René Pleven on the one hand and Kurt Schumacher's successor, Erich Ollenhauer, on the other.[10]

At the same time, the Action Committee was no shapeless coalition of all parties and interests. There was no courting of the extreme Right or the Communist Left. Monnet recruited the men and forces he needed, no more. Remembering the opposition of big business to his projects in the past, he invited no trade association representatives. He did not splinter his phalanx with potential dissidents.[11] As a bold, supremely confident strategist, strengthened by a cause whose success was to be his only reward, Monnet wasted no time building up pressure obliquely and by stealth. He went straight to his goal by approaching the men who counted and on whom he could count. He proselyted neither his enemies nor the masses. The former he discounted, the latter he left to the individual members of the Committee.[12]

The Action Committee held its first meeting on January 18, 1956.

[8] *Bonner Rundschau*, loc. cit.

[9] *Badische Neueste Nachrichten*, October 14, 1955.

[10] There was much favorable press comment on this score: *Rheinischer Merkur*, October 21, 1955; *L'Express*, October 15, 1955; *New York Herald-Tribune* (Paris Edition), October 14, 1955.

[11] *Bonner Rundschau*, October 14, 1955; *La Cité* (Brussels), October 15, 1955.

[12] Writer's interview with Mr. Max Kohnstamm, July 22, 1957.

Its members associated themselves unanimously with the Messina declaration and adopted a joint resolution outlining a European atomic energy authority to meet the critical energy deficit on a supranational basis. Those in a position to act promised to submit this project to the national parliaments and to reconvene in April to evaluate the immediate results.[13]

Monnet obviously intended to prevent the burial of the next major European project in long parliamentary squabbles and procrastinations.[14] He had chosen his ground with imagination. Integration of nuclear efforts violated a minimum of traditional interests. Hence it offered the best chance for success while pointing a path out of the most serious industrial impasse of the hour.[15] The potential dangers of unilateral national nuclear developments, furthermore, accounted for the surprising ease with which the German socialists had been persuaded to cast their lots with Monnet's new European spearhead.[16]

Soon the pendulum of chance was swinging toward Europe once again. Over the April and September meetings of the Action Committee stood the shadow of Egypt's Abdul Gamal Nasser. The Suez Canal had been closed, and more than fifty million tons of oil which had passed through its locks in 1955 had to be shipped around Africa, if they could be shipped at all. To the growing coal shortage of several years' standing was added an oil crisis of staggering proportions. In 1955 Europe had imported 26.5 million tons from the Pennsylvania and West Virginia coal mines. Predictions for 1956, disregarding the Suez developments, had estimated a possible doubling of this volume.[17] Europe was being strangled and the abortive and desperate Suez military measures in October and November sharpened public comprehension of the stakes. To the threat of war were added empty gas tanks and unheated homes. The fact that the Mediterranean issue was settled by the United

[13]Action Committee for a United States of Europe, *First Session, Meeting of January 17-18, 1956,* 3-9.

[14]*Manchester Guardian,* January 24, 1956.

[15]Cf., the interview of a Dutch committee member in *Het vrije Volk* (Amsterdam), January 24, 1956.

[16]*De Maasbode* (Rotterdam), January 17, 1956.

[17]Studienausschuss des Westeuropäischen Kohlenbergbaus, Unterausschuss für Marktuntersuchung, "Bericht über das Problem der Einfuhr amerikanischer Kohle nach Europa." *Doc. Mar 112/3, September 1956,* 2.

States and the USSR, and the coincident Hungarian uprising by the latter alone, impressed upon even the densest observer that Europe had had her last warning.

Meanwhile, Paul-Henri Spaak's intergovernmental committee had completed the technical groundwork for the establishment of the common market and a European atomic energy treaty. On May 29-30, 1956, the ministers met again on Italian soil, this time in Venice, to support the preliminary proposals of this group, and on March 25, 1957, the treaties establishing a common market for all goods and services among the Six, as well as Euratom, were signed at Rome.

Formally these new communities provided for less freedom of action on the part of the executive commissions. The advice and consent of the Council of Ministers had to be sought much more often than under the ECSC treaty. On the other hand the Council's decisions could only follow Commission requests. The ministers had no policy initiative, and their verdicts did not have to be unanimous. Though less independent than the High Authority, the Commission could exert considerable pressure if it chose. Whether the ministers would find it politically expedient to counter in the negative to many or most proposals could be doubted. The Rome treaties went into effect on January 1, 1958, less than nine months after signature. They received a quick and overwhelming mandate from the national parliaments. The electorate apparently supported the new agreements. Public opinion soundings in Germany indicated that 75 per cent of the respondents would vote for a United States of Europe, were the opportunity presented to them. Under these circumstances, the ministers might well hesitate before using their treaty prerogatives indiscriminately, and Commission proposals could at the very least always count on a sympathetic reception.[18]

Events have justified this optimism. The Common Market treaty, for instance, provided that internal import duties would be reduced 10 per cent the first year, and an additional 20 per cent during the ensuing three years. The remainder was to be cut gradually over an approximate span of seven more years. At the end of 1960,

[18]Günther Jaenicke, "Der übernationale Charakter der Europäischen Wirtschaftsgemeinschaft," *Zeitschrift für ausländisches öffentliches Recht und Völkerrecht*, XIX (1958), 175-77.

however, reductions of 30 per cent had already gone into effect, and another cut of 10 per cent was carried through in 1961. In the tariff sector, developments likewise outran the original schedule. At the same time, it was expected that all quota restrictions on industrial goods would soon be abolished. "A schedule that seemed approximate in 1957, appear [ed] out of date in 1960."[19] In January 1962, the second stage in the achievement of full economic union, provided by Article 14b of the EEC treaty, was officially entered under conditions that presaged further acceleration of the original program. Most significant in this respect was the agreement to abolish all national control of agricultural imports by July 1.[20]

Euratom now has three joint research centers in operation. It is building a power plant in Italy which is to begin operation in 1963 with a 149,000 kw capacity, and a 240,000 kw complex is scheduled for completion in France by 1965.[21] This is a far cry from the 15,-000,000 kw output foreseen for 1967, but it must be remembered that Euratom merely retains title to the enriched uranium placed at the disposal of producers. Plant constructions by the agency involve only pilot projects and reflect but a small portion of total production.[22] France alone has plans which promise 4,000,000 kw of atomic electricity at the end of the ten-year period covered by the 1957 report.[23]

With the implementation of the Rome treaties, the ECSC lost its unique status. At the same time, their ratification created the danger of an unwieldy and ridiculous proliferation of institutions whose net effect would fragment rather than unite Europe. "One

[19]European Economic Community, Commission, *Dritter Gesamtbericht über die Tätigkeit der Gemeinschaft* (Brussels, 1960), 29, 33-34; also, *Vierter Gesamtbericht* (Brussels, 1961), 27.

[20]*New York Times,* January 14, 1962; *Bulletin from the European Community,* No. 46 (May 1961), 6-10.

[21]*Ibid.,* No. 44 (February 1961), 8.

[22]See "Target for Euratom. Report submitted by Mr. Louis Armand, Mr. Franz Etzel, and Mr. Francesco Giordano at the request of the governments of Belgium, France, Federal Republic of Germany, Italy, Luxembourg, and the Netherlands." Mimeographed copy, n.l. n.d. 5, 12-13.

[23]Ambassade de France, Service de Presse et d'Information, "Euratom, six nations to pool atomic research and development," *European Affairs,* No. 11 (June 1957), 4.

may well ask whether five per cent of the population of Europe has the slightest idea what the initials OEEC signify or whether they know that the Council of Europe still exists," a speaker opined before the WEU Assembly in 1956. "The public is completely confused by the still growing flow of initials." In addition, he pointed out that Western Europeans were facing the likelihood of six different assemblies speaking in their name on different subjects.[24] This concern, expressed on the floor of every European forum, led to joint remonstrations by the Consultative, Common, and WEU Assemblies, who prevailed on the ministers to agree to a fusion which would establish one European parliament for the ECSC, the Common Market, and Euratom.[25] At the same time, the judicial functions for the new communities were also entrusted to the Court of the Coal and Steel Community.

At the executive level coöperation between the three commissions foreshadows future mergers. Despite the fact that the EEC and Euratom work in Brussels while the ECSC has remained in Luxembourg, several of their service departments (legal staff, statistics, and information) have been unified. Two executive work committees link action by the three communities in the energy sector and on social policies.[26] Sensible streamlining of organizations should be followed before long by arrangements to gather all three communities in one European capital. A merger between the High Authority and the European Commission would likewise eliminate inevitable overlapping and duplication that must result when two institutions, representing partial and total economic integration respectively, operate at the same time.

Integration of the existing communities is one, but by no means the only, remaining item of unfinished business. Another is political integration. Remembering Monnet's attachment to this elusive goal, and Spaak's contention "that March 25, 1957, is from the European point of view, as important a date as July 14, 1789,"[27] one may take it for granted that it has been put off but not forgotten. The redoubtable Belgian statesman, after his success at Messina,

[24] WEU, Assembly, *Second Session, Document 34: Creation of a Fourth European Assembly* (Strasbourg, 1956), 6-7.
[25] ECSC, Common Assembly, *Jahrbuch-Handbuch, 1958,* 160-63.
[26] EEC, Commission, *Dritter Gesamtbericht,* 60-73.
[27] Spaak, "The New Europe," *loc. cit.,* 40.

Venice, and Rome, was temporarily enticed into the secretary-generalship of NATO, where he pursued only phantoms of unity, until recalled to his country's foreign office in 1961. The chairman of the ACFUSE, in his offices at 80 Avenue Foch in Paris, has not only had the satisfaction of leading a European revival; he has also had ample time to reflect on errors committed along the way. It is reported that he would now gladly feed the Common Market to the lions of the National Assembly if he could have his EDC and EPC back, alive and kicking.

But since Monnet cannot live the past ten years over, he may take comfort in an ascending list of accomplishments, stretching from the Marshall Plan to the grand climax at Rome. He may review his history lessons and recall that there has not been a decade of European history in which so much was changed without war. One has to go back one hundred years before encountering a similarly fruitful span of comparable length. But the 1860's, marked by Bismarck and Cavour, saw the death on the battlefield of thousands before uniting the peoples of Germany and Italy. The events of the quarter century which began with the momentous Estates General of 1789 and ended with Napoleon's last hopeless journey to St. Helena likewise wrought great transformations, but again only after continuous recourse to arms. The West European revolution of the 1950's has been peaceful. From American aid to economic union, results have been garnered without direct threats, ultimata, or mobilizations. Future events may prove Spaak's claim for the Rome treaties to have been an understatement. A new Europe is in the making, but the Bastilles of the old *status quo* were not taken by storm: they surrendered to statesmanlike persuasion.

If the foreign offices have themselves not felt the bite of advancing integration, this has largely been due to the fact that their heads have led the march. Adenauer, Brentano, Schuman, Spaak, Stikker of the Netherlands, and Bech of Luxembourg have all been dubbed "great Europeans" at one time or another. They have agreed among each other to pull the rug from under their colleagues in such departments as finance, economics, labor, transport, and agriculture. But their own bailiwicks have remained above the battle. It is unprofitable, therefore, to look back ruefully on plays that might have been called. What lies ahead is a major engagement with the ministers of foreign affairs, who, so far, have espoused integration everywhere except in their own offices.

A meeting of the six foreign ministers, held in February 1961, broached the plan of a loose political confederation but without supranational institutions. They were content to propose that heads of state meet regularly to deal with unspecified common problems. General de Gaulle's formula of a *Europe des patries* satisfied the European ardor of the same diplomats who would be content with nothing less than abdication of sovereignty in the economic sphere. They argued, not unreasonably, that Britain could join such an executive confederation and thus restore a united front of western nations in Europe. An inflexible and dogmatic integrated political community, on the other hand, could not reckon with English adherence, unless recent experience counted for nothing. They also hinted that to find France's Fifth Republic in the vanguard of any "European" project was of itself remarkable enough. It was indeed hard to decide whether the moderate push into the realm of political union or the open acceptance by former foes of economic integration constituted the most remarkable Gaullist reversal.[28]

All is still in flux. A meeting of heads of state and prime ministers held at Bonn on July 18, 1961, made these commitments:

1) "To hold at regular intervals meetings whose aim will be to compare their views, to concert their policies, and to reach common positions in order to further the political union of Europe, thereby strengthening the Atlantic Alliance."

2) "To instruct their Committee to submit to them proposals of the means which will as soon as possible enable *a statutory character* to be given to the union of their peoples."[29]

It would appear from these timid formulae that the United States of Europe are still in the "Council of Europe" stage. They are being talked about, but work has only been countenanced on a part-time basis. Yet there is some ground for optimism.

The Bonn Communiqué speaks of strengthening the Atlantic Alliance. This reflects a desire to search beyond the original bound-

[28]For an interesting and detailed discussion of the French outlook on Europe, see the lead article in Michel Debré's *Echo de Touraine* (Tours), February 17, 1961.

[29]From the text of the Bonn communiqué in *Bulletin from the European Community*, No. 49 (October 1961), 6. Italics supplied.

aries of the Common Market. In this respect 1961 was a year of unprecedented accomplishment. On July 9, Greece signed an agreement of association with the EEC. Three weeks later Ireland made
application for full membership, and simultaneously Prime Minister Macmillan expressed the identical intention on behalf of the
United Kingdom. Denmark followed suit on August 10, and in December Austria initiated negotiations for a treaty of association.

Ireland's and Denmark's action indicated the demise of the
ephemeral Outer Seven, the British attempt to balance the Common Market with a customs union of the remaining free nations
in Europe. The Austrian application was more portentous. Since
the State Treaty of 1955, whose signatories included the Soviet
Union, and which imposed strict neutrality on her, it had been
widely held in Vienna and elsewhere, that any attempt to forge ties
with the ECSC and the EEC would founder on Russian opposition. It was, therefore, obvious that the current Austrian step
would not have been taken without some prior soundings in Moscow. Apparently, and surprisingly, these encouraged Austria to
proceed.

The British initiative generated the greatest excitement. Its results remain quite uncertain. Prime Minister Macmillan indicated
that the time had come to sit down and negotiate for admission
under Article 237 of the EEC treaty. This provides that the Commission will give its opinion on the advisability of accepting an
applicant, who will be allowed to enter only after a unanimous
invitation from the Council of Ministers. Equally important is the
next provision which stipulates that any treaty changes necessi-
tated by an expansion of membership must be ratified by all powers concerned in accordance with their respective constitutions.
Because of the United Kingdom's Commonwealth ties, this second
step will be complicated, and there seems to be relatively little
predisposition among the present Six to agree to an undue number
of treaty amendments merely to facilitate British entry. The feeling in Western Europe today is that they have managed nicely
without the cousins across the Channel so far. They would wel-
come their joining the firm, but this does not indicate a willingness
to sacrifice unduly for that end. Hence a quick consummation of
this union must not be anticipated.

The Europe of the Six has received still other testimonials of success. Ever since they refused to participate in the Marshall Plan, the USSR and her satellites have paid Western European integration the compliment of continuous verbal attack—and the considerably more substantial tribute of imitation. In 1949 the splendid launching of the OEEC gave rise to a pale blueprint which bore the name of Molotov. It brought forth a Council of Mutual Economic Aid in Moscow, no more than "a statistical collecting agency" and "meeting place for the negotiation of bi-lateral trade agreements." From 1950 to 1055 it was completely inactive. Then, possibly in the wake of the WEU treaties, it was revived to spearhead simple integration of socialist planning. The Polish and Hungarian revolts halted operations again, but they also channelled Eastern integration into broader avenues. Moscow has ceased to dominate openly since 1957. Multilateral trade agreements between some satellites, and excluding the USSR, are now possible. In 1959 the CMEA was reconstituted as a multi-powered effort, with a new statute and a convention on its powers, privileges and immunities. Different offices of the agency are distributed among various satellite capitals.[30] There are no signs of multilateral decision-making yet, but symptoms are multiplying that the capitalist and social-democratic entente of the West has given the Communists a lesson in international coöperation which they are not disposed to overlook.

Success of the Common Market and the early inauguration of a common external tariff among the Six will also raise the question of United States association. Since it looks more than ever before to foreign markets, American industry seeks to benefit from the demolition of trade barriers in Europe, but the point has now clearly been reached where these benefits will be limited unless a substantial reduction of American tariffs in all sectors is accepted. Furthermore, the issue involves not merely two markets on opposite sides of the Atlantic. Many African areas, still associated states of the European treaty partners in 1957, have become sovereign. The EEC and the European Parliamentary Assembly have

[30]For the above, see David T. Cattell, "Multilateral Coöperation and Integration in Eastern Europe," *The Western Political Quarterly*, XIII (1960), 64-69.

been quick to recognize that the new situations call for new action in order to maintain strong ties and to prevent the USSR's entering the area as a major consumer of raw materials. As new modes of association and coöperation take shape, notably with the establishment of the Organization for Economic Cooperation and Development on September 30, 1961,[31] the likelihood of American (as well as Soviet) exclusion from the African complex increases. What the significance of such a loss might eventually be is hard to prophesy. But no one is disposed to countenance it without concern. This challenge may be another reason compelling the United States to call in "the Old World . . . to redress the balance of the new."[32]

None of these exciting new steps, whether actual or potential, provide a clear answer to the question: what next? Will Europe's Common Market find application elsewere? Is there prospect of union in Africa; are the Africans convinced that federation is their best hope for survival and progress?[33] Has the time come for an economic union of Turkey, Iraq, Israel, and Egypt? The case for it has been made with intelligence and conviction, but how much of that intelligence is apt to find a "market" in the present Near East?[34] Will the past failures to achieve union in Latin America[35] be put behind to be followed by a new approach and a new era? In all these cases, will we witness the blind adoption of inappropriate solutions merely because they have succeeded in Europe, or will there be intelligent adaptions of basic patterns to the needs of particular areas? Is Jean Monnet right, finally, when he predicts: "Some day the United States will also delegate real, even political, authority to joint institutions."?[36]

These are all questions which ten years ago belonged in the realm of utopian fiction. Today they make sense and contain sub-

[31]With the apparently enthusiastic concurrence of Ludwig Erhard. See his "Die Einigung Europas—eine Lebensfrage," *Aussenpolitik*, XII (1961), 73.

[32]Joseph Kraft, "The Grand Design Takes Shape," *Harper's Magazine*, CC-XXIV (February, 1962), 36; Helmut Allardt, "Praktische Entwicklungsarbeit in Afrika," *Aussenpolitik*, XI (1960), 665-70.

[33]Cf., Donald S. Rothchild, *Toward Unity in Africa* (Washington, 1960).

[34]See David Garnick, "The Economic Feasibility of a Middle Eastern Common Market," *Middle East Journal*, XIV (1960), 270-73.

[35]One sector of which has been ably chronicled by Thomas L. Karnes, *The Failure of Union: Central America, 1824-1960* (Chapel Hill, N.C., 1961).

[36]Jean Monnet, "Une politique de l'Occident," *L'Europe en formation*, II, No. 10 (1961), 1.

stance. They illustrate the scope of our decade of revolution. Whatever the answer to them may ultimately be, that decade has reformed Western Europe: national pride has finally been cut down
to size. Crippled and mutilated, retreating to those ancient centers
whence they long ago set out to conquer the world, the powers of
Western Europe have learned that they must lash themselves se-
curely to each other if they are to keep from drowning in the angry
seas that surround them. The still redoubtable continental fragments of world power can recapture some of the greatness of the
past by rising to new grandeur, but only in a union that surrenders
the most conspicuous luxuries of independence.

There is no other way.

BIBLIOGRAPHY

A. UNPUBLISHED MATERIALS.

EUROPEAN COAL AND STEEL COMMUNITY, Council of Ministers, "Accord rélatif au frets et conditions de transport pour le charbon et l'acier sur le Rhin." *Doc. 416f/57*.

EUROPEAN COAL AND STEEL COMMUNITY, High Authority, "Aufzeichnungen über das Funktionieren des gemeinsamen Marktes." *Doc. 7403/1/56*.

EUROPEAN COAL AND STEEL COMMUNITY, High Authority, "New Deal for French Steel." *Doc. 2684/553*.

EUROPEAN COAL AND STEEL COMMUNITY, High Authority, "Note de la Haute Autorité de la Communauté Européenne du Charbon et de l'Acier concernant l'application de l'Article 69 du traité . . ." *Doc. 5749/55*.

EUROPEAN COAL AND STEEL COMMUNITY, High Authority, "Report on the fact-finding mission to the United States . . . for the purpose of studying anti-trust legislation there, 8.3.-6.4. 1958." *Doc. 5879/58e*.

EUROPEAN COAL AND STEEL COMMUNITY, High Authority, "The Social Mission of the European Coal and Steel Community." *Doc. 1697/57e*.

EUROPEAN COAL AND STEEL COMMUNITY, High Authority, "Les transferts de main d'oeuvre du Centre-Midi vers la Lorraine." *Doc. 2129/56f*.

EUROPEAN COAL AND STEEL COMMUNITY, High Authority, "Transport in the Community." *Doc. 1199/2/55a*.

GEORGES GORIELY, "Naissance de la Communauté Européenne du Charbon et de l'Acier." Unpub. Paper. ECSC, Information Division, Luxembourg, n.d.

RICHARD A. HAMBURGER, "Coal and Steel Community. Rules for a Competitive Market and Their Application." Unpub. Manuscript, Luxembourg, 1960. Writer headed High Authority's anti-trust division from 1952 to 1960.

ORGANIZATION FOR EUROPEAN ECONOMIC COOPERATION, "Plan d'action pour l'intégration économique de l'Europe. Memorandum de la délégation des Pays Bas." *Doc. C(50)159, 1950*.

STUDIENAUSSCHUSS DES WESTEUROPAEISCHEN KOHLENBERGBAUS, Unterausschuss für Marktuntersuchung, "Bericht über das Problem der Einfuhr amerikanischer Kohlen nach Europa." *Doc. Mar 112/3, September 1956.*

"TARGET FOR EURATOM. Report submitted by Mr. Louis Armand, Mr. Franz Etzel, and Mr. Francesco Giordano at the Request of the Governments of Belgium, France, Federal Republic of Germany, Italy, Luxembourg and the Netherlands." Mimeo., n.l. n.d.

UNITED STATES, DEPARTMENT OF STATE, Sub-Committee on European Organization, "Chronological Minutes, 1943-1944."

UNITED STATES, DEPARTMENT OF STATE, Sub-Committee on European Organization, "Analytical Minutes, 1943-1944."

UNITED STATES, DEPARTMENT OF STATE, "The Current Status of the Schuman Plan, PRE Divisional Report 1.6, September 8, 1950."

UNITED STATES, DEPARTMENT OF STATE, "Telegram prepared by ECA for clearance in the Department of State to Embassy Paris, November 10, 1950."

B.   PRINTED SOURCES.

DRAFT TREATY EMBODYING THE STATUTE OF THE EUROPEAN COMMUNITY, (Luxembourg, 1953) prepared by an *Ad Hoc* Assembly instructed to work out a draft treaty setting up a European Political Community.

SUMMARY REPORT OF DEBATES (Luxembourg, 1952-53.) of the *Ad Hoc* Assembly instructed to work out a draft treaty setting up a European Political Community.

BELGIUM, SENAT. *Session 1951-52* (Brussels, 1951-52).

JULIUS BRAUNTHAL (ed.), *Yearbook of the International Socialist Labor Movement,* 1956-57 (London, 1956).

NORMAN CAMERON AND R. H. STEVENS (eds.), *Hitler's Table Talk, 1941-44* (London, 1953).

A. CONDORCET-O'CONNOR AND M. F. ARAGO (eds.), *Oeuvres de Condorcet,* 12 v. (Paris, 1847).

COUNCIL OF ASSOCIATION BETWEEN THE GOVERNMENT OF THE UNITED KINGDOM OF GREAT BRITAIN AND NORTHERN IRELAND AND THE HIGH AUTHORITY OF THE EUROPEAN COAL AND STEEL COMMUNITY, *Annual Reports* (Luxembourg, 1957-).

COUNCIL OF EUROPE, *European Yearbook* (The Hague, 1955-). Bilingual. Includes articles as well as a chronology of European activities and texts of agreements concluded in the course of the year. The latter are reproduced on parallel pages in French and English.

COUNCIL OF EUROPE, Consultative Assembly, *Official Reports* (Strasbourg, 1949-).

COUNCIL OF EUROPE, Consultative Assembly, *Documents—Working Papers* (Strasbourg, 1949-).

DOKUMENTE ZUM EUROPAEISCHEN KONGRESS IM HAAG, vom. 7 bis. 11. Mai, 1948, *Europa Archiv,* III (1948).

EUROPEAN COAL AND STEEL COMMUNITY, *Journal Officiel,* 7 v. (December 30, 1952 - April 19, 1958). Beginning April 20, 1958: European Communities, *Journal Officiel.* Published, like all ECSC publications, in Dutch, French, German, and Italian.

EUROPEAN COAL AND STEEL COMMUNITY, *Décision rélative a l'application de l'Article 69 du traité du 18 avril 1951 instituant la Communauté . . .* (Luxembourg, 1955).

EUROPEAN COAL AND STEEL COMMUNITY, Common Assembly, *Débats,* (Published as part of the Community's *Journal Officiel* in 39 supplements) (Luxembourg, 1953-58). Since March 1958 appears as European Parliamentary Assembly, *Débats.*

EUROPEAN COAL AND STEEL COMMUNITY, Common Assembly, *Annuaire de l'Assemblée Commune,* 3 v, (Luxembourg, 1956-58).

EUROPEAN COAL AND STEEL COMMUNITY, Common Assembly, *Règlement de l'Assemblée Commune* (Luxembourg, 1956).

EUROPEAN COAL AND STEEL COMMUNITY, Common Assembly, Ausschuss für Fragen der Sozialpolitik, *Übersicht über die sozialpolitischen Bestimmungen des Vertrags* (Luxembourg, 1953).

EUROPEAN COAL AND STEEL COMMUNITY, Court of Justice, *Recueil de la jurisprudence,* 4 v. (Luxembourg, 1955-58). Beginning with volume five published as Court of Justice of the European Communities, *Recueil de la jurisprudence.*

EUROPEAN COAL AND STEEL COMMUNITY, High Authority, *Besonderer Bericht über die Errichtung des gemeinsamen Marktes für Stahl* (Luxembourg, 1953).

EUROPEAN COAL AND STEEL COMMUNITY, High Authority. *Exposé über die Lage der Gemeinschaft* (Luxembourg, 1953).

EUROPEAN COAL AND STEEL COMMUNITY, High Authority, *Financial Reports* (Luxembourg, 1956-). Published at irregular intervals, also in English.

EUROPEAN COAL AND STEEL COMMUNITY, High Authority, *Annual Reports* (Luxembourg, 1953-). English translations for the earlier years abridged.

EUROPEAN COAL AND STEEL COMMUNITY, High Authority, *Monatliches Mitteilungsblatt* (Luxembourg, 1954-). Renamed *Bulletin der Europäischen Gemeinschaft für Kohle und Stahl.* Appears at irregular intervals now, approximately three to four times per year. Contains good summaries of annual reports and of salient events of the immediately preceding months.

EUROPEAN COAL AND STEEL COMMUNITY, High Authority, *Report on the Problems Raised by the Different Turnover Tax Systems Applied Within the Common Market* (Luxembourg, 1953), better known as the Tinbergen report.

EUROPEAN COAL AND STEEL COMMUNITY, High Authority, *Statistisches Bulletin* (Luxembourg, 1953-).

EUROPEAN COAL AND STEEL COMMUNITY, High Authority, Consultative Committee, *Manuel*, 3. ed. (Luxembourg, 1956).

EUROPEAN COAL AND STEEL COMMUNITY, High Authority, Information Service (sic), *Bulletin from the European Community for Coal and Steel* (Luxembourg, 1954-). Appeared at irregular intervals, and still does. Beginning with No. 30 (May-June 1955) it became *Bulletin from the European Community*.

EUROPEAN ECONOMIC COMMUNITY, Commission, *Annual Reports* (Brussels, 1958-).

FRANCE, ASSEMBLEE NATIONALE, *Séance de 1951* (Paris, 1951).

FRANCE, ASSEMBLEE NATIONALE, *Séance de 1954* (Paris, 1954).

FRANCE, CONSEIL DE LA REPUBLIQUE, *Séance de 1952* (Paris, 1952).

A. RUTH FRY (ed.), *John Bellers, 1654-1725, Quaker, Economist and Social Reformer* (London, 1935).

GRAND DUCHY OF LUXEMBOURG, CHAMBRE DES DEPUTES, *Session ordinaire de 1951-52* (Luxembourg, 1952).

RESOLUTION ADOPTED BY THE MINISTERS OF FOREIGN AFFAIRS OF THE MEMBERS OF THE ECSC AT THEIR MEETING AT MESSINA ON JUNE 1 AND 2, 1955. *Provisional Translation* (Luxembourg, n.d.).

NETHERLANDS, STAATEN-GENERAAL, ZITTING 1950-51, *Document No. 2228, Goedkeuring van het op 18 april, 1951 te Parijs ondertekende verdrag tot oprichting van de EGKS . . . ; Memorie van toelichting* (The Hague, 1951).

ORGANIZATION FOR EUROPEAN ECONOMIC COOPERATION, *A European Payments Union and the Rules of Commercial Policy to be Followed by Member Countries. Document Approved by the Council of OEEC on July 7, 1950* (Paris, 1950).

ORGANIZATION FOR EUROPEAN ECONOMIC COOPERATION, *European Payments Union*, Managing Board, *Annual Reports*, 10 v. (Paris, 1951-1960).

WILLIAM PENN, *An Essay Toward the Present and Future Peace of Europe by the Establishment of an European Dyet, Parliament or Estates* (Old South Leaflets, No. 75) (Boston, n.d.).

ROYAL INSTITUTE OF INTERNATIONAL AFFAIRS, *Documents on International Affairs, 1929-* (London, 1930-).

ROYAL INSTITUTE OF INTERNATIONAL AFFAIRS, *Britain in Western Europe: WEU and the Atlantic Alliance* (London, 1956).

TREATY INSTITUTING THE EUROPEAN COAL AND STEEL COMMUNITY (Luxembourg, 1952).

UNITED STATES, DEPARTMENT OF STATE, *Germany 1947-1949, the Story in Documents* (Washington, 1950).

UNITED STATES, DEPARTMENT OF STATE, *Outline of a European Recovery Program* (Washington, 1949).

UNITED STATES, 87TH CONGRESS, 1st Session, Senate Committee on Foreign Relations, *Documents on Germany, 1944-1961* (Washington, 1961).

ARTHUR H. VANDENBERG, JR. (ed.), *The Private Papers of Senator Vandenberg* (Boston, 1952).

DIE VERTRAGSWERKE VON BONN UND PARIS VOM MAI 1952 (Dokumente und Berichte des Europa-Archivs, Band 10) (Frankfurt/Main, 1952).

CONSTANTIN FRANCOIS VOLNEY, *Oeuvres complètes* (Paris, 1846).

WESTERN EUROPEAN UNION, Assembly, *Proceedings* (Strasbourg, 1955-). French and English.

RICHARD ZOUCHE, *An Exposition of Fecial Law and Procedure, or of Law Between Nations and Questions Concerning the Same*, tr. by J. L. Brierly, 2 v. (Washington, 1911).

C. BOOKS AND MEMOIRS.

ANON., *Was bringt der Schumanplan?* (n.l., 1950).

KARL ARNOLD, *Deutsche Beiträge zur Verwirklichung der Europa-Idee* (Politeia, Bonner Universitätsreden zu öffentlichen Fragen, I) (Krefeld, n.d.).

RAYMOND ARON and DANIEL LERNER (eds.), *La querelle de la CED* (Cahiers de la Fondation Nationale des Sciences Politiques, No. 10) (Paris, 1956).

M. MARGARET BALL, *Nato and the European Union Movement* (New York, 1959).

JULIUS G. BOETTCHER, *Europa erwacht; die europäische Bewegung von der Utopie zur Wirklichkeit* (Vienna, 1950).

DEREK C. BOK, *The First Three Years of the Schuman Plan.* (Princeton, 1955).

W. A. BROWN and R. OPIE, *American Foreign Assistance* (Washington, 1953).

KARL CARSTENS, *Das Recht des Europarats* (Berlin, 1957).

SIR GEORGE N. CLARK, *War and Society in the Seventeenth Century* (Cambridge, 1958).

ANACHARSIS CLOOTS, *La république universelle ou adresse aux 'tyrannicides'* (Paris, 1792).

RICHARD COUDENHOVE-KALERGI, *Kampf um Europa. Aus meinem Leben* (Zürich, 1949).

COUNCIL OF EUROPE, *The Present State of Economic Integration in Western Europe* (Strasbourg, 1955). Excellent summary of first postwar decade.

LUDWIG DEHIO, *Gleichgewicht oder Hegemonie; Betrachtungen über ein Grundproblem der neueren Staatengeschichte* (Krefeld, 1948).

A. DELMER, *La géographie de la Communauté Européenne du Charbon et de l'Acier* (Brussels, 1953).

ALBERT DELPEREE, *Politique sociale et intégration européenne* (Liege, 1952).

LOUIS DELVAUX, *La cour de justice de la Communauté Européenne du Charbon et de l'Acier* (Paris, 1956).

ERNST DEUERLEIN, *Die Einheit Deutschlands* (Frankfurt/Main, 1957).

WILLIAM DIEBOLD, JR., *The Schuman Plan, a Study in Economic Coöperation* (New York, 1959). Comprehensive and authoritative study of ECSC's policies and operations.

LUDWIG DISCHLER, *Das Saarland, 1945-56, eine Darstellung der historischen Entwicklung, mit den wichtigsten Dokumenten*, 2 v. (Hamburg, 1956).

ROSCOE DRUMMOND and GASTON COBLENTZ, *Duel at the Brink, John Foster Dulles' Command of American Power* (New York, 1960).

ANDRE DUBOSQ, *Le conflit contemporain des houillières européennes* (Paris, 1930).

PIERRE DUCLOS, *La réforme du Conseil de l'Europe* (Bibliothèque de textes et études fédéralistes, Vol. II) (Paris, 1958).

MAURICE DUVERGER, *The French Political System* tr. Barbara and Robert North (Chicago, 1958).

SIR ANTHONY EDEN, *Full Circle* (London, 1960).

H. W. EHRMANN, *Organized Business in France* (Princeton, 1957).

MATTHEW H. ELBOW, *French Corporative Theory, 1789-1948, a Chapter in the History of Ideas* (New York, 1953).

EUROPEAN COAL AND STEEL COMMUNITY, Common Assembly, *Die Debatte über den EGKS-Vertrag in den nationalen Parlamenten* (Luxembourg, 1958).

EUROPEAN COAL AND STEEL COMMUNITY, High Authority, *Entwicklung der Löhne und Lohnpolitik in den Ländern der Gemeinschaft im Jahre 1958* (Luxembourg, 1959).

EUROPEAN COAL AND STEEL COMMUNITY, High Authority, *Hindernisse für die Beweglichkeit der Arbeitskräfte und soziale Probleme der Anpassung* (Luxembourg, 1956).

ANTOINE FERRIER, *La liberté de navigation sur le Rhin de Bâle à la mer* (Winterthur, 1955).

G. LOWELL FIELD, *The Syndical and Corporative Institutions of Italian Fascism* (New York, 1938).

FIFTH PLENARY MEETING OF THE WORLD POWER CONFERENCE, *Power Today*, 3 v. (Vienna, 1956).

WALTER FRANK, *Adolf Hitler, Vollender des Reiches. Deutsche Geschichte und deutsche Gegenwart* (n.l. 1944).

JACQUES FREYMOND, *The Saar Conflict* (London, 1960).

EDGAR S. FURNISS, JR., *France, Troubled Ally: De Gaulle's Heritage and Prospects* (New York, 1960).

OTTO GUGLIA, *Kampf um Europa* (Vienna, 1954).

ERNST B. HAAS, *The Uniting of Europe; Political, Social and Economic Forces, 1950-1957* (Stanford, 1959). A very substantial work in the tradition of V. O. Key. At times more sophisticated but less lucid than the model.

CARL H. HAHN, *Der Schuman-Plan* (Munich, 1953).

C. GROVE HAINES, (ed.), *European Integration* (Baltimore, 1957).

GEORGE W. F. HALLGARTEN, *Hitler, Reichswehr und Industrie* (Frankfurt/Main, 1955).

SYLVESTER J. HEMLEBEN, *Plans for World Peace Through Six Centuries* (Chicago, 1943). By far the most readable and penetrating work on the subject.

PAUL HERRE, *Deutschland und die europäische Ordnung* (Berlin, 1941).

KAREL HOLBIK, *Italy in International Cooperation. The Achievements of Her Liberal Economic Policies* (Padua, 1959).

KENNETH INGRAM, *History of the Cold War* (New York, 1955).

Institut Royal des Relations Internationales, *La Communauté Européenne du Charbon et de l'Acier* (Brussels, 1953).

JOSEPH M. JONES, *The Fifteen Weeks* (New York, 1955).

THOMAS L. KARNES, *The Failure of Union: Central America, 1824-1960* (Chapel Hill, N. C., 1961).

KARLHEINZ KLEPS, *Kartellpolitik and Energiewirtschaft in der Montanunion* (Ökonomische Studien, Heft 7) (Stuttgart, 1961). Best and most complete treatment of the cartel problem in the ECSC.

CHRISTIAN L. LANGE, *Histoire du Internationalisme*, Vol. I (Oslo, 1919).

WILHELM LANGWIELER, *Die sozialpolitische Problematik der Montanunion* (Bonn, 1953).

LASZLO LEDERMANN, *Fédération internationale, idées d'hier, possibilités de demain* (Neuchâtel, 1950).

CHARLES LEDRE, *Robert Schuman, pélérin de l'Europe* (Paris, 1954).

NATHAN LEITES AND CHRISTIAN DE LA MALENE, *Paris from EDC to WEU* (Santa Monica, 1956).

KENNETH LINDSEY, *European Assemblies, the Experimental Period, 1949-1959* (London, 1960). Includes the report of an international study group and a number of excellent papers. Indispensable for the study of European integration.

KENNETH LINDSEY, *Towards a European Parliament* (Strasbourg, 1957).

LOUIS LISTER, *Europe's Coal and Steel Community, an Experiment in Economic Union* (New York, 1960).

ROBERT MARJOLIN, *Europe and the United States in the World Economy* (Durham, N. C., 1953). Penetrating insights by the brilliant former Secretary-General of OEEC.

HENRY L. MASON, *The European Coal and Steel Community, Experi-*

ment in Supra-Nationalism (The Hague, 1955). Pioneer Study in English. Though obviously no longer the last word on a rapidly evolving subject, it remains useful as an admirably concise and authoritative introduction.

JAMES E. MEADE, *The Belgium-Luxembourg Economic Union, 1921-1939; Lessons from an Experiment* (Essays in International Finance, No. 25) (Princeton, 1956).

JAMES E. MEADE, *The Theory of Customs Unions* (Amsterdam, 1955).

LEON METZLER, *Le plan Schuman dans la perspective luxembourgeoise* (Luxembourg, 1952).

BEN T. MOORE, *NATO and the Future of Europe* (New York, 1958).

ELWOOD S. MOORE, *Coal, its Properties, Analysis, Classification, Geology, Extraction, Uses, and Distribution*, 2nd ed. (New York, 1940).

BERTHOLD MOSER, *Die überstaatliche Gerichtsbarkeit der Montanunion* (Vienna, 1955).

Die Neuordnung der Eisen- und Stahlindustrie im Gebiete der Bundesrepublik Deutschland (Munich, 1954).

ORGANIZATION FOR EUROPEAN ECONOMIC COOPERATION, *At Work for Europe* (Paris, 1957).

ORGANIZATION FOR EUROPEAN ECONOMIC COOPERATION, *The Organization for European Economic Cooperation, History and Structure* (Paris, 1953).

RAFFAELE PATITUCCI, *Partito Socialisto Europeo—Unità Socialista—Unità Europea* (Rovigo, 1953).

RUDOLF PETZ AND HELMUT ZÖLLNER, *Die Beschäftigungsfreiheit der Montanfacharbeiter* (Frankfurt/Main, 1956).

PAUL REUTER, *La Communauté Européenne du Charbon et de l'Acier* (Paris, 1953). A thorough and imaginative analysis of the treaty by one of its drafters. As a contribution to the "constitutional" thought of the ECSC, its value stands undiminished. As a forecast, it is very dated, however.

PAUL REYNAUD, *In the Thick of the Fight, 1930-45*, tr. James D. Lambert (New York, 1955). Notable for many questions left unanswered.

JEAN DE RICHEMONT, *Communauté Européenne du Charbon et de l'Acier: La Cour de Justice, code annoté, guide pratique* (Paris, 1954).

HENRI RIEBEN, *Des ententes des maîtres de forges au Plan Schuman* (Lausanne, 1954). An indispensable introduction to the study of integration in heavy industry.

A. H. ROBERTSON, *The Council of Europe; its Structure, Functions and Achievements* (London, 1956). Comprehensive and objective. Still the standard work.

DONALD S. ROTHSCHILD, *Toward Unity in Africa* (Washington, 1960).

ROYAL INSTITUTE OF INTERNATIONAL AFFAIRS, *NATO's Role in the Free World* (London, 1952).

LUCIEN DE STE. LORETTE, *L'idée d'union fédérale européenne* (Paris, 1955).

JEAN SALMON, *Le rôle des organizations internationales en matière de prêts et d'emprunts* (New York, 1958).

ROLF E. SANNWALD AND JACQUES STOHLER, *Economic Integration, Theoretical Assumptions and Consequences of European Integration,* tr. Herman F. Karreman (Princeton, 1959).

HANS W. SCHMALZ, *Versuche einer gesamteuropäischen Organisation, 1815-1830* (Untersuchungen zur allgemeinen Geschichte, Heft 10) (Aarau, 1940).

CARL T. SCHMIDT, *The Corporate State in Action* (London, 1939).

KURT SCHUMACHER, *50 Jahre mit gebundenen Händen?* (Bonn, 1951).

KURT SCHUMACHER, *Macht Europa stark!* (Hanover, 1951).

JOHN L. SNELL, *Wartime Origins of the East-West Dilemma over Germany* (New Orleans, 1959). Best historical synthesis of the German question as it emerged from the collapse of 1945.

ELIZABETH V. SOULEYMAN, *The Vision of World Peace in Seventeenth and Eighteenth Century France* (New York, 1941).

SOZIALE ARBEITSGEMEINSCHAFT DER SPD, *Der richtige Weg? Eine sachliche Würdigung des Schumanplans* (n.l. 1950?).

FRIEDRICH STIEVE, *Deutsche Tat für Europa. Von Arnim bis Hitler* (Potsdam, 1944).

STUDIENAUSSCHUSS DES WESTEUROPAEISCHEN KOHLENBERGBAUS, *Die Anwendung der Kernenergie zur Kraft- und Stromerzeugung und ihr Einfluss auf den Kohlenbergbau* (Essen, 1956).

O. R. TAYLOR, *The Fourth Republic of France, Constitution and Political Parties* (London, 1951).

JACOB TER MEULEN, *Der Gedanke der internationalen Organisation in seiner Entwicklung,* vol. 1: 1300-1800 (The Hague, 1917).

ARTHUR C. TURNER, *Bulwark of the West; Implications and Problems of NATO* (Toronto, 1953).

R. C. VALENTINE, *The Court of Justice of the European Coal and Steel Community* (The Hague, 1955).

RICHARD W. VAN ALSTYNE, *American Crisis Diplomacy, the Quest for Collective Security, 1918-1952* (Stanford, 1952).

S. I. P. VAN CAMPEN, *The Quest for Security* (The Hague, 1956).

KARL VORLAENDER, *Kant und der Gedanke des Völkerbundes* (Leipzig, 1919).

ALEXANDER WERTH, *France, 1940-55* (London, 1956).

ALEXANDER WERTH, *Lost Statesman, the Strange Story of Pierre Mendès-France* (New York, 1955).

PAUL WEYMAR, *Adenauer, His Authorized Biography* tr. Peter de Mendelsohn (New York, 1957).

PIERRE WIGNY, *Rechenschaft über die Gemeinschaft der Sechs* (Luxembourg, 1957).

PHILIP J. WILSON and JOSEPH H. WELLS, *Coal, Coke, and Coal Chemicals* (New York, 1950).

EDITH WYNNER and GEORGIA LLOYD, *Searchlight on Peace Plans* (New York, 1944).

ARNOLD J. ZURCHER, *The Struggle to Unite Europe, 1940-1958* (New York, 1958). A good introduction to a complex subject.

D. PERIODICAL ARTICLES.

HELMUT ALLARDT, "Praktische Entwicklungsarbeit in Afrika," *Aussenpolitik,* XI (1960).

ROBERT ALS, "Le plan Schuman dans la perspective luxembourgeoise," *Société Belge d'Études et d'Expansion, Bulletin Bimestriel,* LI (1952).

ANON., "Le débat sur le plan Schuman au Bundestag," *Réalités Allemandes,* No. 37 (1952).

ANON., "Faut-il élire l'Assemblée de la CECA au suffrage universel?" *France-Europe,* VIII, No. 32 (1955).

ANON., "Fifth Liberal Congress, Strasbourg, 25-28 September, 1952," *World Liberalism,* II (1952).

ANON., "La ratification du traité instituant la Communauté Européenne du Charbon et de l'Acier," *Chronique de Politique Étrangère,* VI (1953).

ANON., "Das Reich und Europa," *Zeitschrift für Politik,* XXXII (1942).

GERHARD BEBR, "The European Coal and Steel Community; a Political and Legal Innovation," *Yale Law Journal,* LII (1953).

GERHARD BEBR, "The European Defense Community and the Western European Union; an Agonizing Dilemma," *Stanford Law Review,* VII (1955).

KURT BIRRENBACH, "Europe, the European Economic Community and the Outer Seven," *International Journal,* XV (1959-60).

JEAN BOULOUIS, "Les rapports de l'Assemblée Consultative et du Comité des Ministres du Conseil de l'Europe," *RDP,* LVIII (1952).

DAVID T. CATTELL, "Multi-lateral Coöperation and Integration in Eastern Europe," *The Western Political Quarterly,* XIII (1960).

FEDERICO CHABOD, "L'idea di Europa," *Rassegna d'Italia,* II, No. 4 (1947).

DAVID E. CHRISTIAN, "Resistance to International Worker Mobility; a Barrier to European Unity," *Industrial and Labor Relations Review,* VIII (1954).

WILL CLAYTON, "Is the Marshall Plan 'Operation Rathole'?" *Saturday Evening Post*, November 29, 1947.

SHEPARD CLOUGH, "Economic Planning in a Capitalist Society; France from Monnet to Hirsch," *Political Science Quarterly*, LXXI (1956).

FERNAND DEHOUSSE, "Belgique," *Notre Europe*, Nos. 11 and 12 (1952).

CHARLES L. DELZELL, "The European Federalist Movement in Italy: First Phase, 1918-1947," *The Journal of Modern History*, XXXII (1960).

H. W. EHRMANN, "The French Trade Associations and the Ratification of the Schuman Plan," *World Politics*, VI (1954).

F. GUNTHER EYCK, "Benelux in the Balance," *Political Science Quarterly*, LXIX (1954).

FRITZ ULRICH FACK, "Wirtschaftsordnung zwischen Freiheit und Bindung," *Die Öffentliche Wirtschaft*, I (1956).

JOHN H. FERGUSON, "The Anglo-American Financial Agreements and Our Foreign Policy," *The Yale Law Review*, LV (1946).

PER FISCHER, "Dreijährige Bilanz der Westeuropäischen Union," *Europa Archiv*, XIV (1959).

KURT F. FLEXNER, "The Creation of the European Payments Union," *Political Science Quarterly*, LXXII (1957).

WOLFGANG FRIEDMANN, "New Tasks for NATO," *International Journal*, XI (1956).

HANS FURLER, "Europäisches Parlament und Europäische Politik," *Aussenpolitik*, XI (1960)

DAVID GARNICK, "The Economic Feasibility of a Middle Eastern Common Market," *Middle East Journal*, XIV (1960).

PIERRE GERBET, "La génèse du Plan Schuman," *Revue Française de Science Politique*, VI (1956). Fine pioneering study.

LINCOLN GORDON, "Myth and Reality of European Integration," *Yale Review*, XLV (1955).

LINCOLN GORDON, "NATO and European Integration," *World Politics*, X (1958).

LINCOLN GORDON, "The Organization for European Economic Cooperation," *International Organization*, X (1956).

ALFRED GROSSER, "Suez, Hungary, and European Integration, *ibid.*, XI (1957).

ERNST B. HAAS and PETER H. MERKL, "Parliamentarians Against Ministers; the Case of Western European Union," *ibid.*, XIV (1960). The authors very fairly present evidence that contradicts their "spillover" or "trickle-down" hypothesis, without abandoning it, however.

FRITZ HELLWIG, "Die deutsche Eisen-und Stahlindustrie innerhalb der Europäischen Gemeinschaft für Kohle und Stahl," *Bergfreiheit*, XLI (1951).

DANIEL HENRI-VIGNES, "Notes sur l'évolution institutionelle de la Communauté Européenne du Charbon et de l'Acier," *Les Cahiers de Bruges*, IV (1954).

GUENTHER JAENICKE, "Der übernationale Charakter der Europäischen Wirtschaftsgemeinschaft," *Zeitschrift für ausländisches öffentliches Recht und Völkerrecht*, XIX (1958).

GEORGES KAEKENBEEK, "The International Authority for the Ruhr and the Schuman Plan," *Transactions for the Grotius Society*, XXXVII (1952).

BASIL KARP, "The Draft Constitution for a European Political Community," *International Organization*, VIII (1954).

U. W. KITZINGER, "Europe: The Six and the Seven," *ibid.*, X (1960).

PAUL KLUKE, "Nationalsozialistische Europaideologie," *Vierteljahreshefte für Zeitgeschichte*, III (1955). Thorough, scholarly demolition of Hitler the "European."

J. F. KOEVER, "The Integration of Western Europe," *Political Science Quarterly*, LXIX (1954).

LEOPOLD KOHR, "The History of the Common Market," *The Journal of Economic History*, XX (1960). Author equates customs union and common market.

MAURICE LAGRANGE, "L'ordre juridique de la CECA vu à travers la jurisprudence de sa cour de justice," *RDP*, LXXIV (1958).

CLAUDE LASALLE, "Aspects institutionnels de la Communauté Charbon-Acier" *ibid.*, LXXIV (1958).

CLAUDE LASALLE, "Contribution à une théorie de la fonction publique supranationale," *ibid.*, LXXIII (1957).

FRIEDRICH LEMMER, "Über den Schuman-Plan," *Deutsche Rundschau*, LXXVII (1951).

CHARLES D. DE LESPAUL, "L'industrie charbonnière et le plan Schuman," *Bulletin de l'Institut de Recherches Économiques et Sociales*, XVII (1951). Deals only with Belgium.

LEO LOUBÈRE, "The Intellectual Origins of French Jacobin Socialism," *International Review of Social History*, IV (1959).

CHARLES G. McCLINTOCK and DALE J. HEKHUIS, "European Community Deterrence; its Organization, Utility, and Political Feasibility," *The Journal of Conflict Resolution*, V (1961).

R. CRAIG McIvor, "Canadian Foreign Trade and the European Common Market," *International Journal*, XIII (1957-58).

WILLIAM C. MALLALIEU, "The Origin of the Marshall Plan; a Study in Policy Formation and National Leadership," *Political Science Quarterly*, LXXIII (1958).

HENRY L. MASON, "The Assembly of Western European Union and European Defense," *Internationale Spectator*, XIV (1960).

JAMES E. MEADE, "Benelux: the Formulation of the Common Customs," *Economica*, XXIII (1956). Meade's work on Benelux is by far the most valuable contribution to the subject.

JAMES E. MEADE, "The Building of Benelux," *The Banker*, CVI (1956).

HENRY J. MERRY, "The European Coal and Steel Community, Operations of the High Authority," *The Western Political Quarterly*, VIII (1955).

A. R. METRAL, "Le Comité Consultatif, chéville ouvrière de la CECA," *Annales des Mines*, CXLIV (June, 1955). Author was chairman of the Committee at the time.

MICHEL MOUSHKELY, "Le mandat des représentants à l'Assemblée Consultative du Conseil de l'Europe," *RDP*, LVIII (1952).

MICHEL MOUSHKELY, "Le président de l'Assemblée Consultative du Conseil de l'Europe," *ibid.*, LVIII (1952).

FRITZ MUENCH, "Die Gerichtsbarkeit im Schuman-Plan," *Gegenwartsprobleme des internationalen Rechts und der Rechtsphilosophie. Festschrift für Rudolf Laun . . .* (Hamburg, 1953).

ALLAN NANES, "The Evolution of Euratom," *International Journal*, XIII (1958).

HEINZ NAUPERT, "Die Grundlagen des Schuman-Plans," *Der Betrieb*, V (1952).

LESTER PEARSON, "NATO: Retrospect and Prospect," *International Journal*, XIII (1958).

CARL H. PEGG, "Die Résistance als Träger der europäischen Einigungsbestrebungen in Frankreich während des zweiten Weltkrieges," *Europa-Archiv*, VII (1952).

FLOOR PETERS, "Benelux—Ideal und Wirklichkeit," *Politische Bildung*, VI (1953).

LISE PFANNENSCHMIDT, "Anti-Democratic Parties in European Politics," *Les Cahiers de Bruges*, VIII, No. 1 (1958).

HEINZ POTTHOFF, "Europäische Investitionspolitik im Kohlenbergbau und in der Stahlindustrie," *Bergbau und Wirtschaft*, X (1957).

HEINZ POTTHOFF, "Von der Ruhrbehörde zum Schumanplan," *Recht-Staat-Wirtschaft*, III (1951).

FRANCO RECCO, "La politica di investimenti dell' Alta Autorità Carbo-Siderurgica," *Rivista di Politica Economica*, XLIV (1954).

HANS ROTHFELS, "Zehn Jahre danach," *Vierteljahreshefte für Zeitgeschichte*, III (1955).

WILHELM SALEWSKI, "Investitionssorgen der Hohen Behörde," *Der Volkswirt*, No. 44 (1956). Author was director of High Authority's division for investments at the time.

JACK SCHIEFER, "Sozialpolitik der Hohen Behörde–Möglichkeiten und Grenzen," *Bergbau und Wirtschaft*, X (1957).

PAUL SCHULZ-KIESOW, "Montan-Union und Verkehr," *Zeitschrift für Verkehrswissenschaft*, XXIV (1955).

FREDERICK L. SCHUMAN, "The Council of Europe," *American Political Science Review*, XLV (1951).

ROBERT SCHUMAN, "Origines et élaboration du 'Plan Schuman'," *Les Cahiers de Bruges*, III (1953).

P. J. S. SERRARENS, "La construction sociale de l'Europe," *Droit Social*, XVII (1954).

FREDERICK SETHUR, "The Schuman Plan and Ruhr Coal," *Political Science Quarterly*, LXVII (1952).

DUSAN SIDJANSKI, "Le Conseil de l'Europe et son évolution," *L'Europe Naissante*, III, No. 2 (1956).

DUSAN SIDJANSKI, "Partis politiques en face de l'intégration Européenne," *Res Publica*, III (1961).

FERNAND SPAAK, "Competition in ECSC," *1960 Institute on Legal Aspects of the European community* (Washington, 1960).

PAUL-HENRI SPAAK, "NATO and the Communist Challenge," *International Journal*, XIII (1958).

PAUL-HENRI SPAAK, "The New Europe," *The Atlantic Monthly*, CCIII (September, 1958).

ERIC STEIN, "The European Coal and Steel Community: the Beginning Process," *Columbia Law Review*, LV (1955). Very competent *and* very readable.

ERIC STEIN, "The European Parliamentary Assembly, Techniques of Emerging Political Control," *International Organization*, XIII (1959).

FELIX STOESSINGER, "Geschichte und Verfassung des Schuman-Plans," *Neue Schweizer Rundschau*, XIX (1951-52).

KURT P. TAUBER, "German Nationalists and European Union," *Political Science Quarterly*, LXXIV (1959). A thorough review of pan-European neo-Nazis in the Federal Republic.

KARL-WILHELM ULRICH, "Réactions Allemandes," *Documents*, No. 6 (1951).

G. VAN BENTHEM VAN DEN BERGH, "De parlamentaire vergadering van de Westeuropese Union," *Internationale Spectator*, XV, No. 2 (1961).

MARINUS VAN DER GOES VAN NATERS, "De huidige staat van het Europese parlamentarisme," *ibid.*, XII (1956).

MARINUS VAN DER GOES VAN NATERS, "L'histoire de la Sarre en documents," *European Yearbook*, II (1956).

ALBERT VAN HOUTTE, "La Cour de Justice de la Communauté Européenne du Charbon et de l'Acier," *ibid.*, (1956). The best introduction.

HERMANN VOLLE, "Die Agonie der Europäischen Verteidigungsgemeinschaft," *Europa Archiv,* IX (1954).

RUDOLF VON ALBERTINI, "Aristide Briand's Union Européenne und der Schuman Plan," *Schweizer Monatshefte,* XXX (1950).

H. W. VON DEWALL, "Schuman-Plan und Bergbau," *Bergfreiheit,* XVI (1951).

ELLINOR VON PUTTKAMER, "Der Entwurf eines Vertrages über die Satzung der europäischen Gemeinschaft," *Zeitschrift für ausländisches öffentliches Recht und Völkerrecht,* XV (1953).

ELLINOR VON PUTTKAMER, "Historische Pläne europäischer Verfassungsbildung," *Völkerrechtliche und staatsrechtliche Abhandlungen Carl Bilfinger zum 75. Geburtstag gewidmet* (Cologne, 1954).

A. VOSEN, "Für und wider den Schuman-Plan: Ökonomische Argumente in der Debatte des Bundestages," *Mitteilungen des Westfälischen Instituts für Wirtschaftsforschung, Essen,* III (1952).

CLARENCE C. WALTON, "Background for the European Defense Community," *Political Science Quarterly,* LXVIII (1953).

CLARENCE C. WALTON, "The Hague 'Congress of Europe': a Case Study of Public Opinion," *The Western Political Quarterly,* XII (1959).

TH. E. WESTERTERP, "Europese fractievorming, een eerste experiment," *Internationale Spectator,* XII (1959).

K. K. F. ZAWADZKI, "The Economics of the Schuman-Plan," *Oxford Economic Papers* (new series), V (1953).

EGMONT ZECHLIN, "Die europäische Ordnung und die Ozeane," *Zeitschrift für Politik,* XXXII (1942). A particularly extravagant pronouncement of Hitlerian *Weltpolitik.*

Index

263

268

Index

International Ruhr Authority, 52, 53–54, 63, 73, 82, 207
International Steel Cartel, 50
Iran, 34
Iraq, 244
Ireland, 22 n., 40, 242
Israel, 244
Italian Blackshirts. *See* Fascism
Italy, 3, 7, 11, 16, 18, 19, 20, 22 n., 28, 38, 40, 41, 63–64, 65, 66, 74, 76, 87, 115, 119, 129, 130, 138, 141, 145, 165, 173, 176, 187–88, 190, 200, 214, 221, 240

Japan, 11
Journal officiel of the European Coal and Steel Community, 100, 128
Juin, Alphonse, French marshal, 217

Kant, Immanuel, German philosopher, 5–6
Kennan, George, U. S. diplomat, 21–22
Keynes, John Maynard, British economist, 53
Kiesinger, Kurt, chairman of foreign policy committee in German Bundestag, 141
Koenig, Pierre, French general, 214, 218, 219
Kohnstamm, Max, secretary of High Authority, 159
Korean armistice, 214
Korean War, 30, 37, 38, 49, 206, 207
Korthals, H. A. Dutch liberal, 139
Kreuger, Ivar, Swedish financier, 56

Labor, 50, 155, 196
Labor mobility, 197–202
Labor party (Netherlands), 65, 137, 142
Ladd, William, U. S. pacifist, 7

Laniel, Joseph, French premier, 214, 217, 218
Lapie, Pierre-Oliver, French member of High Authority, 99, 100, 137
Latin America, 244
League for Peace and Freedom, 7
League for the Union of Europe, 7
League of Nations, 7, 8, 9, 14
Lehr, Robert, German minister of the interior, 70
Leibniz, Gottfried Wilhelm, German philosopher, 5
Lemonnier, Charles, French pioneer of European union, 7
Liberal Group (Common Assembly), 138–39
Liberal Group (European Parliamentary Assembly), 139 n.
Liberalization of trade, 25, 27
Liberals, 42, 142, 145, 150
Lindsay, Kenneth, British M. P., 130
Loewenthal, Eduard, German pacifist, 7
London Conference (1954), 225–29
Lorraine, 170, 184, 201
Low Countries, 18, 28, 29, 63, 68, 145
Luxembourg, 22 n., 29, 40, 64, 66, 74, 76, 77, 83, 113, 115, 129, 137, 141, 144, 173, 186, 190, 212–13

Macmillan, Harold, British premier, 43, 242
Malvestiti, Piero, fourth president of High Authority, 94, 99
Margue, Nicolas, leader of Luxembourg, Christian social party, 137, 144
Marshall, George Catlett, U. S. statesman, 20, 21
Marshall Plan, 20–25, 31, 34, 37, 49–50, 57, 61, 240, 243
Masaryk, Jan, Czech diplomat, 22
Mayer, René, second president of High Authority, 92, 95, 98, 99, 100, 133, 142, 150, 214, 221
Mazzini, Giuseppe, Italian leader, 6–7